DESIGN
CAPABILITY and AWARENESS

JOHN MORRISON and JOHN TWYFORD

LONGMAN

Longman Group UK Limited
Longman House, Burnt Mill, Harlow, Essex CM20 2JE, England
and Associated Companies throughout the World.

© Longman Group UK Limited 1994

The publisher's policy is to use paper manufactured from sustainable forests.

First published 1994

ISBN 0 582 05687 X

Set in 10/11 pt Palatino
Produced by Longman Singapore Publishers Pte Ltd
Printed in Singapore

Acknowledgements

We are grateful to the following for permission to reproduce copyright
material:
Apollo Magazine Ltd for the article 'Duck Fountain' by Anna Somers
Cocks from *Weekend Guardian* 27–28th May 1989; Guardian News
Service Ltd for the articles 'Tower Power' by Brenda Polan from *The
Guardian* 16.4.90 and 'Protect the lie' (author unknown) from *The
Guardian* 30.12.88, (c) The Guardian; Oxford University Delegacy of
Local Examinations for an adaptation of 9883 assessment form (IMS
9883)

We have been unable to trace the copyright holder in the article 'To
hell with Helvetica' by Peter Bonnici and John Willett from *The
Guardian* 2.12.88 and would appreciate any information that would
enable us to do so.

Photographic and other copyright material is acknowledged on the
inside back cover.

CONTENTS

Section Four: The Practice of Design

Section Five: Design Resources

ridge danyers

INTRODUCTION

The study of contemporary life and culture is an essential requirement of design education. It is the main human context from which the examples in this book are derived. Preparation for future living and an individual's choices concerning objects and activities are prime motivators for design study. Such activity should also be related to the needs of communities and a respect for natural life. Knowing about design and designing can provide individuals with the capability to absorb, criticise and evaluate a wide range of influences from society and culture.

   The study of people, including their successes, failures, aspirations and dreams, is also an important feature of designing today. We have the capacity to attach values and meanings to the things that we make and own, some of which are vitally important at one moment and trivial the next. This book is a springboard from which design students, as well as those with a general interest, can design effectively and also develop their awareness and appreciation of design. It is intended to complement the many other resources for design that are already available.

When designing a designer should regard the context of their work as a prime source of inspiration.

Well-designed objects are easy to interpret and understand. They contain visible clues to their operation. Poorly designed objects can be difficult and frustrating to use. They provide no clues – or sometimes false clues. *The Psychology of Everydaythings*, (Donald A. Norman)

A design in its own right should communicate its essential use and allow a user to know what to do with it. How well this is done varies greatly. To what extent should a design make obvious how it can be used?

What is this for? Designs should generate popular and ingenious creations that use materials intelligently and ergonomics effectively.

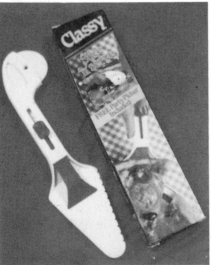

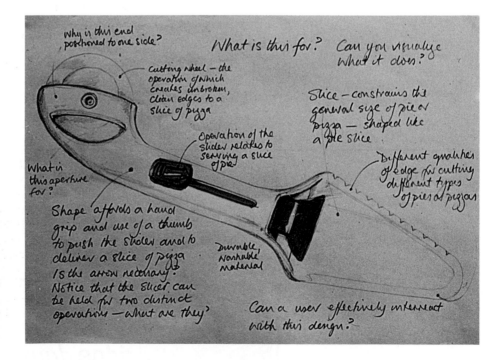

Why is this end positioned to one side?

What is this for? Can you visualize what it does?

cutting wheel – the operation of which creates unbroken, clean edges to a slice of pizza

Slice – constrains the general size of pie or pizza – shaped like a pie slice

Operation of the slider relates to serving a slice of pie

Different qualities of edge for cutting different types of pies or pizzas

What is this aperture for?

Shape affords a hand grip and use of a thumb to push the slider and to deliver a slice of pizza. Is the arrow necessary? Notice that the slicer can be held for two distinct operations – what are they?

Durable, washable material

Can a user effectively interact with this design?

The user's perception of the purpose of a design is based on the concept they have for the design and its task. For new or modified designs this is better formed if the design's use is visible and understandable. Usability and understandability are crucial factors which allow people to know something about what a design is for – its affordance. A designer should aim to be aware of the concepts which a user might form about what the design is intended to do. If there is a mismatch what happens?

How well designers communicate to a user, through their designs, depends greatly upon relating their conceptual model of a design idea to its visible attributes for use. Look at the diagram titled 'what is this for' and use what you find to establish the affordances, constraints and the relationship of one action to another in the operation of the following designs: a digital stop-watch, scissors, a video, a door in a public building and a motorway.

A prepared mind is crucial to lasting design interest and capability. Effective design education is formed in a continuum of experiences and creative attitudes, which result from developing in individuals imagination, the sensitivity to create aesthetic ideals and the personal vitality that will prepare them both technically and culturally to design.

The major objectives of this book are to foster students' understanding and awareness of the processes of design and designing and to enhance their capabilities to create and use the products of design by:

- providing experience of a variety of activities, models, systems, facts, beliefs, values, problems, decision-making examples and technical and expressive issues concerning design and designing.

- presenting issues concerning the way in which students might acknowledge, criticise, reason, comment upon and demonstrate their understanding of how design influences themselves and others.

- enabling them to seek and experiment with their own chosen design propositions, as well as those provided by their courses of study, examinations, teachers, industry or any other suitable source, from both market-led and problem-led issues.

Because design is a human activity, its study should not be concerned solely with processes involving the form, function and costs of artefacts, models, systems or images. Design is also a mixture of trends, tasks, aesthetic ideals, problem-solving and decision-making for use in many fields of knowledge that are historically, socially and culturally located.

This book is designed to develop the many different ways of looking at, knowing about and being sensitive to the power and value of design. It is intended to form a rich source of experiences and examples for students to try and to consider.

Design methods and processes are not unique. They are found in many examples where different forms of technical and creative knowledge and experience are combined across a wide spectrum of human achievements. Invention and creativity have been strong influences on the use and development of design.

It is equally important to acknowledge the reality of how designers work. By revealing and evaluating examples of design, and by analysing and demonstrating designers' working attitudes, procedures, restraints, strategies, products, modelling and systems, this important factor is highlighted throughout this book.

Lenny Henry and Comic Relief.
Design may be concerned with worthy and prestigious schemes.

Design is a field of study that has economic and industrial significance, with regard to its role in promoting flexible and creative attitudes towards industry, as much as towards developing responsible citizenship in our technical and material society.

Masterpiece by Roy Lichtenstein © Roy Lichtenstein/DACS 1994.
Design is a feature of the achievements and 'beauty' of art.

DESIGN: IN PLACE OF A DEFINITION

Design is a factor in every commercial venture. It is inescapable. Small design differences can produce very big results – for better or worse.

Design deals in the issues which come closest to a human being's personal reality. It is about his – or her – needs and desires; about social context, about just how far you can reach and bend.

Design serves to unite the different parts of a varied or dispersed venture. It identifies the venture as a whole, acts as a focus of its reputation, and sharpens its impact in the marketplace.

Design is built on contrasts: disciplined by method, it is also freely inspired. Design uses an extraordinary range of outside influences, most of them strictly practical. It feeds on a radical cross-fertilisation of ideas.

'Good' and 'bad' design are not only matters of opinion. They can also be measured.

In the best companies, design resources are managed with all the seriousness shown to Marketing or Finance. But design can also be fun – it can uplift people. Consistently pursued, good design can help carry an organisation through any number of changes.

Design is durable. It is about gaining more control over your business, and communicating to the outside world the uniqueness of what you do.

Just as much as your conventional investments, good design now will repay you in the future.

Design motivates and enables enterprises to be successful.
Words and artwork from designers Fitch and Co.

The Lloyd's Building, London.
Design supports sound technology, including the many fields of engineering, architecture and industry.

Students will be exposed to issues concerning the commercial significance and costs of design, production techniques, processes and manufacture, concerning both activities that are market-led and problem-led. It is this aspect of design education that needs further development, support and management, as it is as challenging as the creative aspects of design. Such approaches do require from students intellectual self-discipline and an understanding of the relationship between design and production, as well as judgement concerning how to meet market needs and develop consumer products and consumer awareness.

This is a prime test of the value of design, especially as it should not be seen as yet another way of manipulating people commercially. Issues concerning the tastes of consumers and how student designers can anticipate these are all pertinent factors at this level of design.

This book is based upon the promotion of individual awareness of how design affects all our lives, as well as enabling students of design to realise their own ideas and skills by developing personal performance when designing. Designing is a human activity which produces a myriad ideas and objects. Do you agree with these views?

1 The Nature of Design

THE ORIGIN AND PURPOSE OF DESIGN

What is design?

Design and designing are important human skills, especially as good design is not easy. It is hard work. Being aware of the value and wide-reaching effect of design is crucial to our cultural sensitivity, as is its actual use by individuals or organisations.

Design awareness means knowing about design generally and tacitly. It involves knowing how to look at design and understanding our own personal reactions to designs – a knowledge that is achieved through careful study. Design awareness can be fostered through the combination of knowledge and experience of the objects, actions and ideas that are derived from many contexts. Design capability is dependent upon design awareness to inform and inspire fresh work.

Design is an ever-changing and evolving process based upon human achievement and technical prowess. It is what individuals and organisations make of it as they think about and discuss future improvements or change. Designing is an adventure using observation and intelligence to explore new or modified possibilities. It is part of the human imagination, expressed in objects and activities, and represents a powerful method of synthesising many forms of knowledge and experience. The desire to design comes from our need to communicate certain chosen aesthetic ideals, to learn about technical skills and to be cultured and prepared to get things right.

Design is our imaginative life made real. It is a creative and disciplined activity based upon bringing together information, knowledge, skills and sensitivities within a working context. Design is essentially a compromise of factors within a set of constraints.

Design is predominantly a problem-solving activity. The focus of attention for designers is the formation of various propositions, from which a solution can be chosen; there will be no correct solution, but only a selection of the 'best' option. Designing is a creative building up of possibilities rather than a deductive analytical process. Designers are generally constrained by many factors, for example working context, time, cost, materials, their own knowledge and the needs of clients.

Design encompasses, as well as operating within, many areas of knowledge and understanding, especially those of art and technology. It is a multifarious process which has been associated in recent times with the making, selling and using of artefacts, systems and images derived from general manufacturing. However, it originates from many human endeavours, notably the arts, including references to drawing and planning.

A prepared mind is necessary for the adventure of design.
(A wood engraving by Arthur Hughes from *The Princess and the Goblin* by George MacDonald).

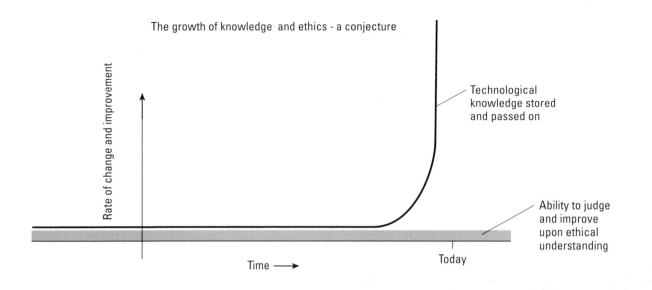

The growth of knowledge and ethics - a conjecture

Rate of change and improvement

Technological
knowledge stored
and passed on

Ability to judge
and improve
upon ethical
understanding

Time ⟶

Today

Today, a product designer might ask what the price of design would be in relation to a manufactured article. What, indeed, would be the price of no design at all, to industry, commercial enterprises or our well-being in general?

Which of the following aspects of design – function, appearance or cost, feature most strongly in: a pump working the bottom of a North Sea oil rig, a hi-tech clothes peg which detects rain and a black bin liner with a hole in it, presented as high fashion? How important would aesthetic considerations be in the design of a pump devised to operate on the sea bed under a North Sea oil rig? Would anyone wearing an *haute couture* garment worry about how well it was made? Would a clothes peg be worth buying if it cost £100?

The versatility of design

Consciously, or otherwise, we learn to be acquisitive and critical of 'things'. The *raison d'être* of work depends on the concept that we need 'things', whether as necessities or as luxuries. The objects we own and use are part of us, and it is the mark of an educated person to know something about how and why designs come about, including why people spend so much time and effort on obtaining them.

Do you try to be critical of how design influences your life, or are you taken in by it all? Should we agree as to which designs are likeable or unlikeable, or whether or not design is for the general good? Enjoying the different possibilities that designing brings is part of its value to us.

Has the development of human capabilities simply been part of general evolution, so that certain designs would have appeared anyway, without designers? Can we accelerate the development of 'better' things through design? Is this in our long-term interests? Are we trying to 'second guess' the future by using design?

Consider the present day. How many household gadgets do you fully understand? Do you know how they work, what they do, how they should be serviced and maintained, and so on? In how many of these things do you appreciate the background to their design? Are you aware of the influence of designers in creating the idea that the future will bring better things? Are there technical remedies for present ills and worries, based on 'better' design? If you have difficulty with everyday things, how would you understand the technicalities of a hi-tech item that is 'clinically superior by design'?

Changing and modifying things to perform various functions are technological acts. The variety of forms of things is essentially an expression of their design. The modification and adaptation of the environment over thousands of years, including its material resources, have become part of the way of life of different peoples, as well as many other living creatures or organisms. Using stone, wood and minerals as well as quarrying, building, farming and harvesting, are essential technological examples in the design and development of homes, food production and communities.

Richard Dawkins, a biologist, defines a living thing as a phenotype. When a phenotype takes some object from the environment to use as an essential item for survival, this object is termed an 'extended phenotype'. A drey is an extended phenotype of a squirrel, and this is what technology is for humans. Squirrels might be technological without knowing it, but are they designers? Has blind chance determined the best type of drey rather than rational, creative or intuitive thought. Is complex behaviour more likely to be the product of heredity rather than learning? If this is true, and design is a complex form of behaviour, would it be true to say that designers are born rather than a product of skills acquired as they learn to design through their experience of other examples of designing?

Squirrels build their dreys 10m up a tree, close to the trunk. A drey has no obvious entrance and is made from a mass of interlaced twigs and branches and lined with leaves and moss. Do squirrels design their dreys?

Our ideas and dreams are projected into concepts which technology makes material, and it is cheaper to produce a design than to experiment by continually making things until they work. Designing is essentially a synthesis of our experiences; the more we find out about things, the more capable we become. Our capability is further enhanced when we fully understand the principles by which things come into being or work.

To what extent should a designer understand first principles? What is the value of collaboration? What is it that drives progress and why do some societies make quicker progress than others?

Design as a human activity

To understand what design is we need to understand something of human capabilities. We seek and achieve our goals and purposes in life through the acquired attributes of reason and intuition. We know about the world through our experience of and creation of actions, images and symbols.

As we design, we orientate ourselves towards the future. Culturally we institutionalise the usefulness of design in the workplace, through professional enterprises and, especially, education. Design is as good for business as it is for developing people's talents through the progressive stages of their education, from elementary forms of knowledge to more advanced forms.

There are strong links between the ideas of design and reason. Consider what Shakespeare uses the character of Prospero to achieve.

> You do look, my son, in a mov'd sort,
> As if you were dismay'd; be cheerful, sir:
> Our revels now are ended. These our actors,
> As I foretold you, were all spirits, and
> Are melted into air, into thin air;
> And, like the baseless fabric of this vision,
> The cloud-capp'd towers, the gorgeous palaces,
> The solemn temples, the great globe itself,
> Yea, all which it inherit, shall dissolve,
> And, like this insubstantial pageant faded,
> Leave not a rack behind. We are such stuff
> As dreams are made on; and our little life
> Is rounded with a sleep. — Sir, I am vex'd;
> Bear with my weakness; my old brain is troubled;
> Be not disturb'd with my infirmity.
> If you be pleas'd, retire into my cell
> And there repose; a turn or two I'll walk
> To still my beating mind.

(Prospero in *The Tempest*, Act IV, scene I, line 146)

By looking carefully at this scene from *The Tempest*, we can experience the richness of design. Does this speech highlight the tensions we might find in ourselves concerning our understanding of dreams and reality? What is the value of ideas or possessions in our lives? How can our understanding of design reveal our interest in things? How is design used in a theatre to make this scene become real?

Prospero's speech concerns the nature and value of human achievements. It tends to argue that human beings, as well as the things that they make and treasure, are of little importance or lasting value. Prospero is reminding us of the differences between our dreams and reality; of how our works will dissolve into thin air.

However, this is not a sufficient explanation of how we live our lives in relation to the things designed to meet our needs for shelter, comfort, safety and general wellbeing. The emphasis made by Prospero is that we should not always take our possessions or our dreams so seriously. Yet, without them where would we be?

Disney World, Florida.
What is the magic of Disney?

This may be a useful starting point to consider what our motives are for being involved with design, especially if understanding human nature is something that intrigues us. We know what the real world is and we also know something of the power of human imagination. We might begin to understand what design can mean to us by considering our powers of creativity and our aspirations in design. Are dreams the stuff of effective designers? Is design the unifying concept that binds together objects and human activities and achievements. It is quite likely that your time as a design student will be the only time you will have to produce your own ideas, as well as to explore outlandish notions. Why is this?

Think for a moment about why people believe strongly in certain ideas or always buy the same type of product. There is a human need to project meaning into things. The meanings that we place on things, including the semantics of objects, are an important consideration in our understanding of design. This strategy is now employed in many product designs.

Klari Engi and Attila Toth, Hungary in the World Ice Skating Championships 1990.

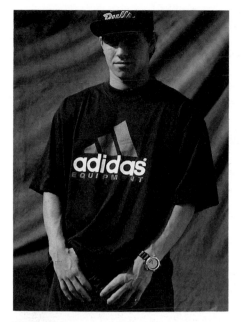

Marky Mark.
Different peoples attach particular meaning to the things they wear. Is this by design or part of being human?

Elderly Masai woman.

We engage in both real and imaginary activities which seem to have a purpose and require planning. We often devise quite artificial schemes, games or simulations of reality. We take both life and our games seriously. Where does designing fit into this scheme of things?

The word 'why' is one of the most important words in our language; the moment we employ it, we become involved in some sort of reasoning which, on many occasions, leads to designing. It is part of our spirit to find meaning in all manner of activities. Designing is one way of giving meaning to our lives. It is most potent when it is employed to benefit people or the natural world; it is least valuable when it is used to manipulate and deceive.

Is there a need to define design?

Naturally, there is a danger in forming too much theory about the products of design, as well as the methods of designing, because once design becomes codified as a set of procedures then it may become deadened. It is crucial that design knowledge remains lively, and that designers remain sensitive to improbable circumstances, as well as opportunities, so that their end products are valuable and useful.

Practically speaking, however, working definitions for design can be effective, especially when working in a team. It is generally valuable to know how to co-operate with other designers, especially when handling and presenting information.

The essence of design is often seen as change for purely human purposes. Most people *recognise* what design is, but generally they have difficulty in *expressing* clearly what it is. The possibilities for establishing different methods of design are infinite. Design processes can be analysed, especially after the event, and there will never be an absolute methodology that can be prescribed for all time. Design arises from problems and issues, not necessarily from any one process of thought or organisation.

Many things can be learned from the ways designers find themselves working. It is vital that awareness of similar examples of design is used to inform fresh judgement and decision-making. This is the importance of knowing about design.

The sport of ice dancing is also a performing art and an entertainment. It is judged by specified rules, which frequently undergo change, and which can be subject to many possible interpretations. Competitors are judged on the technical merit of their performance as well as artistic impression. When is the process of judging an ice dance performance like that of evaluating what a designer achieves, and when is it not?

Probably the most practical way of understanding what design means is to acknowledge what people know it to be, including the context in which the word is used. We can also establish the meanings of terms like design and designing by tracing their origins through studying the history of design and designers.

Look up the word 'design' in a dictionary and note how the word has been used over the years. How far back does the information go? Do you agree that design involves the notions of 'planning', 'purpose' and 'drawing'?

The root meaning of design involves the idea of setting down plans and schemes. Its modern usage has widened, although it still retains the essence of preparation and forethought concerning creative work. Design is essentially change through spontaneous or painstaking action derived from a decision arising from a synthesis of information.

In *A Dictionary of Art and Artists*, an Italian word, *disegno*, is said to

The meaning of the term design

The essential concepts of design given in dictionaries revolve around the notions set out below.

'A mental plan: a plan or scheme conceived in the mind and intended for subsequent execution; the preliminary conception of an idea that is to be carried into effect by action; a project.'

'Purpose, aim, invention, the thing aimed at; the end in view; the final purpose.'

'Contrivance in accordance with a preconceived plan; adaptation of means to ends; pre-arranged purpose; specifically used in reference to the view that the universe manifests divine forethought and testifies to an intelligent Creator'.

'Crafty contrivance, hypocritical scheming; an instance of this.'

'A plan in art: a preliminary sketch for a picture or other work of art; the plan of a building or any part of it, or the outline of a piece of decorative work, after which the actual structure or texture is to be complete; a delineation, pattern.'

'The combination of artistic details or architectural features which go to make up a picture, statue, building, etc; the artistic idea as executed; a piece of decorative work, an artistic device.'

'The art of picturesque delineation and construction; original work in a graphic or plastic art.'

have a variety of meanings, the simplest of which is 'drawing', and the next simplest 'design'. The *arti del disegno* are the visual arts in general, not just drawing alone, and sixteenth-century usage became more and more complicated, involving the idea of 'design [being] the sign-manual of God'.

For Vasari (1511–1574) the first art historian, who wrote about Renaissance art and artists,

> . . . *disegno* meant design, draughtsmanship, or simply drawing according to the context . . . design was the foundation of the fine arts in the philosophical sense that in the creative act the artist has (implanted in his mind by God) an Idea of the object he is reproducing. The figure he draws or carves must reflect both what he sees and the perfect form or design existing in his mind. (Renna, in *Lives of the Artist*, 1568)

It is worth reading Vasari's terms, at least to see how your own values colour *your* judgement about art, beauty or design. Vasari said, 'design is . . . the animating principle of all creative processes'.

So far these ideas about what design means apply to the arts and refer to 'ideal forms' of individual works. However, the essential ideas of preparation and perfection underline what we now understand as design. As the Industrial Revolution came about, the value of design drawing as a means of controlling production and passing on technical information to the different people involved in making and building things became apparent.

> It is the Age of Machinery, in every outward and inward sense of that word; the age which willing its whole undivided might, forwards, teaches and practises the great art of adapting means to end.
> (*The Mechanical Age*, Thomas Carlyle, 1795–1881)

A Victorian porch showing the use of patterns.

The influence of industrialisation on design, architecture, the fine arts and printing was very strong, especially through processes of mechanisation. Design was still considered to be concerned with form and style, especially by the Victorians. Engineers, architects and industrialists were the designers, and the influence of scientific methods also played its part in the invention of machines, products and devices. It was soon found that useful objects made even more money if they were also 'beautiful'. Thus, design was very important to Victorian manufacturing and trading. Design was seen as the necessary ingredient in giving 'mercantile value' to manufactured products – a preoccupation that still exists today.

The idea of design has had a long association with notions of patterning and ornamentation for both aesthetic and functional reasons. The use of drawing to create inventions undoubtedly became a widespread practice, and this was considered the 'art of the engineer', rather than the role of a designer.

In Prince Albert's opening speech at the Great Exhibition of 1851, he stated that the exhibition had been divided into four great classes:

i) raw materials;

ii) machinery;

iii) manufactures;

iv) sculpture and the fine arts.

These were the preoccupations of the Victorians, and it was, as Lethaby says, '. . . one of the first serious attempts to bring design and modern industry together . . .'.

By now people were becoming critical of the influence of design on their way of life. John Ruskin said, 'beautiful art can only be produced by people who have beautiful things about them, and leisure to look at them; and unless you provide some elements of beauty for your workmen to be surrounded by, you will find that no elements of beauty can be invented by them'.

The idea of design being needed so that products should be sound in construction and function soon came about and dominated trade. However, it was hoped that 'men were to be masters of their machines, to save their toil for more useful and rewarding labour' (William Morris).

Then design became divorced from making. In the early twentieth century the 'professional designer' appeared: someone highly trained, adept at using theoretical knowledge, a specialist capable of enhancing styles and tastes. This is an idea that meets with some criticism today. The modern usage of design is very widespread indeed, because it is associated with so many contexts, processes and practices. Design is concerned with preparation and forethought. It is a word that can be used to express the confidence that people have to bring choice and change into their lives.

Technological improvements in manufacturing have brought about mass production and consumerism. In turn, these have, to some extent, improved living standards and created and ensured the need for variety in consumer products and services. Design itself can be bought. Mass production, service industries and leisure industries have enabled design to become professionalised through flourishing studios and agencies.

Mechanisation and functionalism brought about the idea that the form of a product can be determined by its internal working parts. However, it is also possible to make something fulfil its function and yet look like something else. Notions of style and built-in obsolescence became major themes in manufacturing. People were encouraged to buy things not only for what they did but for what they looked like. Due to commercial pressures, this idea tends to dominate people's thinking today. Hence, the idea of the good life, where owning things of quality which represent good taste and fashion permeates people's thinking. Can this be seen in the article quoted below?

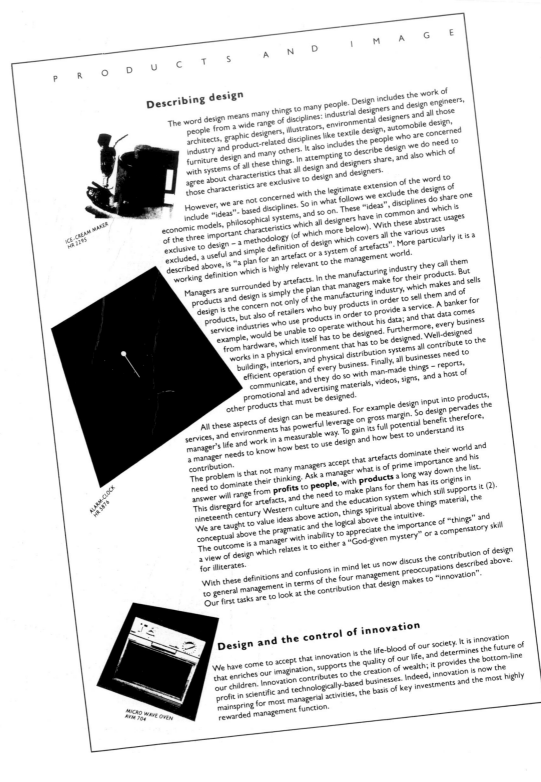

PRODUCTS AND IMAGE

Describing design

The word design means many things to many people. Design includes the work of people from a wide range of disciplines: industrial designers and design engineers, architects, graphic designers, illustrators, environmental designers and all those industry and product-related disciplines like textile design, automobile design, furniture design and many others. It also includes the people who are concerned with systems of all these things. In attempting to describe design we do need to agree about characteristics that all design and designers share, and also which of those characteristics are exclusive to design and designers.

However, we are not concerned with the legitimate extension of the word to include "ideas"- based disciplines. So in what follows we exclude the designs of economic models, philosophical systems, and so on. These "ideas", disciplines do share one of the three important characteristics which all designers have in common and which is exclusive to design – a methodology (of which more below). With these abstract usages excluded, a useful and simple definition of design which covers all the various uses described above, is "a plan for an artefact or a system of artefacts". More particularly it is a working definition which is highly relevant to the management world.

ICE-CREAM MAKER
HR 2295

Managers are surrounded by artefacts. In the manufacturing industry they call them products and design is simply the plan that managers make for their products. But design is the concern not only of the manufacturing industry, which makes and sells products, but also of retailers who buy products in order to sell them and of service industries who use products in order to provide a service. A banker for example, would be unable to operate without his data; and that data comes from hardware, which itself has to be designed. Furthermore, every business works in a physical environment that has to be designed. Well-designed buildings, interiors, and physical distribution systems all contribute to the efficient operation of every business. Finally, all businesses need to communicate, and they do so with man-made things – reports, promotional and advertising materials, videos, signs, and a host of other products that must be designed.

All these aspects of design can be measured. For example design input into products, services, and environments has powerful leverage on gross margin. So design pervades the manager's life and work in a measurable way. To gain its full potential benefit therefore, a manager needs to know how best to use design and how best to understand its contribution.

The problem is that not many managers accept that artefacts dominate their world and need to dominate their thinking. Ask a manager what is of prime importance and his answer will range from **profits** to **people**, with **products** a long way down the list. This disregard for artefacts, and the need to make plans for them has its origins in nineteenth century Western culture and the education system which still supports it (2). We are taught to value ideas above action, things spiritual above things material, the conceptual above the pragmatic and the logical above the intuitive. The outcome is a manager with inability to appreciate the importance of "things" and a view of design which relates it to either a "God-given mystery" or a compensatory skill for illiterates.

ALARM-CLOCK
HR 5876

With these definitions and confusions in mind let us now discuss the contribution of design to general management in terms of the four management preoccupations described above. Our first tasks are to look at the contribution that design makes to "innovation".

Design and the control of innovation

We have come to accept that innovation is the life-blood of our society. It is innovation that enriches our imagination, supports the quality of our life, and determines the future of our children. Innovation contributes to the creation of wealth; it provides the bottom-line profit in scientific and technologically-based businesses. Indeed, innovation is now the mainspring for most managerial activities, the basis of key investments and the most highly rewarded management function.

MICRO WAVE OVEN
AVM 704

New technologies and rapidly changing knowledge are strong features of today's design. More and more things have symbolic significance and this, together with materialism encouraged by financial considerations, is at the roots of modern design. Design is 'a plan for an artefact or a system of artefacts', according to Philips. This article establishes the meaning of design for a very large and successful international company. Notice how the idea of the design of economic models and philosophical systems is covered in the article.

It is vital that other people's views concerning design are appreciated, as well as the views expressed by organisations which, to a great extent, provide many examples of design for our use and pleasure.

Design is inseparable from modern industry and the modern economy, and as a fundamental part of the process which brings mass-produced artefacts to us all it is a significant component of contemporary material culture.' (*The Conran Directory of Design* by S. Bayley)

Wilkinson Sword's disposable razor, using a retractable blade instead of a removable protective covering, evolved from a need to keep the manufacturing costs down, and was designed by Ken Grange.

Study a modern disposable razor and consider the continuum of the following notions concerning invention, design, innovation and diffusion of such a product.

The influence on designers comes not only from their imaginations and expertise, but also from their society, culture and history. The consequences of design are worldwide, and we should not underestimate how design influences our lives.

An early razor design. What are the advantages and disadvantages of this product?

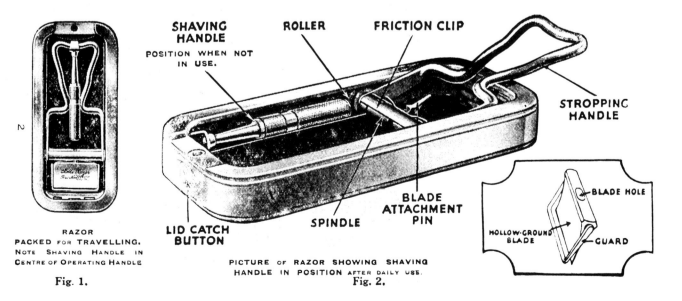

RAZOR PACKED FOR TRAVELLING. NOTE SHAVING HANDLE IN CENTRE OF OPERATING HANDLE

Fig. 1.

SHAVING HANDLE POSITION WHEN NOT IN USE.

ROLLER

FRICTION CLIP

STROPPING HANDLE

LID CATCH BUTTON

SPINDLE

BLADE ATTACHMENT PIN

BLADE HOLE

HOLLOW-GROUND BLADE

GUARD

PICTURE OF RAZOR SHOWING SHAVING HANDLE IN POSITION AFTER DAILY USE.

Fig. 2.

Terence Conran. How has he influenced design?

Why did this logo come about?

Stena Seawell in dock. What happened to one of the most technologically advanced shipyards in Britain at the end of the 1980s? What part did the following play in the demise of the shipyards at Sunderland: politicians, financiers, world market forces, the town, the workforce, other industries, the EC, government, technological trends, enterprise and training initiatives? Why is it that Sunderland cannot build ships on the Wear any more after 800 years' shipbuilding tradition? Who benefits from such large-scale change? Was the quality of design a factor in this saga?

It is necessary to know something of the history of design, especially certain key events, and, more important, the key connections that have brought together many forms of understanding to produce new and exciting designs. Personalities are very important in this regard because they usually provide the driving force and energy to sustain certain developments, and also have the courage to stand behind a good idea and make it work.

Study examples of leading personalities in the design world.

Can you predict an item that we will all be using in ten years time? The story of design is not just concerned with things, facts and systems, it is much more to do with a human desire to improve our quality of life. Such change can be on a small scale or on a grand scale; it may be hardly noticed at all, or come about so quickly that people have their breath taken away.

Did local owners of industry keep the industrial towns alive? Can city bankers and shareholders provide the same level of interest in local enterprises? Having worthy products, based upon excellent designs, and supported by efficient and skilled workforces is crucial to industrial success, but investment plays a vital role as well. Thus, getting things right is of value to national economies, and this is one role of good design. What is the most important change you have experienced or witnessed concerning the usefulness of design?

Being technologically aware has become an instinctive and institutionalised virtue. Today we are immersed in the economic and political troubles of trade figures, balances of payment and market pressures. We tend to think that being more efficient, or able to produce better designs will solve various economic problems. Britain is in competition with other countries, but we should also appreciate that design is part of our national character and that a great deal of what we achieve is derived from our history and individuality, rather than the latest production techniques.

In 1990 the Government predicted that there would be an increase of 142 percent in the number of cars on British roads by 2020. What will this mean for the general quality of life in Britain? Compare the design and development of cars over the last century with the development of roads in Britain. Are the roads adequate for the volume of traffic? There are many issues within this topic, and it might be useful to consider why it is

Accessibilité.

Le matériel roulant mis à la disposition des usagers a été étudié pour satisfaire au confort, à la sécurité et à l'esthétique.

Un de ses atouts : l'accessibilité. Le TAG constitue un pas décisif dans cette direction avec un plancher à 35 cm du sol et l'adoption d'une palette mobile utilisable à la demande pour les voyageurs en fauteuil roulant, etc.

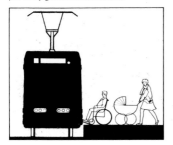

Pollution.

Le tramway entraîne une diminution importante d'émissions de polluants.

D'abord lui-même ne pollue pas. La consommation d'énergie électrique est propre. Mais cette diminution provient de la réduction du passage des bus dans le centre et de leur suppression dans certaines artères.

	Nombre de passages de bus diesel par sens à l'heure de pointe du soir	
	Réseau 1984	Réseau avec tramway
Rue Poulat	49	0
Avenue Alsace-Lorraine	54	0
Rue Lesdiguières	68	27
Boulevard Agutte-Sembat	30	30

Le tramway et la rénovation des lignes électriques du réseau SEMITAG entraînent une réduction sensible des véhicules thermiques.

Bruit.

Le tramway réduit le niveau sonore moyen de la circulation.

Voici deux exemples comparant le bruit émis par le passage du tramway à celui d'autres véhicules en situation de superposition au bruit de la circulation générale.

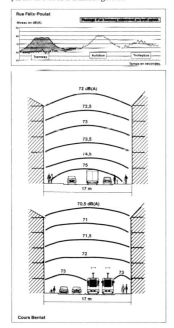

Many original ideas are the result of perceiving familiar things in a new way, for example, trams.
'Une ville et un tramway', SMTC Ville de Grenoble.

that on the one hand we have very fast and efficient vehicles, but on the other hand seemingly inadequate roads. This problem has much to do with the fact that an overall design strategy was not employed.

Total design is what is required here, so that all the relevant systems are taken into account together and not in isolation. Do we reason out all the factors required to solve major problems, or do we just let things happen? How would trade and communications benefit from one comprehensive design of Britain's transport system? Why do we continue to improve vehicles beyond the capabilities of the transport system that carries them?

Consider the relationship between support and investment strategies for public and private transport in Britain and Europe. Grenoble, in France, has invested in an efficient tramway system called TAG, which achieves *un impact économique et social* of genuine value to its citizens. Are trams an old solution to a new problem? Can they, through design, provide an important asset to a city and improve the quality of life for people through efficient city-wide mobility without congested streets? What are the economic advantages of public transport based on tramways? Cost is always an important consideration, especially with regard to energy consumption. Consider an energy audit for a city's use of a particular transport policy.

We have seen that design is intrinsic to technology, and both are elements of thought and accumulated experience. They are the mainstream of human history. They affect our daily lives in travel, leisure, housing and the workplace.

Le TAG, un matériel d'avant-garde

Le TAG répond à un cahier des charges très complet. Il doit satisfaire des attentes de confort et d'esthétique, des attentes de service et de sécurité et des attentes économiques.

Une esthétique de pointe.

L'esthétique générale du véhicule a fait l'objet d'une étude très poussée d'ergonomie et de confort. Le matériel possède une grande transparence intérieure, une finition extérieure soignée, et des aménagements fonctionnels et agréables pour le voyageur.

Les formes arrondies, les faces galbées, l'avant avec pare-brise panoramique, les grandes baies, participent avec les contours bleus et gris argenté, les teints aux vitres des portes et fenêtres à donner au tramway un "look" moderne et séduisant.

L'architecture du mobilier urbain et notamment des stations est dans le ton de ce design et conçue pour s'adapter agréablement au paysage urbain.

Design can be defined by the different contexts for human purposefulness, as much as through the form and function of things. It involves reason, intuition and discernment.

THE EVOLUTION OF AN INDUSTRIAL CULTURE

The origins of industrial design

Man is a social animal, distinguished by 'culture': by the ability to make tools and communicate ideas. Employment of tools appears to be his chief biological characteristic, for considered functionally they are detachable extensions of the forelimb. (*Man the Toolmaker*, Kenneth Oakley)

This anthropological view of human development is central to the evolution of art, design and technology, which can be traced back to the dawn of civilisation. Down the centuries many different individuals, civilisations and cultures have made their own unique contributions to the collective knowledge, skills and understanding, which we freely apply to our own contemporary requirements.

The Egyptians, Romans and Greeks influenced early European art and architecture and the style and form of everyday objects. Other civilisations such as the Incas, Chinese and the North American Indians created their own particular artefacts and environments,

Reconstruction of a carpenter's shop in the Housesteads Settlement on Hadrian's Wall, c. AD 125.

Ceramic jar in the shape of a female head, second or third century AD.

influenced by their lifestyle and beliefs, as well as by the materials and processes at their disposal.

The story of these great achievements has been the subject material of many commentators and critics throughout the ages and it is not the purpose of this book to trace all these developments. However, it is important that we try to understand the factors that have influenced the evolution of our contemporary environment, as well as the objects, images and systems contained within it.

It is clear that prior to the Industrial Revolution the visual appearance of artefacts was specifically related to the community from which they emerged, and they thus echoed the values and beliefs professed by that community. These values often manifested themselves in architecture, clothing, furnishings and religious works of art that were frequently interpreted in a slightly different way depending on climatic or nationalistic trends which could influence the use of materials or the symbolism deployed.

As Britain approached the eighteenth century, it did so with an air of optimism and commercial confidence. Overseas trade in products such as wool had accrued large profits and this was reflected in the growing affluence of the emerging middle class. Artist-designers such as Chippendale, Wedgwood and Minton catered for this élite market. Architects of the period also inspired many of the craftsmen of the day. The great eighteenth-century country mansions such as Blenheim, Harewood and Burleigh provided the perfect setting for the art, furniture, textiles and ceramics of the period as well as a showcase for artefacts collected from around the world, following the growth in trading, which were also to influence taste and fashion in their own particular way. Items collected by the upper classes were soon sought by the aspiring merchants and bankers of the middle class for use in decorating and furnishing their town houses, while the majority of the population made do with simpler and more utilitarian products.

A silver swan automaton that employs a complex mechanism to move the neck of the swan and catch the fish below. Produced in the workshop of James Cox c.1773.

While more artefacts were being produced in greater variety, there was still not the means of production to increase output significantly. As the eighteenth century unfolded, the nature of work and the techniques of manufacture began to move slowly away from a 'craft' based method of production, where the 'designer' and maker were usually the same person, to a gradual separation of these two tasks. Indeed, the term 'designer' is reported to have appeared in an English

In 1759 Edwin Lascelles commissioned Carr of York and Robert Adam to build Harewood House in Yorkshire.

dictionary as early as 1662, where it was defined as meaning: 'One who makes designs or patterns for the manufacturer or constructor'. Textile, ceramics and furniture producers were among the first to explore more sophisticated methods of production, embracing the division of labour and an increased use of mechanisation.

With these pressures for change, the Industrial Revolution gained impetus. It was centred around an unprecedented flood of technological developments and the organisational and social changes which resulted from them. Once begun, the upwardly spiralling momentum was concerned with speeding up production, meeting new demands and increasing profits. These new objectives inevitably resulted in the roles of designer and craftsman drifting apart, with the change from a home-based method of production to manufacture in a factory. From this time, mass production encouraged, and began to rely on, mass consumption, to the point where, today, they are mutually dependent. Despite these pressures, there still exists a strong 'craft' tradition in certain artefacts.

The rapid growth of industrial developments and inventions during the eighteenth and early nineteenth centuries

The Industrial Revolution was characterised by an impetuous growth in new inventions and processes and the harnessing of energy. In particular, the increased demand for iron and steel prompted new metal finishing processes and machine tools. This required craftsmen and engineers to look more carefully at exact measurement and accuracy of working and all of this greater output was made possible by the more efficient use of wind, water and steam as sources of energy.

The following list indicates a few of these developments and the personalities involved in them.

1709 Abraham Darby made cast iron using coke instead of wood, which significantly increased the output of the material and its availability.

1712 Thomas Newcomen's heat engine utilised steam to move a piston, which in turn worked a giant rocking beam that pumped water. Despite patent squabbles with Savery and although Newcomen's device was slow and inefficient, it was the first to harness power in a cylinder with any practical success.

1733 John Kay, a weaver and mechanic from Bury, developed the 'flying' shuttle, which enabled a single weaver to propel the shuttle through the shed and increased the efficiency by which broadcloth could be produced.

1739 Nasmyth invented the steam hammer, which greatly increased the size of forgings that could be produced.

1765 James Watt, an instrument maker at Glasgow University, decided to try to improve upon the efficiency of the Newcomen engine. This resulted in his version of the engine, with a separate condenser, eliminating heat loss, and allowing the cylinder to remain as hot as the steam throughout every stroke.

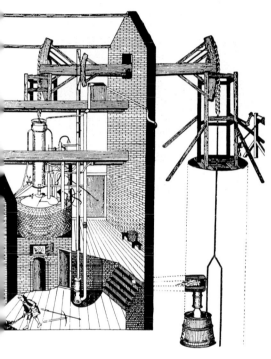

Thomas Newcomen's engine.

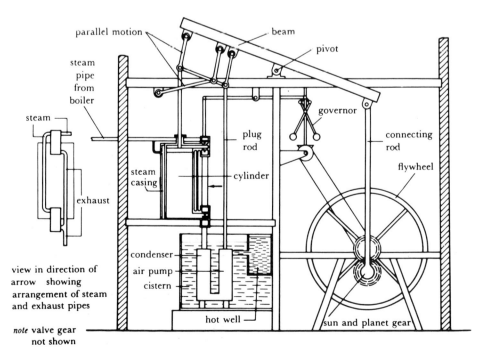

The Watt double-action engine.

1768 James Hargreaves's 'spinning jenny' increased the production of thread. Even the smallest jenny was capable of producing more thread in a day than six human spinners and their handwheels.

Hargreaves spinning jenny.

1769–75 Arkwright's patented water-frame for spinning cotton was much faster than the old spinning wheel and also spun a far stronger thread. This enabled cloth to be woven from pure cotton, rather than cotton mixed with flax as in the past.

1788? Watt's device of the 'sun and planet gear', consisting of two meshed cog wheels, enabled the up and down (linear) motion of the steam engine to be converted to a circular (rotary) motion, thus enabling the engine to replace water power as the method of driving belts, lathes, wheels and other types of machinery. The steam engine emerged as the workhorse of the Industrial Revolution.

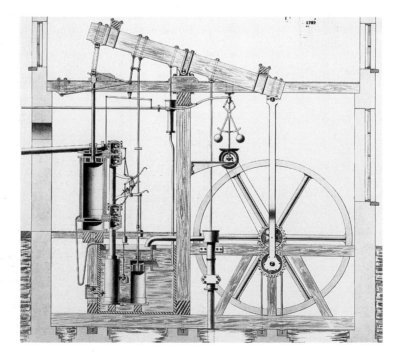

Watt's sun and planet gear.

A Jacquard loom.

1799 The Jacquard loom used a card program to lift individual warp threads in order to create complex patterns. This has been recognised as the forerunner of modern Jacquard computer systems, representing an early breakthrough in simple automation.

1829 George Stephenson's *Rocket* won the Rainhill trials for the right to work on the new Liverpool and Manchester Railway, at times attaining speeds of just over 30 mph (48 kmph)!

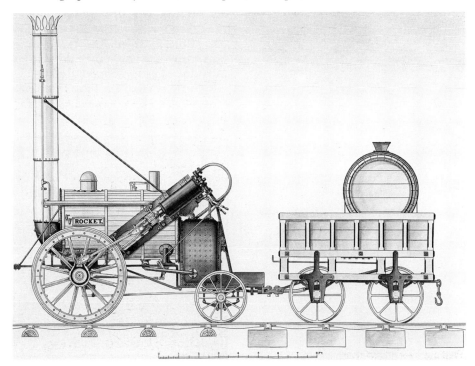

Scale drawing of Stephenson's Rocket, 1829.

Josiah Wedgwood, painted by George Stubbs.

Pioneers of early industrialisation

Josiah Wedgwood (1730–95) and the transformation of an industry

The existence of a ceramics industry in north Staffordshire was due to the abundance of both a suitable pottery clay and the necessary supply of coal needed to fuel the numerous small family-owned kilns that scattered the area. In the seventeenth century the products of the region were mainly functional dishes and pots made from coarse clays with little thought given to ornamentation. Indeed, it was only towards the end of the century that the quality of the wares gradually improved, partially as a result of the import of white clays from Devon.

Into this environment Josiah Wedgwood was born, the youngest son of a large family who were already established in the pottery trade. In 1744, at the age of fourteen, he was apprenticed to his eldest brother, Thomas, who had taken over the family business on the premature death of their father. Having 'served his time', Josiah then worked with a number of different partners in the local area. During this period his interest in experimenting with different clays, body glazes, colours and forms convinced him that commercial success would be based upon two important principles.

1. He had to produce products that would please the buyer, particularly the growing and affluent middle class.

2. Falling sales due to imported ware and the competition from porcelain could only be reversed by achieving an output of consistently high quality, using more sophisticated materials and processes.

When he eventually set up in business on his own, his commercial sense, coupled with his practical understanding of the industry, was to prove invaluable. He recognised the advantages of transfer decoration developed by the Liverpool-based firm Sadler and Green, which allowed the fine detail of a woodcut or engraving to be transferred to the glazed surface of the object to be decorated. He used slip casting and lathes for turning work, to improve steadily the quality of his goods.

Wedgwood worked tirelessly to improve his products and he introduced a durable lead glaze, resulting in his cream-coloured pieces, which he wasted no time in commercially renaming 'Queensware'

QUEEN's WARE and ORNAMENTAL VASES, manufactured by Josiah Wedgwood, Potter to her Majesty, are sold at his Warehouse, the Queen's Arms, the Corner of Great Newport Street, Long Acre, where, and at his Works at Burslim in Staffordshire, Orders are executed on the shortest Notice.

As he now sells for ready Money only, he delivers the Goods safe, and Carriage free to London.

☞ His Manufacture stands the Lamp for Stewing, &c. without any Danger of breaking, and is sold at no other Place in Town.

Advertisement from a newspaper of 1769.

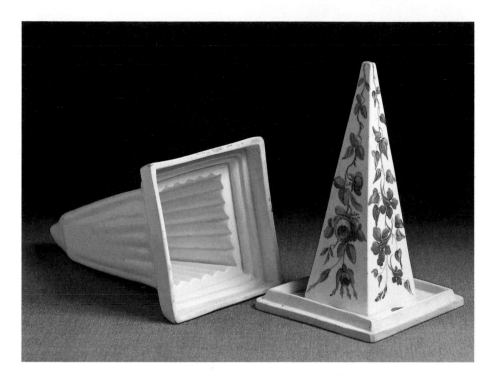

Queensware jellymould and cover, c. 1790.

following orders from the royal family. His black basalt ware and his green glazed ware were further outcomes of his developments. However, today Wedgwood's work is most easily recognised by the general public in the more expensive jasper ware, which depicted low-relief Greek and Roman themes, selected as a result of his recognition of the vogue for neo-classical decoration in the second half of the eighteenth century.

In his book *Wedgwood*, Geoffrey Wills considers his influence.

Few potters have created wares of such variety and beauty as typified by the Wedgwood pieces in private and public collections all over the world. Even fewer have established a style with such vigour that the impetus is being maintained over two centuries later.

Wedgwood's commercial vision included the following:

- He commissioned fine artists of the day, including George Stubbs, John Flaxman and Joseph Wright, who worked on designs for the top end of the market.

- His keen sense of designing for the customer included his recognition of the potential of neo-classical forms and decoration and their application to his wares.

- He established sales outlets in London as well as in his local area and he exported his wares to America, France, Spain and Italy.

- He successfully campaigned for new roads and canals, including the Trent and Mersey Canal, to assist with the distribution of materials during production as well as the transporting of finished goods.

- He recognised the need for a well-organised workplace employing a division of labour and mechanisation wherever it was appropriate.

Blue Jasper vase and cover with white relief, 1786.

Wedgwood's vision lay in his total approach to the design, production and marketing of his goods and he laid the foundations of a very successful industry which has survived the test of time.

Chippendale's letter to prince William Henry.

Thomas Chippendale (1718–79)

Thomas Chippendale was by trade a master wood carver and master cabinet maker; he was also an excellent designer and a shrewd businessman. He was responsive to the emerging styles of the period and consequently his designs reflect a variety of influences. It is estimated that Chippendale's premises in St Martin's Lane, London employed over 40 men, although many who left his employ set up their own businesses, including a group of Philadelphia cabinet-makers who were still producing typical Chippendale designs in the late 1780s in America.

Chippendale circulated his designs through his publication *The Gentleman and Cabinet-Maker's Director*, which was published in 1754 and 1755 and finally in a much enlarged version in 1762. Although the catalogues of designs were created for the wealthy upper classes, Chippendale was sufficiently shrewd to be aware of the emerging middle class and always offered to produce simpler designs for the less opulent householder.

Chippendale design influences

Early Georgian
The early part of the eighteenth century was characterised by heavy, chunky furniture. Decorative features included human and animal faces, lion heads, carved shells, sturdy pilasters and animal paws. Chippendale lightened these designs by using thinner sections, pierced backs and the ball and claw foot.

French taste – rococo
This was influenced by the style of Louis XV. The introduction of mahogany to the Western world allowed for the carving of the ribbon back chair, with all its extraordinary detail.

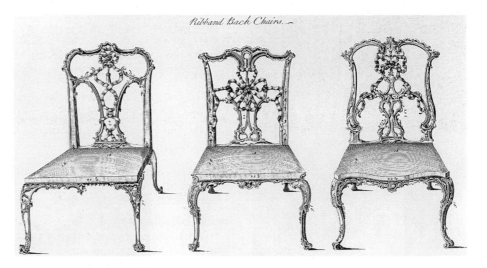

Chinoiserie
When traders from the Far East began to publish pictures and accounts of the strange and fascinating land of China, Chippendale, inspired by these accounts, created Chinese Chippendale furniture with its decorative framework and pagoda motifs.

Gothic

During the romantic revival of ancient gothic styles, this influence can be seen in Chippendale chairs, tables and bookcases with details and motifs including arched windows, carved pinnacles, trefoil motifs and other details found in medieval church architecture.

Classical

Can you identify the influences upon these design drawings for Chippendale furniture?

This was influenced by Robert Adam around 1760. Adam had returned to features found in classical Greek and Roman architecture, including columns, urns, swags of husk and other details.

Hall Chairs.

XVII.

T. Chippendale invt et delt.

Pubd according to Act of Parliamt 1759.

J. Taylor Sculp.

Mahogany

At the beginning of the eighteenth century walnut was still the most popular hardwood in use since its introduction in 1660 by Charles II following his period of exile in Holland. However, in 1720 a wood famine in France lead to an embargo on the export of walnut, which forced furniture manufacturers to look for alternative timbers. Spanish mahogany had been known in England for some time and it had gained in popularity thanks to the abolition of high tariffs in 1733. By 1753, 500,000 tonnes of mahogany were being exported through Jamaica, with additional supplies arriving from San Domingo, Cuba and Puerto Rico. The dark-reddish timber soon gained in popularity as the timber of the day, its strength and hard, heavy close grain allowing it to be carved with precise detail. The Cuban variety was outstanding as its hardness meant that it did not easily scratch, crack or warp, as well as making it resistant to attack from woodworm.

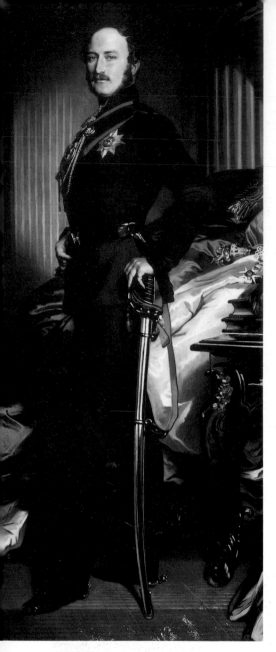

Prince Albert by F. Winterhalter.

Victorian lifestyles and the Arts and Crafts Movement

The Victorians were not looking for sameness or uniformity. They reacted in their literature, as much as their visual arts against what they saw as the dullness of the Georgian town, with its repetitive houses and streets. They wanted not uniformity but more variety, more diversity. They therefore searched in the past for inspiration for a future which would have not one face but many. (*Influences in Victorian Art and Architecture*, edited by Sarah Macready and F. H. Thompson)

When Queen Victoria's reign began in 1837, many of the key developments that were to drive the Industrial Revolution had already emerged. However, several of these changes took place at different times in different places. Consequently, Victorian Britain was the stage upon which most of these technological developments and the resulting social changes were to become consolidated. The growth of the great cities, shaped by the art and architecture of the time, was powered by steam and gas and serviced by railways and trams. Unfortunately, the rapid and massive increases in population in the new industrial centres caused a severe deterioration in living conditions for the masses. An extract from *Cloth for All* illustrates the problems of one typical mill town.

Between 1834 and 1836 a survey was carried out in Bury covering the living conditions of the working classes. 2,755 working class dwellings were examined of which 2,641 were houses, 46 single rooms and 68 cellar dwellings (at this time in Bury most of these cellar dwellings would be flooded by sewage in wet weather). These 2,755 dwellings housed 3,001 families totalling 14,322 people. It was calculated that the working classes formed 71% of the population of Bury and Bury's population had risen from about 7,000 in 1801 to 20,472 at the time of the survey. Out of the 3,001 families; 1,512 had members sleeping 2 or 3 to a bed; 773 families had 3 or 4 to a bed; 207 families had 4 or 5 to a bed with 15 families having 6 people in a bed. *Cloth for All*, Jennifer Bolt)

Critics today look back upon Victorian lifestyles and artefacts with mixed emotions, some extolling the virtues of Victorian enterprise, solidity and inventiveness, while others criticise the overelaborate use of applied ornamentation or the crude forms of many objects determined by the unrefined application of mechanisation.

Cutlery and razor by Mappin. An illustration from the 1851 Great Exhibition catalogue.

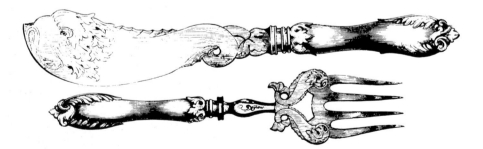

However, the Great Exhibition of 1851, skilfully organised by Henry Cole and Prince Albert, became the shop window of the world. It allowed the Victorians to celebrate their ingenuity and industry, and by inviting international involvement it signalled the outward-looking nature of the Empire and all the commercial implications this implied. Industrial output and commercial optimism were at a peak, although

'King Cole'; caricature of Sir Henry Cole (1808-1882), founder of the Victoria and Albert Museum and organiser of the Great Exhibition of 1851.

the social conditions that supported this growth, and the living conditions of the workforce, were quite miserable. It is therefore not surprising that questions should be asked about the value of this new way of life and whether industrialisation had been a terrible mistake from which there might still be some form of escape.

The Arts and Crafts Movement

The Arts and Crafts Movement led the crusade against the materialism and ugliness of Victorian England. This influential group, which included such scholars, artists and academics as William Morris, Dante Rossetti, Edward Burne-Jones and Ford Madox Brown, advocated a return to craftsmanship in preference to the mass-production processes of the time. They viewed the craftsmanship of the Middle Ages (prior to the artist Raphael), as free from the corrupting influence of capitalism and machinery and held the nostalgic view that the independence of the individual worker, operating once again in a small rural cottage and free from the division of labour, would be a practical solution to the problems of the day and a positive force in man's spiritual fulfilment. However, they were not just political philosophers, they were also a very committed and intense group of artists and designers.

William Morris and Edward Burne-Jones.

Sources of inspiration for their work

Romance
A great deal of pictorial work, including book illustration, tapestries, murals and ceramics, depicted Arthurian legend and typified their yearning for the Middle Ages.

Pomona, a silk and wool tapestry designed by Burne-Jones and woven by Morris and Co, 1890.

William Morris wallpaper showing designs of fruit, seaweed and daffodils.

Nature
The Movement saw flowers, leaves and the realism of nature as something that should be observed with pleasure and applied to all aspects of design work. Henry Wilson, a silversmith and jeweller, described how to design a pendant to be made in the form of a nightingale: 'First go and watch one sing. There are happily numerous woods and copses near London in which the nightingale can be heard and seen at almost any time of day . . . Take an opera glass'.

Materials and techniques

The group set about reviving the craft techniques of the past and returned to using traditional materials such as oak and natural stone from the locality in which a building was to be constructed.

Gothic style

In 1854, Morris and Burne-Jones undertook an 'aesthetic pilgrimage' to Belgium and northern France where they marvelled at the cathedrals of Rouen, Beauvais and Amiens. Morris recorded: 'I think these churches of northern France the greatest, the kindest and most loving of all the buildings the earth has ever borne'.

The Arts and Crafts Movement cannot be assessed briefly and is worthy of further study. It comprised many talented individuals covering a wide range of disciplines and expertise. It is easy to dismiss the movement as a progressive élite minority who saw themselves set apart, as artists, from the bourgeois philistines; however their work has made a lasting contribution to the evolution of design in the twentieth century.

Unfortunately, their mission to reverse the trends of mechanisation was, perhaps, an impossibility from the start. As John Gloag observes, their activities diverted a considerable amount of time and energy which could perhaps have been more profitably used in reforming the system and its artefacts rather than totally rejecting it. 'The Arts and Crafts Movement captured the interests of so many artists who might otherwise have been attracted to industrial design.'

Research the Art and Crafts Movement in greater detail and establish your own views about its contribution to twentieth-century design.

The quest for a modern style

One of the consequences of the Industrial Revolution had been to replace muscle power with machine power. However, as the twentieth century began, Britain, and for that matter the rest of the world, was still grappling with the difficult task of designing for mechanisation. In the aftermath of the exhibitions of 1851 and 1862, considerable debate had taken place surrounding the need to avoid vulgar and inappropriate ornamentation being applied to the industrial output of the day. When, in 1899, the South Kensington Museum was renamed the Victoria and Albert Museum, it was remarkable for the fact that Henry Cole chose to display badly designed objects so that their study might 'excite some higher ambition', thus promoting discussion and learning.

As part of this search for a new beginning, the roots of the Art Nouveau Movement lay in the rebellion against the classical and gothic revivals of the Victorians. However, the Art Nouveau movement did not herald a direct link with the Modern Movement that was to emerge later, as its many followers still championed a belief in individual creativity and handwork rather than the standardisation of a particular style focused upon machine production methods.

In his book *In the Nouveau Style*, Malcolm Haslam explains some of the influences that directed the movement:

Turning their backs on classical art, the artists who created Art Nouveau sought inspiration in nature. The flower was the motif probably used more than any other for the style. Poppies, roses, orchids, cyclamens, fuchsias and lilies were among the blooms most frequently depicted. They covered the façades of buildings and grew out of pieces of furniture, they were found on glassware and pottery, they were cast in bronze and carved in wood. Indeed one of the names given to Art Nouveau in Italy was *Stile Floreale*.

The majolikhaus, with its tiled facade, was built in Vienna by Otto Wagner in 1898.

While the Art Nouveau movement was particularly influential on the European continent, many of its devotees still looked to Britain as a fountainhead of ideas. Unfortunately, this period represented a missed opportunity as British artists and designers failed to carry this influence into the new Modern Movement. The pioneering work of experimenting with new materials and machine techniques in the true spirit of 'industrial design' passed to the Germans who established the *Werkbund* in 1907 and the Bauhaus in 1919. For this lost opportunity, the influence of the Arts and Crafts Movement has to be partially blamed. Through their antipathy to mechanisation, they failed to realise that machines, harnessed under skilful and sympathetic control, had the potential to produce well-designed products at much lower costs than hand-production methods, and by so doing offered the opportunity to raise the living standards of the very classes the Arts and Craft Movement was seeking to protect.

The growing influence of the Modern Movement

Much of the built environment in which we now live and the products that surround us owe their style to the philosophy of the Modern Movement. With its origins centred around the teaching of the Bauhaus, this new breed of architects, artists and designers looked

Joost Schmidt's poster for the Bauhaus exhibition in Weimar in 1923.

upon the creative use of materials such as steel, concrete and glass and the growth of modern machine processes as an opportunity to integrate aesthetics and mechanisation. Peter Behrens (1868–1940) symbolised this new thinking. He saw the potential for a natural harmony between art and technology, which he summarised in his book *Art and Technics* (1910). In 1907 he had joined the expanding German electrical products company A.E.G. He entered the organisation with a brief to establish a corporate design image for its buildings, brochures, advertisements, kettles, fans and lamps. As such, it was perhaps the first example of industrial design methods being applied as part of a total company policy. The reforms that the *Werkbund* had been established to enact were beginning to take place, and the momentum begun by Behrens was continued by Walter Gropius, Mies Van Der Rohe and Le Corbusier with enthusiastic vigour. The new movement was to have a profound influence on European and, later, American design practice. It preached the values of simplicity of form, following the function of the design. Applied decoration was abandoned and the aesthetics of the design were to be cultured from the technologies of production and a fidelity to the materials that were being used. The students of the Bauhaus studied elements of shape, form and colour as part of their foundation course and much of this learning can be recognised in the use of geometric elements to be found in their designs for architecture, graphics and products.

There can be little doubt that the Bauhaus and the Modern Movement led the way in a more harmonious integration of people and machines than the Arts and Crafts Movement would ever have considered possible. However, like any major cultural movement, its fortunes ebbed and flowed, particularly in the area of architecture where its ideas have been diluted for reasons of cost as well as quality, so that some of the practical implementations of modernist design principles have been far less successful than earlier theories suggested.

Experimental chair 1917 by Gerrit Rietveld © DACS 1994.

37

The Princess of Wales wearing a Bruce Oldfield dress, 1991.

Designing and making products for a mass market

When I asked an American money trader 'How far ahead do you plan?' the reply was '10 minutes'. A 10 minute profit cycle economy does not permit companies to invest in long-term development . . . We Japanese plan and develop our business strategies 10 years ahead. There are few things in the U.S. that Japanese want to buy, but there are lots of things in Japan that Americans want to buy. (Akio Morita, Chairman of Sony)

With the advent of the twenty-first century, it is perhaps beneficial to take stock of the present role of design within both a national and international perspective. This is a very complex subject, which today embraces economics as much as aesthetics.

The pioneering work undertaken by early production engineers, such as the American small-arms manufacturers Eli Whitney and Samuel Colt, and the automobile industry led by Henry Ford, pointed the way to increased output and efficiency through the use of interchangeable parts and the introduction of a production line. In due course, the American method of manufacture was copied and applied all over the world, leading in many cases to increased output efficiency and lower prices. This, in turn, meant that the products of industry became more accessible to a larger section of the population and created a gradual increase in living standards.

In our contemporary society the majority of products of design can be classified under three broad headings:

1. Individual or 'one-off' designs
   These are individual commissions such as jewellery, paintings, furniture or other craft-oriented design. They include individual fashion designs for famous people and prestigious buildings, often sponsored by individual or corporate patronage, for example the Lloyds of London Building designed by Richard Rogers.

2. Products made in small quantities or 'batches'
   These might include limited edition prints, small production runs of prestigious motor cars, some types of housing, and the manufacture of glass-reinforced plastic (GRP) boats on a small scale.

3. Mass-produced items, which may include thousands or even millions of a similar or identical design.

This range of products is enormous and includes international designs such as the Sony Walkman which currently has 89 models on offer and during its first eight and a half years of production sold 35,000,000 units worldwide! Our homes are filled with other consumer goods such as carpets and wall coverings, refrigerators and stereos, clothes and magazines, all produced by specialist companies hoping to reap the benefit of their investment from the high sales potential of a national and international market.

Industrial competition

The advanced manufacturing nations are now competing in world markets where characteristics such as the performance of the product, its customer appeal and selling price are all closely linked factors which can determine the commercial success or failure of a product with small margins for error. In Britain it is significant that in 1983 the trade in manufactured goods went into deficit for the first time since the Industrial Revolution. In 1990 that deficit was running close to £20 billion annually. If this trend is to be reversed, then a number of

Harrier jump jet.

strategies will have to be recognised and implemented across a range of disciplines. In a report on *Design and the Economy*, published by the Design Council in 1990, many of these strategies were identified and these are summarised below:

- Britain must produce goods that are not only competitive in price but are also competitive in terms of their appearance and reliability, quality of manufacture, materials and finish, as well as in their safety and ease of use and after-sales service. These 'non-price' factors are becoming increasingly important as the market demands more sophisticated products.

- There is a need for greater market awareness, which involves keeping in touch with the customers during both the initial design and developmental stages of a product as well as after they have bought the product.

- There is a significant need to improve the management of the design process in industry and to ensure that design and innovation have the right climate in which they can flourish. Peter Benton, Director General of the British Institute of Management, makes the following observation:

For too long, people have been aware that scientific ideas originating in Britain, or from British scientists, have found their economic exploitation elsewhere. Perhaps if we in Britain were better at using the technology we have invented so creatively, there would be a stronger case for spending more to generate future seed corn for economic growth . . . Technologists are often ignorant of business strategy and managers innocent of scientific education, so the transfer of technology faces special difficulties in Britain. Similar gaps in culture exist between suppliers and customers; government and industry; academia and the trading world; and – most significantly for Britain's economic growth – between the financiers and the companies that need their money.

It would be wrong to give the impression that all British industry is failing to compete successfully; many companies have invested considerably in research and development. However, as the statistics revealing the number of research and development (R&D) scientists and engineers employed as a proportion of the labour force shows, in 1986 Britain was bottom of the league of major competitors in this respect.

For Britain to reverse this decline, greater efforts must be made by all business, financial and educational sectors of the community, encouraged by a supportive political environment.

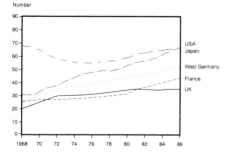

The number of research and development scientists and engineers employed per 10,000 labour force in USA, Japan, West Germany, France and the UK.

THE URBAN DESIGN CONTEXT

The built environment – its evolution and design

The aim of this chapter is to identify and explain the more recent social, economic and cultural factors that have influenced the evolution and planning of many of the towns and cities we now inhabit.

Most urban areas are composed of a wide variety of buildings designed for different purposes and usually belonging to a number of architectural periods and styles:

1. Domestic accommodation: private housing, public sector housing, (including flats)

2. Commerce and trade: offices and shops

3. Transport: bus and railway stations, airports and ports, garages and service areas

4. Cultural and religious: churches, cathedrals and temples

5. Recreational: cinemas, theatres, sport centres, restaurants, public houses, stadia and leisure parks

6. Public buildings: schools, hospitals and local authority offices

7. Historic and symbolic: castles, palaces, halls and museums

Bowes Museum, built by the Bowes family and opened in 1892.

This list is not definitive nor exhaustive and is presented merely to illustrate the diversity of buildings that begin to make up the built environment. Indeed, many buildings may have more than one function, for example a museum may perform both a recreational and educational role, and also be of historical or architectural significance as a building in its own right. However, as much as we may be interested in the architecture of an individual building, it is when large numbers of buildings are grouped together into towns and cities, and have to interface with one another, as well as meeting the expanding needs of industry, transport and a large urban population that the difficulties inherent in urban design or 'planning' become evident.

Patrick Nuttgens proposes that:

Planning might be defined as the study and control of factors physical, social, economic and aesthetic with a view to their integration and improvement for the benefit of the community. As such it is not a fixed or once and for all activity. It is an organic process. The planner casting his synoptic eye over the terrain for which he is responsible is like an artist struggling with a work of art which is different every time he looks at it. The subject matter changes as it is observed; the problem is indeterminate. (*Living in Towns*, Patrick Nuttgens)

This concept of urban planning is not a modern phenomenon; indeed, all great civilisations, including the Chinese, Greek and Roman, planned towns and cities to meet different demands. These might be for military or strategic purposes to defend certain routes or frontiers. In this way Berwick-on-Tweed guarded the English border with Scotland, while Lincoln was planned by the Romans as a centre for retired soldiers. Versailles was planned by Louis XIV as an architectural showpiece for his court and the centre of administration of France during the eighteenth century.

The evolution of the urban landscape

We can trace the origins of several of our towns and cities back through many centuries. However, as we have already seen in the chapter on the evolution of designed products, the catalyst that lead to the most significant transformation of our urban landscape was the Industrial Revolution. In particular, the eighteenth and nineteenth centuries saw massive population shifts as people poured into towns, either drawn by the prospects of employment or driven from the countryside where agricultural changes made them either landless or unemployed.

In his book *Understanding Towns*, David Stenhouse illustrates the problems created.

> Life for the poor in 1800 was short and unpleasant. This applied particularly to those living in the new industrial towns; in the market and county towns a community still provided some help for its less fortunate. The worst conditions were in the largest towns and cities. In Liverpool in 1840, the expectation of life at birth for a labourer's child was fifteen years, and sixty-two per cent of all children died before the age of five. In Bethnal Green, the poorest district of London, the expectation of life was sixteen years.

As the living conditions in the centres of most towns became desperate, and inner-city slums developed, those sections of the population in the emerging middle classes who had the means to escape, moved to the periphery of the towns, or the 'suburbs' as they were to become known. These occupations included engineers, managers, financiers, bankers and insurance salesmen supported by large numbers of accountants and clerks. This shift was assisted by the growth of public and private transport and the financial capacity of this section of the population to absorb this additional burden.

Towards the middle of the nineteenth century, it became clear to many politicians and civic leaders that there was an urgent need to improve the housing of the poor. The 'back to back' developments lacked basic sanitation and were overcrowded. These houses were characterised by having no running water or sanitary arrangements, little ventilation or natural light, and might be shared by up to eight

Campbell's Flags in about the year 1900: This squalid tenement was in Davies Street off Greengate, Salford. It was not demolished until 1911.

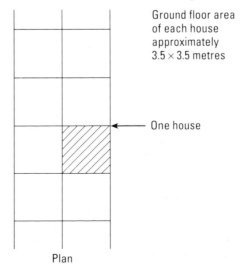

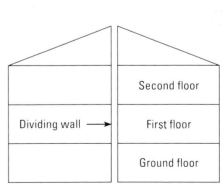

Ground floor area of each house approximately 3.5 × 3.5 metres

One house

Dividing wall →

Second floor

First floor

Ground floor

Section of three-storey house

Plan

Arrangement of 'back to back' dwellings in the mid-nineteenth century.

families, often being built around enclosed courtyards. In 1849, Dr John Snow proved that cholera in a London district was related to polluted water, due to the seepage of human waste through earth closets into underground water supplies. This sent a signal to the more affluent members of society that even they could not escape the consequences of the squalor and that reform was needed. In 1861 Prince Albert died of typhoid, and support for housing reform grew with each fresh outbreak of cholera.

A slum street, Manchester.

Throughout the nineteenth century a succession of Public Health Acts were passed, from 1837 onwards. Most of these acts gave powers to local authorities to deal with a variety of deficiencies, including surface drainage, street cleansing, street lighting, building bylaws and the appointment of Medical Officers of Health. Unfortunately, with the exception of the 1872 Public Health Act, which made the appointment of Medical Officers of Health compulsory, most of this legislation was permissive, i.e. it gave local authorities the powers to pass bylaws to enforce these Acts if they wished. The reality of the situation was that very few authorities took powers and reform was slow. An example of this is that although attempts were made to outlaw 'back to back' housing from 1840, it was not actually prohibited in Britain until the 1936 Housing Act made its construction a criminal offence.

Workhouse paupers hardly registered as human beings at all.

Aerial view of Salford.

The interior of the Eccles New Road workhouse in 1900.

The philanthropic businessmen

While many low-income families lived in rented houses that had been cheaply built by factory owners and were situated within walking distance of their place of work, there emerged a number of wealthy philanthropic industrialists who believed, often allied to their strong religious conviction, that their workers had the right to decent housing conditions and social amenities. During the nineteenth century a number of model communities were established that offered some hope for future generations.

1800 Robert Owen took over the management of cotton mills at New Lanark in Scotland, providing health and welfare provisions, a shorter working week and the first infant school in Britain.

1850–63 Titus Salt, a Bradford mill owner, commissioned the architects Lockwood and Mawson to plan and build 850 dwellings and additional community buildings including schools, public baths, wash houses, alms houses and a local institute on a 25-acre site near Bradford.

1888 William Lever, later Lord Leverhulme, a soap manufacturer, built Port Sunlight, providing a range of low-density housing as well as a full range of community facilities.

1893 George Cadbury started work on the new village of Bournville near Birmingham. It was designed around a central green with shopping facilities and other community buildings.

1902 Joseph Rowntree commissioned the architects Unwin and Parker to design the model village of New Earswick, York, intended for the workers of the Rowntree chocolate company.

Unwin and Parker were also involved in the design for Letchworth, the first garden city. Unfortunately, only a few thousand people benefited from these benefactors and the vast majority of the population was subjected to terrific hardship. By the turn of the century, the standard type of low-income dwelling in most towns was the 'bylaw terrace'. These were houses built after 1859 by speculative builders, and were subject to certain regulations that were laid down to control minimum requirements for street widths, heights of

'The war is over...'

buildings and other factors affecting house layout and structure. Many terraces are still in evidence today, being notable for their backyards, outside toilet and coalshed. Many of the superior type also had bay windows at the front, and have since been modernised to include baths, inside toilets and central heating.

A land fit for heroes

At the end of the First World War, promises were made to provide 'a land fit for heroes'. Part of this initiative was the 1919 Housing & Town Planning Act, which required local authorites to produce schemes for house building, and established central government responsibility for providing financial assistance towards this. This was the advent of 'council housing', with a new style emerging, based around the three-bedroomed, semi-detached house, with kitchen, bathroom and garden. These were planned at a much lower density than terraced housing and they appeared in crescents and closes as well as in a linear formation. From 1919–25, 200,000 of these houses were built.

The urgent need for a large number of acceptable homes after the First World War meant that, for the first time, the state became involved both by building houses and by creating conditions to encourage the private sector.

The growth of middle-class housing

The 'suburbs' were to emerge as the main residential area for the aspiring middle class, with access to nearby centres of industry and commerce and efficient transport systems to help the 'commuter' if required. The Industrial Revolution had sponsored considerable upward social mobility, and while many of the new professions did not pay their members significantly more than many artisans, the new emerging middle class had a different set of aspirations, often centered around the status symbol of the home.

Children at one of Salford's dock strikes in 1907.

Towards the end of the nineteenth century there also emerged the notion of the house in the suburbs as a retreat from the town – a 'cosy' country cottage ideal. These influences were partially a result of the Arts and Crafts Movement, and they had a significant influence on the 'country' features that appeared in house designs and manifested themselves as imposing, steeply pitched roofs, windows placed to suit the internal layout (rather than in a set pattern to reflect the building's façade) and the use of local bricks, tiles and timber weatherboarding. Often, structural beams would be left exposed, chimney stacks would be high and some walls pebbledashed and rendered.

An additional catalyst to the growth of the suburbs was the existence of a reasonably efficient transport system. This was particularly true in London which, in Victorian times, was the largest city in the world. Initially, much of the demand was met by privately owned horse-drawn buses, and followed by the introduction of trams in 1870. The train system was at first slow to react to the potential commuter market, but in 1890 the first tubes began to appear, and by 1910 London had quite an extensive underground network. With further expansion of the tube to the suburbs, builders eager to sell their houses planned developments around the extensions of existing lines and the opening of new stations.

Suburban housing in the inter-war period still tried to fulfil the romantic images of the home (often depicted in stained glass and other features), but the functional requirements of families had changed. While the middle class as a group was still expanding, the average family size fell from 5.8 in 1871 to 2.2 in the 1930s. The group was also poorer than its Victorian counterparts, so these people would not have servants. Their needs were for a cheaper, smaller house that could be easily maintained. Demand was high as mortgages were plentiful, with low interest rates.

Suburban style – the British home 1840–1960.

The style chosen by the builders – mock Tudor or 'Jacobean' – satisfied a curious ambivalence towards the home among the middle classes of the day. The typical mock Tudor semi with its rose-filled front garden was highly functional and modern in some respects, particularly in the kitchen and bathroom, but at the same time cosy and cottage-like, much more rural in atmosphere than any previous speculative housing. Half-timbering, perhaps with herringbone brick infill, leaded lights, inglenooks, tile-hung bays, red brick or pebbledash walls and gabled roofs all combined to give a picturesque if not positively romantic image of a country cottage. (*Suburban Style*, Helena Barrett and John Philips)

In 1801 the population of England and Wales was just under nine million, with only 17 per cent of this number living in towns of over 20,000 inhabitants.

In 1901 the population had more than trebled to 32.5 million, and of these over 50 per cent lived in towns of over 20,000 inhabitants.

The garden cities movement

The idea that our towns and cities needed to be thought out anew was proposed by Ebenezer Howard in his book *Garden Cities of Tomorrow*, published in 1902. The main thrust of his proposals were that:

- Industry should be decentralised from the inner zoned areas, which should consist of parks, houses and gardens.

- The size of the town should be limited to between 30,000–60,000, with the ultimate size of the development being restricted by a green belt of rural land around the city.

- There would be a predominance of family housing with relatively large gardens.

- These new developments would be built on completely new sites to cope with the growth of and overspill from larger cities.

This philosophy was to influence the building of a number of garden cities including Letchworth and Welwyn, as well as all of the subsequent new towns that have been built (see page 55).

Yesterday

Living and Working in the Smoke

To-day

Living in the Suburbs – Working in the Smoke

To-morrow

Living & Working in the Sun at WELWYN GARDEN CITY
Houses for immediate occupation have been built and
are now for sale. Sites for Factories and Industrial
purposes are also available.
Apply to Estate Office: WELWYN GARDEN CITY, Herts.
and at 5 GRAY'S INN PLACE GRAY'S INN W.C.1

High-rise development

The devastation created by bombing during the Second World War left many of our inner cities desperately short of homes. This was further exacerbated by the 'baby boom' of the 1950s, when servicemen returning home got married and started families. Added to this, much of the existing housing stock of Victorian and Edwardian design was in very poor condition and greatly in need of 'modernisation'. Towards the end of the 1950s as the population density of towns increased, many local authorities looked at alternative ways of housing families quickly and economically. As the price of land increased, architects and planners looked to the ideas and proposals of European architects such as Le Corbusier, who saw the idea of high-rise development as a way of solving many of the housing needs, as well as the social ills of the day.

The feature on Le Corbusier (page 51) outlines what were perceived to be the social and practical advantages of high-rise development. However, in retrospect it has to be said that this type of development has not proved popular for a whole variety of reasons. In particular, communities were broken up during rehousing. Families with young children were often placed on higher floors within the block, creating access problems for parents with prams and young toddlers. The older children often had nowhere to play and became a nuisance to neighbours. Lifts frequently broke down, making access almost impossible for old people. Vandalism seemed to increase, and while this was not totally due to the building design, many landings, corridors and lifts were vulnerable. In addition to these problems, many blocks had been built in a very shoddy way, which lead to dampness and a deterioration of the concrete and other materials used

On January 11 1969 Victor and Audrey Johnson, a quiet couple in their 50s, spent the evening at home as they usually did. They watched the television and then went to bed. In the early hours of the following morning two teenagers, to be described later by a judge as "not the brightest of fellows", used a washing-up liquid container to squirt petrol through the letterbox of the Johnsons' 17th floor flat. Then they poked lighted matches through and into the puddle of petrol.

The emergency operator who took Audrey Johnson's 999 call heard her coughing and calling out to her husband to break the door down. His fingerprints in the soot showed that he tried but he could not. Nor could the fire brigade. The Johnsons, afraid of the burglars, muggers and gangs of drug-excited youths who roamed both the streets of Stockwell and the concrete corridors of the tower block in Grantham Road, had turned their maisonette-style flat into a fortress.

There was a heavy-duty steel grille bolted over the front door and steel bars screwed into the frame of the door which led from the upper floor of their flat to the fire-escape corridor.

Last autumn their next-door neighbour, 23-year-old Mark Allan, with whom Audrey Johnson had remonstrated about playing loud music all night, was convicted of manslaughter and incitement to arson and jailed for 12 years.

Journalists who followed up the story found that many of the residents in Pinter House and other Sixties tower blocks had similarly fortified their homes. Lambeth Council, which had, in response to pressure from the residents' organisation, agreed to install entryphone systems just two days before the fire, said no permission to fit steel doors had been requested. A spokesman for a security firm said that steel doors and grilles especially designed for tower blocks were " A real Eighties boom industry".

Not for the first time the press and public wondered at the lack of imagination and the financial niggardliness which had turned the promise of high-density, modern housing for all into a nightmare of vertical mean streets where decent people scurried furtively in their front doors and barricaded themselves in.

Not for the first time the architects took the blame. For weren't the soaring monoliths and the romantic sounding "street in the sky" their panacea? What were they going to do about it? Some blocks were deemed beyond rescue and blown up to general applause. But lack of resources means that cheaper and more thoughtful solutions must be found. The fire-trap doors have now gone from the Grantham Road Estate, replaced by toughened wood multi-lock security doors (smart natural wood with brass knockers and letter boxes), and work is proceeding on the rest of a £2 million package to make the three towers not only safe but attractive places to live. The architect is Cathy Salisbury of Floyd Slaki, a Clapham-based practice which specialises in Multi-Storey Block Improvements (MSBI).

"It's important," says Cathy Salisbury, "that a tower block resident feels at home and safe as soon as he or she enters the building's front door. The corridors are corridors, not dark streets where strangers can hide and menace you. All the surfaces in the Grantham Road blocks were rough-faced concrete, a very inhospitable material."

She indicated the narrow dank ground-floor entrance to Pinter House, more like the way into an underground carpark that to a dwelling. "This was not intended to be the main entrance," she explained.

"Back in the Sixties, when the three blocks were built, Lambeth planned a much larger estate and all the towers were to be linked by walkways at first-floor level where the entrances were to be."

The Grantham Road towers will soon have much more impressive entrances. Cathy Salisbury has designed single-storey extensions to house a reception area for each block. In this spacious, well-lit brick and glass, tiled lobby, a concierge will sit behind a large security desk with a bank of closed circuit television screens which give views of strategic points in and around the block. Visitors have a long walk from the street door around the curve of the desk and under the eye of the conceirge to the steps and ramp to the locked door which gives access to the lifts. There will be two concierges working a shift system and when they are not on duty an entryphone system will operate.

"A serious problem with the tower blocks has always been ease of access," says Cathy. " Not only are the external pathways often used as thoroughfares but very often people use the buildings themselves as short cuts or places to loiter. The new scheme means there will be only one entrance to each building and only people who have business in the block will be admitted.

"Then there's the problem of the surrounding areas. The Grantham Road towers are built around a small green but, since it is the only green patch in the area strangers bring their dogs there to walk them. Not only is the grass fouled with dog dirt but the dogs themselves are menacing, pit bulls and the like. So we are fencing off the green to emphasis that it is a private area and it will be monitored for trespassers."

The "blueprint" for Floyd Slaski's MSBI work is the neighbouring Westbury Estate. Here Cathy Salisbury's colleague, David Whitestone, incorporated the reception areas in the buildings, giving them bright, smart new entrance and an entryphone system. Both here and at Grantham Road the unfriendly concrete exteriors have been covered in brickwork for two storeys.

"High quality materials are very important," he says, indicating the tough damson coloured carpet and the smart quarry tiles on the floor of the top-storey lobby. "People seem to respond well to good, expensive-looking materials; they take a proprietary pride in them and look after them." As if to prove his point, he opened the new wooden fire door to the unchanged concrete back stairs - and a litter of fag ends and empty crisp packets.

Each front door now has a porch flush with the wall which, together with the much higher level of lighting, means there are no hiding places.

There are well protected cameras in the lifts but, says David Whitestone, mirrors are an effective deterrent for spray-can doodlers and muggers. "It's interesting psychologically," he says, " the people do not like to watch themselves doing unpleasant things."

There will be concierges and every resident will be able to tune into the closed circuit surveillance system on their own screen.

Floyd Slaski's client on both projects is Lambeth Council but its brief comes from the residents. "The most common problem," says Cathy Salisbury, "is violence. Beyond that, however, each estate is different and calls for different solutions. Only the residents know what they need.

"There is usually a residents' association to deal with because it is usually only because of pressure from them that the client is commissioning the work in the first place. They are without exception well organised and representative."

Dave Hirst is chairperson of the Grantham Road Residents' Association. He lives on the floor beneath the Johnsons' flat, on a sparklingly clean corridor with polished linoleum floor, freshly painted walls and hanging baskets of silk flowers at every chic new brass-knockered door. "Over the years," he says, "standards in the blocks had declined dramatically. There were break-ins, vandalism, threatening strangers in the corridors. The tenants were terrified."

The residents started to demand changes from the council four years ago but found the way through the various levels of the bureaucracy complicated, time-consuming and frustrating. "It took us three years to get the security doors," says Dave Hirst, "and at first they offered us 80. There are 252 households on the estate. What good are 80 doors? How do you choose who gets them?"

The fight is won, yet attendance at the residents' meetings has hardly flagged. Fighting the council for acceptable surroundings and adequate level of personal safety may finally have achieved what the buildings' original architects thought they were designing: a community in the sky,

But you cannot have that cut-price. As Cathy Salisbury says:"People recognise cheap and tacky, you know."

Tower Power. The Guardian, April 16, 1990.

in construction. The article 'Tower Power' illustrates a particular example of these problems, and explains what architects are trying to do to improve the situation.

In recent years there has been considerable debate not only about the planning of our towns and cities, but also the conservation of the countryside from the growing pressure to develop more roads, homes and commercial properties. Large retail developments have been established on the fringes of towns, allowing for easy access and parking while taking precious trade away from many traditional town centres. There has been considerable investment in inner-city regeneration, of which, perhaps London's docklands have been the most notable example. Housing styles have varied from the single storey, three-bedroomed, semi-detached house to the refurbishment and domestication of converted warehouses and granaries on wharfs.

The pace of change in our urban environment continues to accelerate, and there is concern that commercial interests may override the social, aesthetic and environmental concerns of the individual. HRH the Prince of Wales entered this debate in 1989, with his 'Vision of Britain' campaign. This involved a TV programme, an exhibition at the Victoria and Albert Museum and a book based on the Prince's concern:

> For a long time I have felt strongly about the wanton destruction which has taken place in this country in the name of progress; about the sheer, unadulterated ugliness and mediocrity of public and commercial buildings, and of housing estates, not to mention the dreariness and heartlessness of so much urban planning.
>
> . . .
>
> The fashionable architectural theories of the 50s and 60s, so slavishly followed by those who wanted to be considered 'with it', have spawned deformed monsters which have come to haunt our towns and cities, our villages and our countryside. As a result of thirty years of experimenting with revolutionary building materials and novel ideas, burning all the rule books and purveying the theory that man is a machine, we have ended up with Frankenstein monsters, devoid of character, alien and largely unloved, except by the professors who have been concocting these horrors in their laboratories – and even they find their creations a bit hard to take after a while.

The Prince of Wales 'Vision of Britain' campaign.

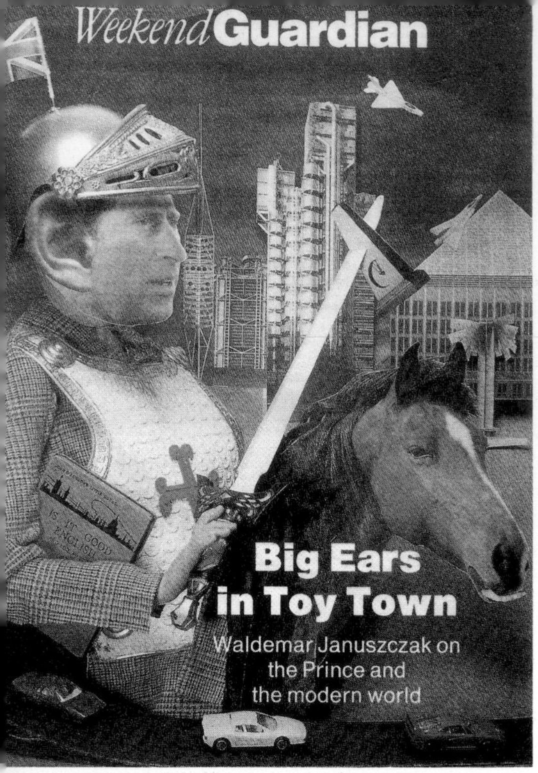

**Big Ears
in Toy Town**

Waldemar Januszczak on
the Prince and
the modern world

The Prince's campaign received a mixed
reaction.

As a positive way forward Prince Charles proposed 'ten principles' that architects and planners should reconsider. 'What follows, therefore, is not new. It is a simple extension of the rules and patterns that have guided architects and builders for centuries. I hope it may be a timely reminder.'

- The place: don't rape the landscape.

- Hierarchy: if a building can't express itself, how can we understand it.

- Scale: less might be more, too much is not enough.

- Harmony: sing with the choir and not against it.

- Enclosure: give us somewhere safe for the children to play.

- Materials: let where it is be what it's made of.

- Decoration: a bare outline won't do; give us the details.

- Art: Michelangelo accepted very few commissions for a free-standing abstract sculpture in a forecourt.

- Signs and lights: don't make rude signs in public places.

- Community: let the people who will have to live with what you build guide your hand.

The prince's criticisms and proposals received considerable popular support, while many architects and critics viewed his comments as retrospective and narrow-minded. Carefully consider the ten principles outlined by Prince Charles. To what extent do you agree or disagree with his arguments for change?

Planning

Planning is defined in the *Oxford English Dictionary* as the 'controlled design of buildings and the development of land'.

Architects are mainly concerned with the detailed design of individual buildings.

Planners are interested in the overall design of groups of buildings.

Developers are concerned with the process by which new buildings, roads, railways, parks, recreational facilities and industry can evolve into a community.

The term **community** can either have a specific geographic meaning or can be used in a social context.

Le Corbusier.

Pavillon Suisse, 1930–1933.

Le Corbusier

In March 1987 an exhibition organised by the Arts Council of Great Britain, in collaboration with the *Fondation Le Corbusier*, Paris was staged at the Hayward Gallery in London to commemorate the centenary of the birth of Charles Edouard Jeanneret – Le Corbusier. The exhibition was entitled 'Le Corbusier, Architect of the Century'.

While many critics and observers would begrudge Le Corbusier this accolade, there can be little doubt that this controversial artist and architect has had a profound influence upon our towns and cities, as well as on a generation of architectural students who identified him as their modernist role model.

When, in 1917, he moved from his home in the Suisse Romande to Paris, he had already gained experience of reinforced concrete and was well acquainted with many of the great names of the European Modern Movement, including Peter Behrens, Walter Gropius and Mies Van Der Rohe. Le Corbusier was deeply committed to the idea that architecture was not just a practical or decorative art but also had the capacity to win over the human spirit, and that this could be harnessed for the good of society. His early work was geometric, hard-edged and functional and his designs for the Villa Savoye introduced 1920s architects to a whole range of new features including plain white walls concealing reinforced concrete and blockwork, flat roofs, thin horizontal windows, long ramps and free-standing staircases.

His work as an artist continued alongside his architecture, and he appeared to use his painting as a way of interpreting and referencing his ideas for architecture. The source material for this work was rarely abstract, making reference to natural materials and objects as well as the female form, and in his designs for the Pavillon Suisse of 1930–33 there is a unity of square geometric concrete forms and curved surfaces using natural stone.

As the 1930s approached, Le Corbusier had begun to establish an international reputation, and he became interested in architectural solutions that might be employed anywhere in the world. He believed that he knew how to resolve the conflict between people and machines, and that the dreariness and drudgery created by the first machine age could be transformed into a more harmonious industrial culture – the second machine age. His philosophy that 'a house is a machine for living in', was not meant to imply that houses should look like machines, merely that houses should serve their inhabitants in the same way any other machine might serve its user. Consequently, houses need not represent any preconceived idea of what a house should look like.

The Cité de Refuge building in Paris, completed in 1933, confirmed Le Corbusier's passion for glass curtain walling. Unfortunately, in this project the windows were sealed, causing the building to overheat, partially as a result of the installation of a cheaper air-conditioning system than had been specified by the architect. Le Corbusier learnt valuable lessons from this experience and on many of his other buildings he incorporated integral sun shields or *brise soleil* as they were known. Other features to emerge from his designs included the use of *piloti*, short vertical columns at the base of his buildings, as well as *aeraturs*, which were large ventilation points fitted with insect filters.

Cité de Refuge, Paris 1933.

One of the architect's most influential pieces of work was the Unité d'Habitation in Marseilles, completed in 1952. It contains a multi-storey block of flats with other amenities, set in open parkland. This, perhaps more than any other building, pointed the way to the much-copied high-rise housing schemes that were to become a feature of most European cities in the 1960s. There can be little doubt that Modernism was pilloried for the simplistic way in which its ideals were often copied in inappropriate and insensitive ways. That many of these subsequent hybrids have totally failed to meet the practical and emotional needs of families and individuals would have been a complete contradiction of Le Corbusier's intentions.

Unité d'Habitation, Marseilles, 1952.

Notre Dame de Haut, Ronchamp 1950–1955.

In his exhibition guide, *Le Corbusier, Architect of the Century* Colin Davies makes the following observation:

> Moreover, the social and urban problems that the modernist pioneers set out to solve are still with us. There is still a chronic housing shortage and our cities seem to be in continuous crisis. The new revivalist architecture has nothing to say on these subjects. If architecture is to face up once again to its social responsibilities, then the example of Le Corbusier will be instructive – in both the positive and negative senses.

Timber and brick house.

Brick and block house.

Modern housing – construction and styling

Modern housing in Britain is dominated by two constructional techniques: brick and block, often referred to as the traditional method of building houses; and timber-frame construction, more accurately referred to as timber and brick.

On an international basis, 70 per cent of low-rise family housing in advanced Western countries is built using timber frame. In the last 30 years some 600,000 such homes have been built in Britain and currently 35 per cent of all new house-building employs this technique. Timber and brick has the advantage of being quick to build and is as reliable as traditional brick and block construction, providing good site management is employed during storage and assembly. In the late 1980s timber-framed housing in Britain received poor press and TV coverage, when numerous examples of poor site management and incorrect assembly procedures were highlighted. These malpractices resulted in the panels becoming damaged by rain, creating dampness problems for the new householder. Unfortunately, the industry had introduced a system, the subtleties of which its traditional workforce did not fully comprehend. There has been considerable effort to redress the damage caused by this episode, and there is today a greater awareness of the need to adopt a more cautious approach on site and during construction if the benefits of the technique are to be fully realised.

Construction methods – carrying the loads

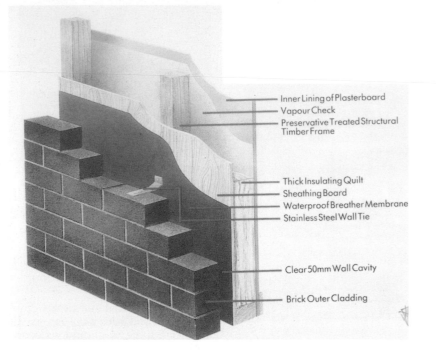

Inner Lining of Plasterboard
Vapour Check
Preservative Treated Structural Timber Frame

Thick Insulating Quilt
Sheathing Board
Waterproof Breather Membrane
Stainless Steel Wall Tie

Clear 50mm Wall Cavity

Brick Outer Cladding

In the traditional brick and block house, the internal wall of concrete blocks and the external wall of facing blocks support all the loads in the house. In the timber and brick house, the internal wall of concrete blocks is replaced by a structural timber frame. These frames are usually made up of modular wall panels constructed in a factory under strict quality control and then assembled on site. This frame is so strong that it carries all the loads of the house itself, without relying on the external brick wall.

The benefits of timber and brick
- The thermal insulation properties of timber and brick houses are significantly higher than those currently advocated by building regulations. The thermal performance of a timber-frame wall is about one third better than a traditional masonry construction.

- The inner frame is a much drier construction than traditional brick and block. Far less moisture is used in the construction, allowing the house to be decorated as soon as it is finished. The average semi-detached house consumes approximately 2,500 litres of water in its construction, and time is required for this to dry out, with all the additional problems of the plaster cracking.

- The modular nature of the frames allows the dimensions of the rooms to be far more accurate, with walls meeting at 90 degrees and fitted furniture actually fitting!

Modern houses – old-fashioned styles
Modern house construction employs numerous examples of materials selected for their outstanding properties. The use of PVC in drainage, gutterings and double-glazed window frames brings a tough light-weight plastic into situations where its weather-resistant properties, coupled with its ease of use, make it an ideal material for the job. Despite the appropriate use of many advanced materials, most house styles are retrospective in their design. They include examples of

The Banbury

(H401T) Four bedroom detached house with double garage

DAVID WILSON HOMES

DAVID WILSON HOME CENTRES
LEICESTER · OAKHAM · NOTTINGHAM · BOURNEMOUTH
NORTHAMPTON · SOUTH MIDLANDS

In keeping with our policy of providing individuality, external treatments often vary from one plot to another. We therefore recommend that purchasers ask our Sales Advisors for details of the treatment specified for individual plots.

black and white 'plastic Tudor' façades, 'plastic leaded' windows and GRP Georgian pillars.

Why has the hi-tech or post-Modern influence of many public buildings not really filtered down into the conservative housing market?

How many builders market nostalgia in their house styles and advertising?

Why does the customer want to own something new that looks old?

Garden cities to new towns

To develop a balanced community enjoying a full social, industrial and commercial life.

During the nineteenth and twentieth centuries we have seen how the evolution of towns has been influenced by three main factors:

1. The relationship between home and work, and the need for community services and shopping facilities to be readily available.

2. The growing demands for recreation and leisure facilities, coupled with the desire to live in a 'pleasant' environment.

3. The influence of transport systems, in relation to the growth of the suburbs as well as to the problems of congestion created by the car.

The approach used to resolve these particular constraints was often piecemeal, and very little progress had been made in producing a more holistic overview of planning. Many of the ideas pioneered by the philanthropists such as Salt, Lever and Rowntree were brought together in 1898 by Ebenezer Howard in his book *Tomorrow: A Peaceful Path to Real Reform* (republished in 1903 under the now-famous title *Garden Cities of Tomorrow*). Howard's proposals included plans for a number of developments where the needs of the whole community were to be planned for in an integrated way. His ideas influenced the building of Letchworth, the first garden city, begun in 1903, Hampstead Garden Suburb (1907) and Welwyn Garden City, begun in 1919.

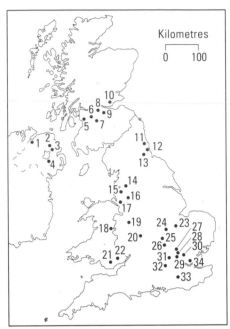

Designated New Towns in the UK

N.IRELAND	NORTH-WEST	SOUTH-EAST
1. Londonderry	ENGLAND	ENGLAND
2. Ballymena	14. Central	23. Peterborough
3. Antrim	Lancashire	24. Corby
4. Craigavon	15. Skelmersdale	25. Northampton
	16. Warrington	26. Milton Keynes
SCOTLAND	17. Runcorn	27. Stevenage
5. Irvine		28. Welwyn
6. E.Kilbride	WEST MIDLANDS/	Garden City
7. Stonehouse	MID WALES	29. Hatfield
8. Cumbernauld	18. Newtown	30. Harlow
9. Livingston	19. Telford	31. Hemel
10. Glenrothes	20. Redditch	Hempstead
		32. Bracknell
NORTH-EAST	SOUTH WALES	33. Crawley
ENGLAND	21. Llantrisant	34. Basildon
11. Washington	22. Cwmbran	
12. Peterlee		
13. Aycliffe		

The Second World War saw the publication of a number of reports looking forward to future social and economic development. In particular, the Barlow Report made proposals on 'The Distribution of the Industrial Population', recommending national planning, limitations on the size of cities, dispersal to smaller towns and government guidance on the location of industry. The New Towns Act of 1946 provided for the designation of land for proposed new towns and the setting up of Development Corporations to carry the proposals through. New towns were seen as the answer to many urban problems, bringing together houses, jobs, services and efficient transport within a pleasant environment.

The Town and Country Planning Act of 1947 became the most influential piece of planning legislation this century. It brought almost all building construction under national control and thus requiring planning permission. Regional plans were prepared for all parts of the country, national parks were proposed and new towns were to be built.

As the designs for these new towns emerged, one of the important features was seen to be the need to create a substructure of smaller neighbourhood communities within the town. Patrick Nuttgens explains:

In order to foster the life of the community, it was necessary to break down the total size of a new settlement into smaller groups which were small enough to acquire a sense of local identification. The key to the size was the number of people necessary to support a secondary school, the school being (as theorists before the war had pointed out) an essential community nucleus.

Washington – study of a new town

I have always regarded the legislation to establish new towns as one of the great imaginative ideas of the post-war Attlee government. I am glad to recall that I was a member of the House of Commons when Lewis Silkin brought forward the bill in 1946 which established the idea of building new towns mostly on green field sites. Our intention was that those who lived in the towns should enjoy a high standard of housing, modern factories would be built, there would be an absence of pollution, as well as access to the open country. They would include convenient shopping centres, sports centres, new libraries, and schools. (Rt Hon. James Callaghan, former British Prime Minister, 1976–79).

The aim of this study is to look at an example of one particular new town and identify some of the factors that influenced its development and eventual success. Since 1946 over twenty new towns have been established in Britain and among them the success of Washington, originally in County Durham, now in Tyne and Wear, stands out. On 24 July 1964, 'The Washington New Town (Designate) Order' was passed in Parliament and a Development Corporation was charged with the task of transforming ideas into reality.

In the early 1960s the area was dominated by a collection of mining villages, accompanied by considerable industrial dereliction. Unlike many new towns, Washington was not to be established on a green field site but on a landscape that had suffered spoil and neglect. However, since this time the Development Corporation has cleared away the pit heaps, laid drains, planted 3.5 million trees, 30 tonnes of bulbs, trebled the population to approaching 60,000 and won 26 architectural design awards. The need to create new jobs was essential to the success of the town and the Development Corporation has attracted over 300 companies to an area with a reservoir of technically skilled workers.

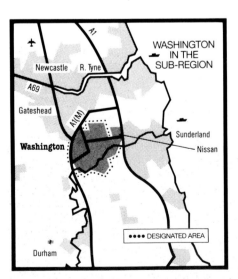

Washington New Town.

The growth of the new town also provided residential and shopping facilities and a diverse range of leisure activities, including a number of sports centres and a wildfowl park. The growth of the town has not always been smooth and the recession of the mid-1980s created unemployment and factory closures. However, the diverse nature of the industry and services provided by employers in the town, coupled with the success of attracting the giant Japanese car manufacturer Nissan to the area, has created an optimistic air for the future. The first chairman of the Washington Development Corporation, Sir James Steel, outlines some of the initial problems he faced in 1964.

Creating a new town may be considered as massive development within a brief time scale. But it is more than just roads, open spaces and buildings. A town consists of people and the success of a new town is measured by the contentment of its inhabitants.

Despite my dedication to attracting new industries to the north east and my awareness of the potential magnetism of a new town, I was appalled by the enormity of the task. I knew of so many spacious sites in beautiful country west of the A1 (M), free from dereliction, that it seemed crazy to build a new town in a welter of industrial waste instead of on a 'green field site'. Of course, I was wrong! The strategic position of Washington, the proximity of big and overcrowded conurbations, at the centre of what was to be the best network of motorways in the country – all these considerations made it an ideal location.

At my first meeting with the Minister I accepted the Chairmanship and asked for my instructions. The response was brief indeed – it was to build a new town for 70,000 inhabitants (to rise to 80,000 by natural expansion) within the designated area of 5,325 acres [2,156 ha] in the most cost-effective manner. The Corporation had to attract new industries, provide employment and raise by example the quality of life in the region. I would be consulted on the appointment of the other eight members of the Corporation and would borrow funds from the exchequer for repayment with interest over 60 years.

I was on my own, without an office or staff or funds. I found an office, opened a bank account, borrowed a small sum, engaged a secretary, met the other Board Members and advertised for a General Manager.(*Washington: Quicker by Quango, The History of Washington New Town, 1964–1983*, Stephen Holley)

From these very modest beginnings a new town was to emerge that has proved to be one of the most successful of the post-war era. The design and planning of Washington have tried to fulfil all of the criteria for providing a sound base from which a community can evolve.

These photos show how reclaimed land was used in the Development of the new town.

Aerial view of Washington New Town.

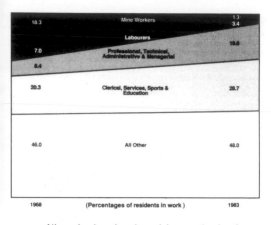

1968	(Percentages of residents in work)	1983
18.3	Mine Workers	1.3 3.4
	Labourers	18.8
7.0	Professional, Technical, Administrative & Managerial	
8.4		
20.3	Clerical, Services, Sports & Education	28.7
46.0	All Other	48.0

Nissan's plans involve raising production from 20,000 to 200,000 cars a year by 1992.

Employment

Washington has a diverse range of manufacturing and service industries including electronics, precision engineering, textiles, plastics and data processing. Many of these are also integrated in the Nissan car plant, which boasted the most advanced car production facility in the world when it was opened in September 1986. In 1992, the plant was responsible for the creation of 3,400 jobs, a figure that does not take account of the opportunities created in the support and services trades to the plant, including car seats and trims, radiators and tyres. From their initial output of 20,000 cars per year, Nissan hope to produce 200,000 cars per year in 1992.

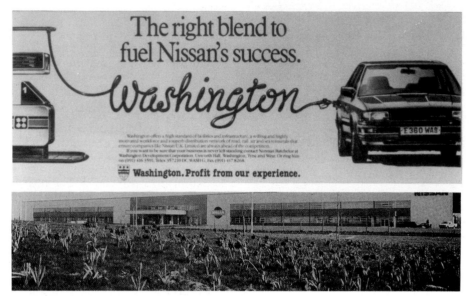

Nissan site in spring.

The Nissan Primera.

Residential areas

Within the boundary of the town there are eighteen villages, each with a target population of 4,500 people. Every village has its own primary school, shops and village hall, all within walking distance. This attempt to build smaller communities as part of a much larger new town population has been a distinctive feature of many other new towns and appears to be a positive way of promoting communal identity. The villages are segregated from the main road communications by virtue of a squared grid system. These grids are

approximately half a mile (800 m) square, enclosing 160 acres (65 ha), and contain each village with a housing density of approximately 50 persons to the acre. Housing is a mixture of public sector and private sector developments, with 70–80 self-build plots having been sold in the late 1970s. There has been a positive attempt to meet the needs of individuals and families at different stages of their life cycles: the singles, the couples, the young and growing families, the retired and elderly.

All these houses were designed by the corporation's architects and received design awards.

The commercial centre

The town centre offers a mix of offices and extensive shopping facilities in addition to a bus station, free parking for 3,000 cars, a leisure centre and swimming pool. The shopping centre of 'The Galleries' is a climate-controlled, indoor, pedestrian precinct. Two large stores, Asda and Savacentre (Sainsbury's and BHS) offer diversity supported by 60 specialist outlets. There are also plans to connect Washington to the Tyneside Metro rail system.

2 Design Issues and Influences

THE CONTEMPORARY PRACTICE OF DESIGN

Design strategies and influences

Design can be studied through revealing typical strategies that designers use, as well as by being aware of the different influences which motivate and interest them. Knowing how popular taste determines design outcome is also important. Does popular culture drive design ideas, or is it left to dominant individuals to lead the way? The best way to learn something about the practice of designing is to do it, and to study what other designers do.

Design for Coventry Cathedral by Basil Spence. The success of a design is the result of a designer employing an aesthetic ideal which is in turn made real through technical judgement. Does this vision match the real thing?

"There are only the three regulars left now, Sir."

Designing involves varying degrees of creativity and the imagination, especially in the promotion and use of human innovation and ingenuity. These are crucial factors in the way designers communicate their sense of responsibility, their persistence to achieve effective results, and their abilities to co-operate in teams and attain success.

Popular notions of design

What do people usually think design is? Do they, for instance, see it as something that only talented and gifted people can do? Is it seen as an intellectual pursuit? Is it slightly cranky? What is the difference between invention and design? What cartoon would be applicable today to present a commonly held view of what design is?

Is there a general feeling that design is an expensive item that only fashion-conscious people enjoy, including the idea of exploitation through expensive shops and agencies? Is design a commercial 'confidence trick'? An advertisement for *Streets of London* – 'Get the unfair advantage' could be seen to take advantage of certain people's desire for high fashion and luxury goods.

Consider what is meant by 'designer lifestyle', a term often used today. Is there any real value in 'one-yupmanship'? How would you score in a quiz on the latest fashions, based on your knowledge of what is 'chic' or 'cool'? Consider the fashions of your friends and peers. What expression do you use to reflect being 'fashionable', especially if you laughed at the term 'chic'!

THE UNFAIR dvantage

Which image is the theme of this advertisement?

What is the place of nostalgia in design? An advertisement might tend to reinforce the notion that design is concerned with maintaining a rather sentimental and sanitised existence, cluttered by things that we don't really need. Yet, isn't design concerned with trying to improve our lives?

We are fixated by the past in many design examples. The present does not seem to hold much interest, although it is the time when these things are required. However, the future holds considerable appeal for designers. Vauxhall cars used the slogan 'Step into the Future' to advertise a contemporary car which suggests that the future is somewhat better than the present. The spoof was that it relied upon a 1950s concept of a 1990s vehicle as the creative narrative of the sales promotion. Do we spend too much time trying to live in the future before it has actually happened? Is the idea of a 'better' future at the heart of commercial design?

Merchandising is another feature of design that is often easily recognised and accepted as a commercial function of design. Some examples are timeless, or at least appear so, others are ephemeral. Why were the Teenage Mutant Hero Turtles so successful, or have you never heard of them? Do you think Batman will last longer than the Teenage Mutant Hero Turtles?

Nutty and natty ideas are often seen as what is meant by design. Imagine a hexagonal potato chip. The idea is that the hexagon provides a small surface area, per volume, through which fat can be absorbed into a chip. It also means that the chips can be cut without waste. Cylindrical chips allow the least amount of fat absorption, but they would leave too much waste. Is there anything wrong with oddly cut chips? Why should there be a new concept of chip? Where is the sense in all this design?

Part of the range of Batman merchandise. What is the commercial significance of merchandising?

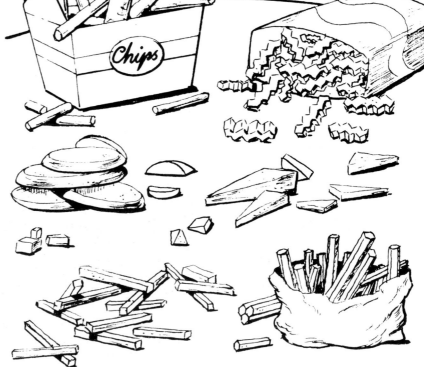

What is the best design of chip?

Simple, practical, easily made ideas often bring a great deal of pleasure and are a very strong feature of what design means to us all. Could you build a barbecue stand?

Design your own barbecue stand.

Designing involves setting down certain schemes for change in the near future. A Napoleonic plan to invade England in 1803 demonstrates that the preoccupations of the present time can be projected into possibilities for the future. Such schemes can be thought through without much cost and somewhat more safely in our imaginations. Drawings and models are very important decision-making devices. Consider the amount of modelling and planning that has gone into the real Channel Tunnel. Would you be happy to travel through the Channel Tunnel when it is completed?

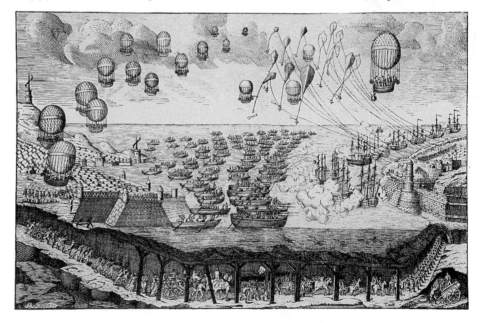

Designers can present fantastic ideas before their time. A scheme for the invasion of England by balloon, tunnel and cross-channel fleet, c. 1803.

Practically, design can be seen as the arrangement of things, whereby the whole tends to be greater than the sum of its parts. Thus, the unity of the design is formed by its constituent parts as a system of 'things'. This combination, together with the relationship of the components, which give it form, including their strength and action together (especially the way in which certain parts can be reached and changed), is the design. These issues are essential requirements for the use and function of the article. This is often termed 'fitness for purpose'. Further, the cost of the design should be a consideration, and this notion relates to the design's value and economy of use. The appearance of the artefact, system or image is also a function of design. Why is this?

However, this cannot be all that design is! It must mean more to us all than the mere function, cost and appearance of things.

> . . . design start from the premise that living is more than just a matter of existing, and that everyday things which are both effective and attractive can raise the quality of life. (Conran)

A great deal of pleasure can be obtained from choosing and owning well-designed things. It is pleasant to visit an attractive house or to read a colourfully illustrated book. When we design, it becomes an extension of ourselves. Designing gives purpose to our lives because we need more in our lives than mere actions based on subsistence and survival. Thus, design and designing can be important to our creativity, but even so we need to maintain a commonsense view of the practical value of design.

Could you design a low-cost house that would withstand a hurricane-force wind?

How important are these designs? Would you object to living near a wind farm?

Most of the things that we encounter everyday are designed, not just in their own right, but according to where they are used and how reliable they are. We are involved with decisions about design not only through the choices we make when buying things, but also in how we perpetuate bad designs.

Very often things do not work very well. Have you ever changed a light bulb only to find that you cannot get the bulb out of its socket because the plastic lampholder has deteriorated and broken due to the heat of the bulb! Is design at fault here, or is it something else? Poor designs create more problems if they are not corrected. Look around for things that work well and those that do not.

Something gone wrong – why is there tape over the sash window?

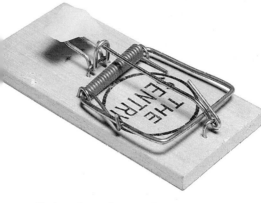

Design a fantastic mouse trap.

Good design does not come about by accident. It is the result of getting many things right: fitness for purpose, performance, appearance, good manufacture and materials, value for money, durability and safety. (Design Council)

What designers do

Designers think about future objects or schemes. When designing, they are aware of the essential issue that originated the need for design, and also the context and nature of the problem posed, all of which form the essential character of designing. Designers create designs, not necessarily the finished article, and there is no one correct way to design or to solve problems.

Designers have to satisfy many criteria in their work, some of which will be open to them to choose and suggest, while others will be determined, for example, by a client or the particular issue. Stopping a tap from dripping is a plumber's job, but ensuring that there are better taps available for use is a design issue. Very often a design problem is raised by someone other than the designer, especially in industry and manufacturing. The success of many designs, and also the designer's career, are dependent upon the personal creativity and the negotiating powers that so many designers exercise.

Designers tend to be orientated towards the general solution of a problem in their work. Naturally, the more designers understand why a problem has occurred, the more likely they are to propose valid solutions or uses for their findings. Designers should also aim to keep their designs simple!

Each example of design is unique because it has arisen from particular needs, opportunities or desires. A design may be formed from traditional craft methods and techniques, or derived from advances in technology. It may be a modified version of something already in use. It may be hand-crafted, mass-produced or the product of large-scale production based upon teamwork and careful, detailed analysis of market trends. Can you tell when things have been designed?

Design is a feature of human thought and acquired knowledge. It is a product of imaginative thinking and problem-solving, and is often the means by which new information or understanding can be discovered and used.

Genius has been defined by George Bernard Shaw as 90 per cent perspiration and 10 per cent inspiration. Design may well be an act of genius, especially if it results in the production of an original creative idea, a new machine or device, a fresh image or picture, or a better way of seeing or understanding life. What is the difference, if any, between a design created from an inspired idea and one derived from long, painstaking research? Is design simply a function of the evolution of human knowledge?

Many design strategies and issues initiate design possibilities. Think of a problem that needs solving. Are design ideas given to you or do you have to find your own brief? Are you a designer looking for a problem? Which field of knowledge would your design issue belong to?

It is doubtful whether any designers are given a clean slate in their work. Some designers draw, some do not; some use calculation, others do not; and a great number of designers think with their hands, designing as they go along. What do you do when you begin to design? Do you make sure of the merits of your task? Specifying and originating design ideas is the crux of designing.

'A Deed of Christmas Kindness' by Heath Robinson.
What has the artist designed in this image?

Consider how the following examples were started and why. Remember, a designer produces a design, not always the final item. All that is required here are your notes and sketches, especially those that highlight the different strategies and issues that have initiated designing. Also try to think about the type of personal qualities that are required for effective design.

Problem-solving activities

- Look at the different strategies employed by leading tennis players for carrying the second service ball. Miss A. Sanchez Vicario uses design to aid her game, but why are different players' techniques so different? How would you solve this problem if you were to play tennis?

An excellent method of judging the quality and effect of any design is to consider what could be added to it, or taken from it, to improve the design. This simple idea may be very useful in problem-solving, if only because it is a clear starting point in designing. Use this technique on the examples given. What exactly do we mean by 'problem-solving'?

- How would you find out how many spines a hedgehog has? How might design help with this problem? The design problem here is the designing of an instrument to measure the number of spines.

- Build a house of cards and observe the way you go about this task. Are you actually designing?

'Scientists can tell you precisely why the structure they have just made has fallen; and technologists have no idea why the structure they made is still standing.' What would be the role of a designer in this example? Are you a scientist, technologist or designer? By way of a strong contrast, compare the building of a card house with the installation of a nuclear power station. Are such buildings designed to outlast the toxic substances they contain and create? How can this problem be solved?

Designers reveal and combine many forms of information. How would a designer work on the following puzzle.

- The problem is to cut an equilateral triangle into four pieces which can then be reassembled to form a square.

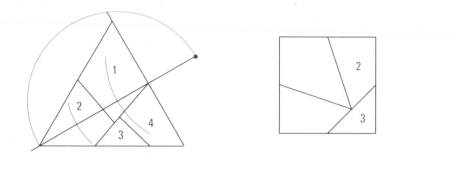

Dudeney's four piece dissection of equilateral triangle to square.

How would different people solve the Dudeney puzzle? What are its properties? Scientists explore and analyse why things are what they are and what they do. In this sense a mathematician employs similar techniques. This type of problem would not be given to designers, but its solution might be offered as a possibility for a toy or game. What is the potential of this puzzle for a designer? Can it be utilised or applied? Would an artist be interested in it at all? Could a designer use the idea of the puzzle for some other purpose?

What is the difference between analysis and synthesis as processes of human thought and endeavour? Compare scientific analytical thinking with design problem-solving thinking? Think about the notion of contrariness, whereby several unrelated ideas or facts might combine to form a powerful solution to a problem.

Applying knowledge, theories and concepts

Consider the relationship between the techniques of holography and the commercial proposition of an anti-forgery device for a credit card? Initially, these ideas seem quite unrelated. When brought together they become effective as holography brings to the credit card an important function of security for each user.

The uses of holography are being researched in many ways. The idea of animated holography, which produces optical, moving sculptures of original design ideas, through a system of computerised video techniques, might well have a future use. For example, interactive simulations in CAD, medical X-rays and architectural modelling are but a few applications of moving, three-dimensional holograms. Are these ideas achievable?

Imagine that you have been commissioned to design shoes for someone living in a different country. What sort of things will you want to know before you can start designing? Are the technical and factual elements of this design activity all that are required? Being creative and intuitive, having a feeling for something and using your design know-how add to the idea of applying knowledge. It is vital

Security conscious banks have looked to the hologram as an integral part of credit card security.

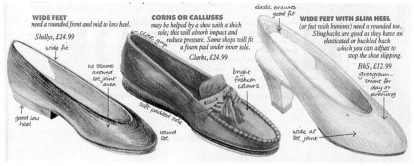

From an article in *Family Circle* magazine.

that designers are prepared for many eventualities.

When reading Vasari's criteria for Renaissance art, you will often find a clash between the notions of realism and idealism. Ideal beauty is meant to be convincing and natural.

> Art, in fact, can and must improve on nature, although nature remains both a starting point and a constant reference. (Vasari)

Vasari used various keywords in his description of artistic creation, as well as the qualities to be looked for in a perfect work of art, for example, *disegno*. Can you see this in Michaelangelo's *Pietá*?

How creative are designers? Are they free spirits, able to conjure up and work towards the best solutions to problems? When is a designer allowed to use his or her creativity and ingenuity to the full? Are all designs a compromise of one sort or another? Is design a highly constrained process? Should a design student be allowed to create outlandish things?

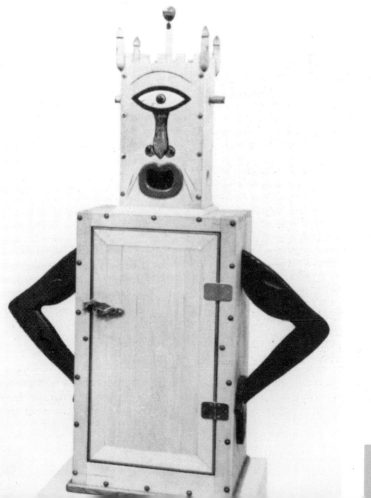

'Pieta' by Michelangelo (1475–1564) Compare this Florentine work with other Pieta's, by Michelangelo, especially his early St. Peter's, Rome example. Vasari said of this: "it is certainly a miracle that a formless block of stone could ever have been reduced to a perfection that nature is scarcely able to create in the flesh."

Memorial for the idea of man if he was an idea.

Where should a designer start designing? Some tend to make arbitrary choices related to particular kinds of solution, so how precise is any designer's start to his or her work? For example, a designer might decide to adopt a certain type of configuration for a structure, for example a table with no legs, or a conventional table with four legs. Many different ideas are brought together by designers, sometimes to provide an impact through putting together contrasting forms or simply to be contrary.

Sometimes designers make things fit their ideas: at other times they bring about new versions of things; but mostly they are concerned with the costs involved. Why would a blister pack be preferable to a cardboard box for a particular type of packaging? How often do we make things fit our needs, or make do, or simply produce things according to our limited experiences? Does a house owner really need to cut the tree to follow the line of the fence?

Design know-how and getting things right

- Study the design of a British Rail tea beaker and consider how many problems have been solved. Study the fins at the top of the cup. What problem do they solve?

Personal qualities concerning responsibility, co-operation and persistence, especially when overcoming the frustration of difficult work, are important characteristics in successful designing. Design know-how can be further developed through the use of basic organisational and planning skills. Did Intercity buy in the beaker design or is it a product of their own improvements to customer service?

Aesthetic judgements and technological issues

- Study a Chinese paper flower. Then, by trial and error use drawing to design an imaginary flower. This might be one way to apply your experience, but could you make a paper cut-out flower? Where could this artwork be used? Do all designs have to be useful?

Consider the Platonic view of someone who loves fine and beautiful things, someone who regularly goes to the theatre, art galleries or concerts and who enjoys fashionable clothes. We might call such a person cultured.

Such a man is not a philosopher, because they love only beautiful things, whereas the philosopher loves beauty itself. The man who only loves beautiful things is dreaming, whereas the man who knows absolute beauty is wide awake. The former has only opinion; the latter has knowledge.
(Bertrand Russell's summary of an aspect of Plato's theory of ideas in *History of Western Philosophy* George Allen & Unwin)

(a) The medieval ideal. The perfectly proportioned face could be divided into sevenths – one each for the hair, the chin and the space between nose and mouth, two each for the forehead and the nose.

(b) The Greek ideal. In the perfect face of 'golden' proportions, the ratio of the whole face (x) to the eye-to-chin section (y) should be equal to the ratio of the eye-to-chin section to the forehead section (z).

In which ways, and for what reasons, would designers design 'beautiful' things? Is a philosopher a designer? What is beauty, and how are designers involved with such a notion, if at all?

Judgement about the human environment is always a facet of a designer's thinking. In the very last scene in *Manhattan*, a monochrome film by Woody Allen, he says, 'This is beautiful', referring to Manhattan. How can this be? Is his opinion objective? What do you think of the image of Paris in the early 1980s?

Urban beauty?

George Pompidou Centre, Paris
How would you demonstrate the 'beauty' of Paris?

Technical judgement is another concern of designers. Things that are well made also tend to be pleasing to look at and easy to use.

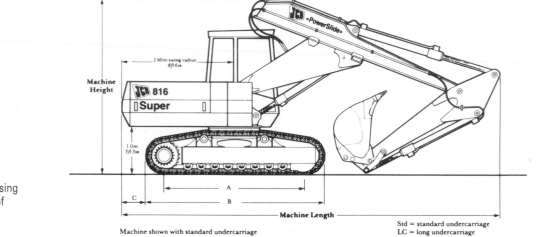

Machine shown with standard undercarriage

Std = standard undercarriage
LC = long undercarriage

JCB – 'great emphasis is placed on using design to improve quality and ease of manufacture'.
How can this be confirmed?

Semaphore car signal system.
Why did this form of direction signalling last so long?

However, attitudes to change are more problematic, especially because it takes time for some ideas to become accepted. Innovation is the key issue here, as worthwhile design ideas need to be accepted and made to work. Consider the development of vehicle signalling devices. Early in the development of cars, electronic signalling systems could have been introduced but because hand signals were the norm, they were retained far longer than necessary. When the idea of using a 'winker' was presented to the British motor industry in the 1950s, there was still some resistance to the idea.

Criticising and understanding the development of various designs can enable the process of innovation to proceed with understanding. Ingenuity feeds this process as well.

Economic judgements and technological issues

In the early 1970s a French journalist first thought of the idea of incorporating a microprocessor on a pocket-size bank card. The microprocessor is a single silicon chip which combines not only program and data memories but also a central processing unit – in effect a pocket-sized computer or smart card.

Having a memory size as great as the personal computers of the early 1980s, the potential applications of a smart card are limited only by one's imagination. The storage of information concerning medical records, financial details or monetary values are typical examples.

Barclays Bank are currently testing smart cards at the Dallington Country Club in Northampton (The Dallington Smart Card Project, from the Barclay/Bull H/N Dallington Smart Card Project), where members have personalised cards that enable them to book and pay for squash courts, pay for drinks and meals and store fitness and medical records. Considering the sophistication and flexibility of smart cards, what other potential applications can you think of?

Increased competition, technology and the effects of deregulation are changing the face of retail banking in the UK and elsewhere. Diversifying into new markets and investing in advanced technology will form an integral part of successful retail banking strategies through the 1990s. These developments will enhance customer services and bring to the market innovative products targeted at today's customers.

This project 'is designed to address the major needs of Leisure Service Administrators and the customers they serve. Significant

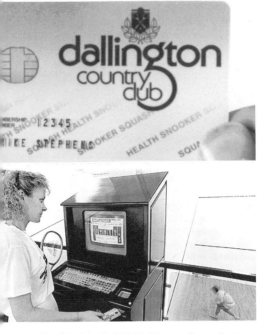

The Barclays/Bull HN Dallington Smart Card Project.

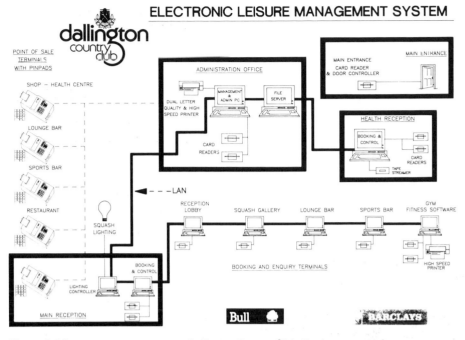

Electronic leisure management system, Dallington Country Club, Northampton.

benefits in improved cash handling, efficient administrative systems and enhanced consumer services are among the features included in this development'. As well as the many features described in the examples there is an 'unassigned area of memory within the microprocessor [which] will be activated whilst the cards are in circulation – this will be the fitness assessment profiles'.

Moral and ethical issues concerning design

Are the 'daring' pictorial images in Picasso's *Guernica* of 1937 constructed into a traditional composition? The idioms used by Picasso were devised to draw our attention to war, but the mural is structured, classical and controlled. Its composition can be analysed into triangles, golden sections and other geometrical devices of the Renaissance.

Guernica by Pablo Picasso.

Thus, the mural has a formal structure and images that are symbolic rather than based upon accurate visual representations.

Are these 'simple' images easily recognised and remembered? Is this work designed to enable each viewer to find out about war, personally or generally? The possibility is that such art enables us to remember what war can mean to us all. Does 'great art' enable us to develop knowledge and feelings as yet unknown to us, or which might be rekindled? Does the frightened horse remind us that innocent things suffer in war? Does the electric light remind us of how dependent we are upon technologies which are themselves easily destroyed, indicating how fragile our way of life can be? Does the image contain a mysterious presence of beauty?

It is . . . largely due to [Picasso] that the conception of art as a powerful emotional medium, rather than a search for the perfection of ideal forms of beauty, has become accepted among artists of our time. The return to a fundamental belief that art should spring from a primitive need to express our feelings towards the world around us in strong emotional terms makes us more prone to value a work of art for its vitality than for its perfection. (*Picasso*, Phaidon)

Art has the potential to communicate very powerful messages through images which can be easily remembered. This is because symbols, not words, can be retained as guiding principles for our experiences and thoughts. Photographs and television images may not be as powerful. They are certainly arresting at the moment they are seen, but are they remembered? These images are distanced from you, but works of art are immediate; they demand personal involvement; they do not have to be profound, but they do invite onlookers to imagine themselves in the situation the artist has presented. In *Guernica*, who attends to the horse, and can the horse understand what is happening? Is the man with out stretched arms dead? Compare Picasso's image with a more recent photograph showing bloodshed in warfare or civil unrest.

Clashes in Tienanmen Square, 1989.

To summarise, developing effective design attitudes based on personal qualities of responsibility and co-operation and complemented by the skills of organisation, decision-making and planning are crucial acquisitions in design work. Your values and sense of purpose will aid your approach to your work and will affect your analysis of situations or contexts for design.

The designer at work

Your task is to experience design and to be able to say something about it, as well as to experiment with your own design ideas. Study the examples of designers at work here and in the following case studies and note how the idea of synthesis operates, as well as the effects of constraints on a designer's work.

A practising designer: Sally Anderson

The following examples of design work are kindly supplied by Sally Anderson (Ceramics) Ltd, Parndon Mill, Harlow, Essex. They are included so that you might experience the work of a professional designer. Aim to distinguish between ideas and issues that are specific to Sally Anderson's work and those that are not. Use the generalised notes given in this section to help you.

Sally Anderson (Ceramics) Ltd has produced tiles since 1970 and Sally Anderson studios have developed an expertise that affords the opportunity for an individually designed scheme to suit any tiled area. From a selection

Constructing a model of a swimming pool scheme for a Yorkshire home. The balance of real and illusionary architectural feature is worked out at this stage. Working three-dimensionally gives the designer the opportunity to balance tone and colour to the customer who can instantly understand what the finished scheme will be like. Photographs courtesy of Sally Anderson.

Painting the last wall of the model of a swimming pool scheme for a home in Lancashire. Several of the architectural features of the house shown on the photographs in the foreground are incorporated in the tile design.

of 50 colours, ranging from subtle Eau-de-Nil to rich Aubergine, many contrasts or sympathetic complementaries can be chosen with the guidance of the designer herself. Units from the system murals can be combined as lavish decoration or simply grouped as a focal point, using themes ranging from tranquil swans and watermeadows to classical figures.

In order to plan a scheme, diagrammatic illustrations of the various designs and mural units are available in black and white. These can be cut out and rearranged, or traced onto a grid of half-inch squares, each one representing a 6-in (15.24 cm) tile.

Natural minerals suspended in a traditional glaze form all the designs and colours. The background tiles used with the murals are referred to as 'plain tiles', but are really not at all plain. Their subtle variation of colour and tone create a lively textural depth. A feature which is simple yet effective, such as a linear frieze or a bold diagonal stripe, can be added.

Slip-resistant floor tiles, suitable for light domestic use, are available in all colours and a few simple designs.

All the tiles are produced to order, usually within 4–6 weeks. Mural displays, colour samples and patterns are readily available through Sally Anderson agents.

Probably the most difficult, and certainly the most important stage of the design commission, is establishing the precise size and shape of the 'canvas'.

In the domestic building industry the length of a wall, floor or ceiling data, or the position of doors and windows may change during construction and the last person to be told is generally the interior designer!

The following check-list is discussed prior to the design of mural works:

Data: Finished floor level and finished ceiling level.

Heating and ventilation: This involves ducting, vents and grilles and is rarely shown on initial drawings; the aesthetics of an area can be destroyed if this is not carefully considered.

Lighting: Early consideration is essential, as the necessity of impervious membrane ceilings puts serious limitations on the choice of fittings. It is often prudent to plan the lighting scheme together with the ceiling structure.

Establishing a design for a swimming pool

The objective of the first site visit is to clarify the following information:

1. To establish the aspect of the pool building — whether it is a converted basement or has windows on to a garden or a landscape. [In previous commissions, Sally has designed an illusionary landscape with the horizon lining up with the actual scene through adjacent windows.]

2. To assess the general shape of the pool, the proportions of the pool hall, as well as considering whether the design should emphasise vertical or horizontal features, including whether the room needs the illusion of space or to be drawn as 'cosy'. Other aspects, such as the division of a long wall into sections, possibly complementing windows and other openings, or the repositioning of some doors, windows and vents, may also be considered.

3. To define the purpose of the pool, for example whether or not it will be used for leisure, 'serious' swimming, entertaining with drinks, for children only, or the whole family.

4. To collect the customer's ideas. Sometimes these are quite positive although based on preconceived notions that do not suit the site. Other customers have no ideas. General conversation establishes tastes and attitudes.

5. To obtain a guide to the customer's tastes and colour preferences from looking around his or her house and furnishings.

Before colour is applied to the model, each wall is photographed and the scale increased slightly so that a numbered grid can be applied. This is the working drawing and will become the tiler's fixing diagram. (At this stage a further check is made of site dimensions as by now rendering has usually been completed.) Here Sally Anderson works out a perspective mural on the full-scale tiled grid.

The completed model ready for presentation to the Yorkshire clients.

The purpose of building the model

1. To check all the dimensions taken on site and find any discrepancies.

2. To work out the setting-out. For example, how the tiles are to be placed on the walls and floor and where cutting will occur.

3. To give an obvious and clear view of the proportions of various parts of the building.

Designing the scheme now takes place using all these considerations. Because designing tiles requires a certain formality relating to the tile grid, symmetry is important. A basic design structure related to the building is worked out. Often this is difficult if, for instance, the pool is not central to the building, windows are at different heights and so on. Strong horizontal bands of frieze give unity. Columns or arches create a structure within a structure. Natural features, for example trees or bushes, are asymmetrical. Their different shapes and sizes can be used to fill awkward areas so as to distract the eye from any asymmetrically placed windows and doors.

When this structure has been modelled and established, the customer's preference for subjects becomes incorporated and our interpretation of preferred colours is used. They may emphasise, play down where necessary, or complement existing colour within the scheme, such as that which might be seen in water. [Sally's Yorkshire client liked birds and figures and suggested she might include her dog.]

When all this is done it should look comfortable, even obvious, and not prompt the customer to ask for an alternative scheme!

Each tile is numbered on the back to correspond to the tiling diagram. The original model is used along with this as a colour guide. The tiles are laid on the bench for the design and colour to be applied, then put into tile ranks for firing. It is essential they are numbered correctly!

The ranks of tiles are fired in the kiln – heating for approximately eight hours, cooling for around 30 hours. Here, George is unloading the kiln and Brenda is checking the tiles. Even the plain tiles are individually checked. Frieze tiles for the Yorkshire pool are laid out on the bench.

All the pictorial mural tiles are set out on the raked wall for checking and criticism. It is possible to apply more colour to parts of the mural if necessary. The tiles must then be refired. Tomo takes the completed murals off the wall and packs them in numerical order, clearly labelled to correspond to the tiling diagram.

DESIGN CASE STUDIES

The purpose of a case study

Case studies will invariably involve liaison with industry or commercial organisations, including some work experience if required. Case studies are concerned with products or systems and processes; they should explore some sort of proposition from which certain critical judgements and analysis can be established and presented. It is important that these studies are both descriptive and analytical; they are not simply historical statements, but detailed investigations which require thought, sensitivity and thorough research.

Generally, these studies are presented in a two-dimensional format, and rely upon a substantial written content, for example between 3,000 and 4,000 words. Full academic procedures should be adhered to, including acknowledgements, bibliographies, references and a diary of visits and contacts. Quotations should be referenced and indicated in the text, and the study folder should employ design throughout.

Clarify and identify the issues or topics to be investigated and set out a proposition for the study.

It is vital that you plan your study with special regard to the overall constraints of the topic that interests you. Know which data you require, and how they will be found. Your decision-making in this regard is crucial.

Be flexible about what you discover and learn to adapt to different situations. It is important that you demonstrate your skills of analysis of the information that you find and show that you know how to draw conclusions and make recommendations.

Your report should be addressed to an appropriate audience and should show good standards of design.

Throughout the exercise try to be aware of your own reactions to design, as well as the reactions of others, from friends to established experts. Above all, aim to interpret what you find through systematic analysis, as well as using your own intuitive judgement.

The purpose of a case study is for you to focus on a particular design issue which will enable you to reveal and reflect upon the nature and value of design.

Selling images, dreams and products

Advertising is the industry of our time. Whether it is called 'the permissible lie', 'the only true new artform' or 'the lifeblood of capitalism', it increasingly influences the whole of our lives – from the toys our children demand to the TV programmes we watch, from the drugs our doctors prescribe to the way we vote. It is pervasive, global and growing. There are three times as many advertisements now as fifteen years ago – but in the new age of satellites and electronic wizardry, the real explosion is yet to come. At the same time, with vast computerised information banks and new psychological techniques, the industry comes closer and closer to its target of persuading us to act as it wants when it wants. (*The Want Makers*, Eric Clark)

Eric Clark's view of advertising is quite prophetic and rather worrying. However, we cannot ignore the fact that persuading people to buy products and services is an essential link between mass production and mass consumption. We use advertising because there is something we want to sell or something we want to buy. We need to maintain employment, but there is no future in having factories working at full capacity if markets cannot be found for their output to maintain this demand. However, advertising is an emotive issue and a subject about which you must develop your own opinions. Is the industry 'a necessary evil', 'a positive force for human and economic advancement' or 'the opium of capitalism'? The only thing that is certain is that you cannot ignore it or shut it out of your senses.

It would be an extreme generalisation to say that advertising *per se* is bad or even harmful. Think of the support generated for famine relief through advertising, or the way many of us found out about the jobs we now occupy. However, there are more vulnerable members of the community, such as children, old people, those in debt, or even people suffering from medical disorders and waiting for a 'cure', who are all potential 'soft targets' for unscrupulous promoters. Between these two extremes, the consumer needs to feel secure while being bombarded with messages to spend more and then borrow to spend again.

World events such as the Olympic Games and football's World Cup become world advertising events. Through the power of television, hidden advertising, in the form of the logos or names of official sponsors, beams its message into over 150 countries, to millions of viewers who are convinced that they are immune to the power of advertising. However, the messages have been received and lie dormant, waiting to be triggered at some time in the future.

Creating the image

During the last twenty years there has been an explosion in the range of goods and services available to the consumer. For the seller this has sometimes meant greater competition, while for the consumer it has often resulted in a wider choice. Technical advances have brought quality and value for money. This leaves the advertising executive with the problem of how to ensure that the product he or she is promoting has an edge over the competition. The response has been to create an image to surround the product or service and give it a unique selling feature that will enable it to stand out from the rest. Hence, Heineken lager is claimed 'To refresh the parts other beers cannot reach', although in practice it is probably no more refreshing than any other similar drink. Carling Black Label drinkers seem to possess special powers, discerned by genial observers who proclaim 'I bet he drinks Carling Black Label'.

The Code of Advertising Practice defines advertisements as 'paid-for communications addressed to the public (or some part of it) with the purpose of influencing the opinions or behaviour of those to whom they are addressed'. It must be remembered that advertising is expensive and is perceived by those who pay for it as a form of investment.

The UK advertising magazine *Campaign* revealed that in 1992 the two leading soap giants, Procter & Gamble and Unilever Lever Brothers, who already share 90 per cent of the total market, spent around £70 million on battling to convince us of the virtues of their products. At the same time, Pedigree Petfoods splashed out £25 million on persuading us that their products would be much better for our cherished animals than those of their rivals. Back in 1986, as British Gas once again raised its prices to customers, it was able to scrape together £21 million to spend in less than three months on promoting its privatisation campaign. Investment on this scale has to be cost-effective, although advertising agencies claim that their campaigns cannot be expected to sell a product that is no good, nor can it change people's views unless they are ready for their views to be changed. However, the growing influence and recognition of the power of advertising mean that these choices may vary from the purchase of a chocolate bar to the way we might cast our vote in a general election. Advertising is at the cutting edge of marketing, although it has been absorbed into our culture as a popular art form that we pass off as amusing and innocuous.

Advertising is planned to achieve the best results for the least cost. It has to be targeted at the particular group of people identified as the most likely potential consumers. This identification is done by a number of different techniques in a variety of countries. One of the more simple, and therefore perhaps least sensitive, forms of target identification combines two pieces of information:

1. The age-group of the potential target audience, which is normally categorised as

   under 15
   15–24
   24–35
   35–55
   55 plus

2. The social grade of the audience as listed below, based on the occupation of the head of the household, which is usually indicative of the spending power of the household.

		%
A	Higher managerial, administrative and professional	2.7
B	Intermediate managerial, administrative and professional	14.0
C1	Supervisory or clerical and junior managerial, administrative and professional	26.3
C2	Skilled manual	24.9
D	Semi-skilled and unskilled manual	19.1
E	Casual labourers, state pensioners and the unemployed	12.9

From this information, advertising agencies charged with the task of managing a company's advertising account will study audience profiles to identify those who can be most closely linked with their client's needs. It should then be possible to pick the type of publication or even a specific television programme that your target audience is most likely to be watching. If you wanted to advertise a luxury executive car, you would select a newspaper, magazine or TV programme looked at by a high number of AB 35- to 55-year-olds. This need to target the right audience is very important when you consider the cost of advertising.

What this and other systems have in common is that it is perceived that people in the same group have a number of similar characteristics and aspirations which the advertisers can tune into in order to sell their products. Another system, called ACORN, divides Britain into 38 groups of people according to their neighbourhood, from which it is hoped to identify who might be interested in borrowing money and where it might be best to target double-glazing sales.

The selection of which media outlet to use will not only be influenced by costings and audience targeting but will also be partially determined by the type of advertising campaign you wish to mount. Billboards, which are often adjacent to roads, usually carry simple messages that the passing motorist or commuter can quickly interpret. However, detailed statistics relating to the performance of a new car would be more appropriate in a newspaper or magazine where the potential buyer could refer to the advertisement in a more leisurely way.

Are some of our national newspapers primarily concerned with conveying news, or are they simply vehicles for advertising?

How advertising pays for the media		Revenue
Type of publication	% from advertising	% from sales
National dailies (e.g. *The Sun*)	44	56
National Sundays (e.g. *The Sunday Times*)	61	39
Regional dailies (e.g. *Yorkshire Post*)	65	35

(Source: Advertising Association, April 1990)

When the statistics on cost are viewed against the total revenue from advertising as a percentage of income, it can be seen that advertising and the media need one another. Advertising must have an outlet for its message and at the same time the media are dependent upon advertising to stay in business. This really begs the question of whether daily newspapers with a mass circulation are seriously in the news business or whether they are primarily in the business of carrying advertising messages and will therefore go to great lengths to increase their sales and hence their attraction to the advertisers. In recent years we have seen the growth of free local newspapers, pushed through our doors, which rely totally on advertising revenue.

With large advertising concerns investing heavily in the media (hence the media's reliance on the advertiser's goodwill for their survival), there are concerns that the independence of the media could be compromised. There exists the fear that the advertisers may begin to exert pressure on TV programmers and newspaper editors regarding the content and even the tone of their output. This potential abuse of power cannot be ignored as it has the ability to hit at the roots of free speech.

Eric Clark makes the following observation:

Advertising exists to inform – but even more so to persuade. It sells goods and services by turning them into images and dreams. As a discipline it is a curious mixture. It is not really an art, nor a science, although it has something of both. The science is there in the form of research, but it is a science with a small 's' although the 's' is growing larger, helped by huge computer data bases and electronic developments. Nor can it truly be called an art, although many of its practitioners would vehemently dispute that. But art is an end in itself; art in advertising is simply a means to an end. (*The Want Makers*)

Legal, decent, honest and truthful . . . control by consent

We have already seen that a competitive market can give advertisers the impetus to make false claims for their goods and services. In the early 1960s, as industries began to extend their product range to cash in on the more affluent consumer, so public opinion voiced its concern over the fear that advertising would be used to manipulate the customer, unless the industry was subject to some form of control. Previous experiences in the USA, which had been graphically documented in Vance Packard's *The Hidden Persuaders*, encouraged consumer pressure groups in the UK to press for control. In 1961 the advertising industry decided to institute a formal, but voluntary, code of standards which would apply to press, poster and cinema advertising (excluding TV and radio which were governed by the Independent Broadcasting Authority).

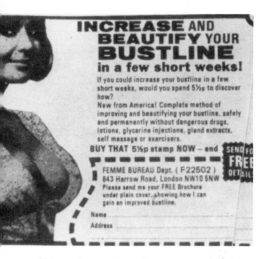

INCREASE AND BEAUTIFY YOUR BUSTLINE in a few short weeks!

If you could increase your bustline in a few short weeks, would you spend 5½p to discover how?
New from America! Complete method of improving and beautifying your bustline, safely and permanently without dangerous drugs, lotions, glycerine injections, gland extracts, self massage or exercisers.

BUY THAT 5½p stamp NOW – and SEND FOR FREE DETAILS

FEMME BUREAU Dept. (F22502)
843 Harrow Road, London NW10 5NW
Please send me your FREE Brochure under plain cover, showing how I can gain an improved bustline.

Name
Address

Claims of cosmetic products are unacceptable if they cannot be backed by medical evidence. What vulnerable section of the community might this advertisement be aimed at?

The British Code of Advertising Practice was followed by the establishment of the Advertising Standards Authority, whose job it is to pursue complaints as well as to monitor a selection of published advertisements. It also receives about 6,000 enquiries per year from advertising agencies requesting prepublication consultation in an attempt to avoid costly and damaging publicity should a campaign be requested to withdraw its advertisement because of a breach of the code.

In 1987 a national newspaper publicised its general election coverage with an advertisement designed for billboards and asking the question, 'Would Britain be better off with a hung Parliament?' This wording was superimposed on a visual that showed the three leaders of the main political parties being hanged. The advertisement generated the greatest volume of protest the ASA has known, and it acted quickly to ensure the advertisement was immediately withdrawn. This decision had nothing to do with politics; the advertisement was simply judged to be in very poor taste and an unnecessary portrayal of violence.

While the code requires that all advertisements should be legal, decent, honest and truthful, in practice interpreting these criteria can be quite difficult. There is also some criticism that a self-regulating watchdog such as the ASA, which is paid for by the advertising industry, will not give the public the protection it deserves. Indeed, in 1974 the government made it clear, through its consumer protection minister, that the code had to be toughened, otherwise the government would introduce its own rules. As the ASA silver jubilee publication pointed out, 'The industry responded rapidly. A tougher code emerged almost overnight, and a more elaborate mechanism to administer it vigorously was set up with funds drawn from a levy (also voluntary) on advertisers'.

As we near the end of the twentieth century, advertising continues to grow and influence our thinking. What is required is that we all develop a greater awareness of its potential power and influence. While some protection can be afforded through voluntary control, it will be interesting to see whether governments resist calls for legislation. How long will the BBC retain its independent status, free from advertising? Will education be able to play its part in making consumers more discriminating and less open to persuasion?

How concerned would you be if the BBC became a commercial television station? Do you feel this could limit the BBC's independence, or would you be pleased to save the licence fee?

Can you believe all the advertisements you see?

Advertising Standards Authority ✓

'Advertising is the art of teaching people to want things', H.G. Wells. What images are being created for the Rover car in the advertisement and which groups do you think may 'aspire' to own such a car?

Advertising rates

The media fix their advertising rates according to the size of their audience and its age and social profile. Some examples of 1993 rates are as follows:

	£
The Daily Telegraph Full page	34,500
The Sunday Times Full page (section 1)	47,000
Radio Times Full page (black & white) (National)	12,700

Informative advertising is best placed in a newspaper or magazine where it can be read at a more leisurely pace and can also be referred to again, if necessary.

The power of advertising. What product do you associate with this couple?

THE LIGHT BULB THAT SAVES THE EARTH.

By using a standard light bulb not only are you throwing money out of the window but you could also be causing needless damage to the environment.

The electricity generated for domestic lighting alone accounts for the emission each year of about 7 million tonnes of "greenhouse gas", carbon dioxide.

Replacing our standard light bulbs as they expire, with energy efficient bulbs, would halve this figure.

Now is your opportunity to do something positive. Next time a bulb blows, replace it with an electronic OSRAM DULUX EL bulb. For the same light output, it uses 80% less electricity. It also lasts about eight times longer – 8000 hours on average.

OSRAM DULUX EL
THE ELECTRONIC ENERGY SAVING LAMP

OSRAM DULUX EL energy-efficient bulbs are available with standard bayonet or screw caps, to fit your existing lampholders.

For every 20 W electronic OSRAM DULUX EL bulb you fit, you will save something like £45.00 in electricity bills, during its 8000 hour life. Ten 20 W electronic bulbs save £450. OSRAM DULUX EL electronic bulbs are a bright investment – for you, and for the planet we all live on.

	£
London Weekend Television 30-second evening spot (7.00 – 11.00 pm)	2,500
Scottish Television 30-second weekday peaktime spot (5.15 pm – close)	20,000
BRMB Radio Birmingham 30-second spot, Monday–Friday 3.00 p.m.–6.00 p.m.	484
London cinemas (395 screens) 30-second spot (each day for one week)	33,726

(Source: BRAD, March 1993)

'No standing, please!'

A stadium seat

A company statement from the stadium seat manufacturer Tubular Edgington Group PLC, read: 'Launch of a safer stadium seat'.

Tubular Engineering is a Washington- (Tyne and Wear) based company which operates in many engineering fields. It began life as Tubular Barriers Ltd in 1955 and, as its name suggests, manufactured (on a subcontract basis) and hired out crowd control barriers. By 1977 the company had increased its output to such a rate that work began on a factory in Birtley, Co. Durham for the manufacture of Tubular's own products.

Tubular Engineering Ltd is one of four companies within the Tubular Edgington Group. It manufactures a range of products where metal fabrication forms the basis of a structure, for example bridge parapets, pedestrian guardrailing and crush barriers and architectural metalwork such as the new Dome Leisure Centre at Doncaster. The company installed a roller coaster in the Metro Centre at Gateshead, where it also designed, fabricated and erected a children's playscheme comprising a variety of slides, climbs and chutes.

Tubular Engineering has been responsible for the design, development and marketing of the new stadium seat. This is a product that meets market needs at the right time, for the right reasons.

There have been many regrettable accidents at football grounds, in recent years, and the need for safe seating has been much debated. Tubular Engineering had begun the design of a durable, safe stadium seat in the mid 1980s. The design ideas were thus well in progress two years before Lord Justice Taylor's Report of 29 January 1990, showing that the company had anticipated the long-awaited recommendations for all-seater football stadia. Many sporting events attract large crowds,

and it is envisaged that in a large stadium being seated, is a more comfortable and civilised way of enjoying sport.

The launch of the safer stadium seat followed the Taylor Report's call for all-seater football grounds. A company statement reads:

Following three years' research and development, the Tubular Engineering division of Tubular Edgington PLC has announced the launch of a new concept in stadium seating – a seat manufactured completely from engineering polymers. It has features, particularly relating to safety and spectator comfort, that are well in advance of conventional seats currently in use in many stadia and other venues.

The new seat is named the 'Durham 2000'. It is designed to be used in all types of venue, indoors as well as outdoors. It goes beyond the current recognised standard to withstand very high pressure and impact. It contains a greater degree of fire resistance than most traditional polypropylene seating currently used by many football league clubs. It also closes automatically to just 200 mm (less than 8 in) – flatter than any other in current use – a feature designed to help speed up emergency evacuation.

For league clubs – and other venues – concerned about costs, Tubular has also devised a demountable system to upgrade terraces at a fraction of the cost and without the inconvenience of rebuilding. Incorporating the new 'Durham 2000' seat and using the existing terracing as its base, Tubular says it can be installed at competitive costs compared to those of rebuilding standard terracing.

The 'Durham 2000' is the successful result of three years of research collaboration between Tubular's development engineers, Durham University and Teesside Polytechnic.

As well as safety, comfort has been enhanced with air cushions built into the seat pan and backrest. This has the added effect of reducing body heat loss, an important factor in chilly stadia. The seat pan and back rest also fit snugly to reduce draughts which cause back pain.

The polymers used allow the seat to stand up to all the everyday hazards of fizzy drinks, atmospheric acid pollution and the sun's ultra-violet rays, making maintenance simple and economical.

Tubular are offering the 'Durham 2000' in a variety of colours. It has a single baseplate to facilitate tread or riser mounting and to prevent the accumulation of inflammable rubbish.

The managing director of Tubular's Engineering Division, Owen Craggs, said: 'Safety at our sporting and major entertainment venues – not just at football grounds – has taken on far greater urgency and must be a top priority as a result of Lord Justice Taylor's Report.

Fortunately, at Tubular we anticipated some time ago the growing demand for increased safety and greater comfort for spectators. Calls for more and better seating, especially from football spectators, encouraged us to begin research into a safer, stronger and more comfortable seat. The result, I believe, is the best seat available anywhere in the world.'

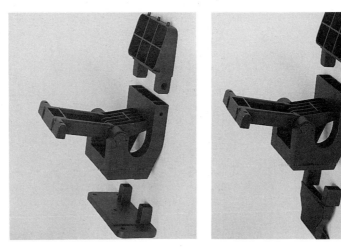

FEATURES
The forum has been ergonomically designed for comfort: stress analysed for warmth. Completely made from engineering polymers for durability

Special features are:
● Maintenance free
● Flexible mounting positions
● Resistance to vandalism
● Fire resistance – to meet regulation CRIB5
● Blow moulded method of manufacture creates air cushion for extra comfort

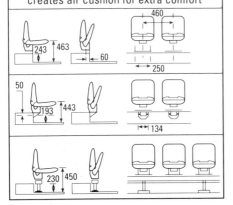

A concept sketch outlines the style of the seat, including a general impression and the function of the seat. These drawings can also be useful when modelling a design and they enable designers to think through different possibilities.

The design and development of a sports stadium seat for both permanent and temporary installation

Before manufacture

The decision to develop the idea of a new stadium seat arose from a perceived opportunity in an expanding leisure industry marketplace. This gap in the market was spotted ahead of time. All-seater stadia are intended to be civilised and comfortable environments where spectators can enjoy entertainment and sport within large public arenas. There is now a growing need, certainly in the football industry, to reduce crowd standing. The Taylor Report recommended a reduction of 20 per cent standing capacity per year, to be enacted by football grounds, hence moving towards an all-seater sport in the near future.

The designer's drawing, testing, selection of materials and production organisation are the essential issues during the initial stages of design in an engineering context.

The drawings and models shown here were used in the design of the 'Durham 2000' seat. They are examples of engineering design and relate to the initial stage of development when the engineer is considering the general proposition and broad outline of alternative schemes.

Anthropometric data concerning the seating position was also considered in the case of this seat design. Detailed information relating the percentile ranges between 2.5 and 97.5% of the adult population was also studied. Further reference was given to the variety of clothing worn at different seasons of the year, to indicate the range of use of the seat by different people.

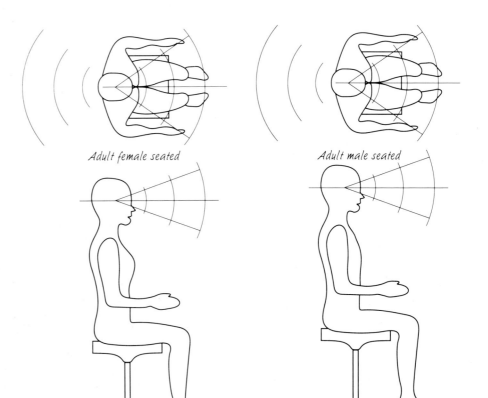

Adult female seated   Adult male seated

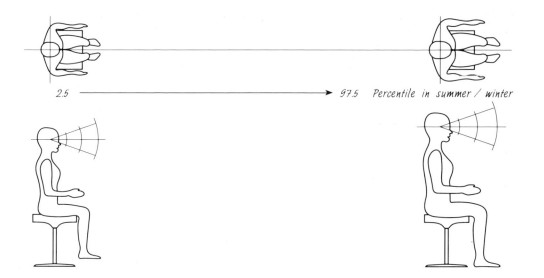

2.5 ——————————————→ 97.5   *Percentile in summer / winter*

Small-scale drawings are also produced at this stage to outline the overall scheme; they are sometimes called project drawings, and are used to present ideas to the team working with the designer, as well as to present information about how components can be assembled. The modular seating system designed by Tubular requires such data to be used and presented through many drawings.

The design organisation for manufacture and the technical qualities of the seat are achieved through the co-operation and subcontracting of the many requirements, requests for information and acquisition of research data from different company and/or university inputs to the design.

The frames and structure of the original seats were made from aluminium. The aim of this new concept is to use plastic for the frame and the seat in the form of an engineering polymer.

The seat was sent to FIRA (Furniture Industry Research Association) and achieved a 'crib 5' rating for its performance in fire. This means that the seat is capable of maintaining appropriate safety requirements in the event of fire in a public place. During these tests it was found that the quality of the final design prevented fire from easily catching hold. Furthermore, the seat material contains a flame-inhibitor substance.

The choice of colour for the seat is an important issue. Ultraviolet stability is a feature of the properties of the polymer used. This is important when considering the effects of the sun on external surfaces, especially its tendency to 'bleach' out colours. Colours are thus steadfast in this new seat. However, the actual colour of a seat performs a function of its own. Colours can be used to mark out certain areas in a stadium. It has been shown in Scandinavia that if a combination of colours is used for seating, when events are televised a speckled effect is achieved, creating the appearance of a crowded stadium even when all the seats have not been filled. White seats can be used for cricket grounds to help the batsmen to see the bowler's arm and the ball. If the stadium uses the same colour throughout, for example orange, red or blue, then footballers merge into the crowd and it becomes very difficult to see the action of the game.

The design also needed to take into account the possibilities of fixing new seats into existing grounds. The main problem here is that many grounds have uneven terraces. In this case Tubular use their demountable system. The life expectancy of this seat is very good, making it a design ahead of its time.

During manufacture

During manufacture it was found that the draft angles achieved on the seat's form for moulding proved to be an aesthetic feature of the overall design. The ergonomic factors concerning comfort and warmth are also essential features of the high quality of the seat's design. The seat contains an air pocket which provides good insulation and retains body heat, thus creating a warm seat to sit on. This warming effect also softens the material, so that the seat 'accommodates' the individual's body shape. The thickness of the material also means that the seat is durable, vandal-proof and has many features that prevent anyone from tampering with the fixings. There are no sharp edges and the seat is safe.

Engineering drawings form essential production information. These are the drawings that help to create the design, resolve the information required for manufacture and help in the organisation of manufacture. They are drawn up as full size or scaled and employ orthographic projection as well as many forms of perspective drawing, including many different forms of three-dimensional representation. Common examples are engineering drawings and prototypes at different stages of development, including views of components which required design in their own right.

Modern design and production generally involve CAD and computer graphics.

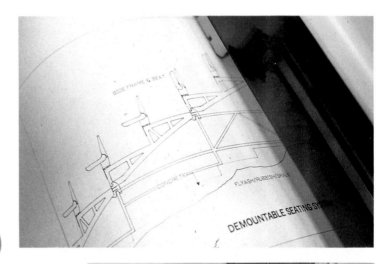

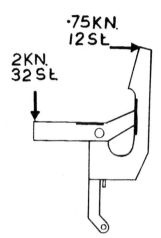

HIGH STRESS AREAS

·75KN.
12St.

2KN.
32St.

·75KN.
12St.

2KN
32St

·75KN.
12St.

2KN
32St

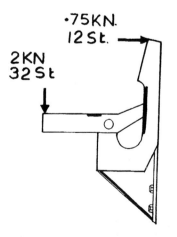

After manufacture

Many aspects of design drawing support the promotion and maintenance of objects once they have been made. These drawings use technical illustration techniques, especially those that are easy to follow. They are intended as technical information for the workforce supporting, servicing and installing the seat.

Promotional artwork involves the use of graphic design treatments aimed at 'selling' the product to an appropriate audience, either the general public or specific clients. The essential aim is to popularise the design and prove its worth in the marketplace. Clarity of communication at this stage is crucial to the success of any product or system.

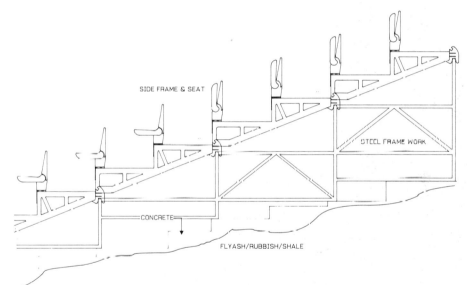

SIDE FRAME & SEAT

STEEL FRAME WORK

CONCRETE

FLYASH/RUBBISH/SHALE

DEMOUNTABLE SEATING SYSTEM

89

Technology in the Press

Introduction

This case study is based on a critical, professional analysis of the influence of technology upon the production of a regional newspaper. It concentrates upon improvements in the design of the newspaper because of the many technological changes that have occurred in the newspaper industry. The article was written by David Kelly, General Manager of *The Northern Echo*.

Design analysis and criticism are concerned with the way in which modern technologies overcome problems or create difficulties for people and society. You should aim to establish which technology has been employed and for what reasons. You should also consider which concepts, theories or facts have been employed as well as how well they have been used.

Collect your own examples of the influence of technology on design, and outline major areas of concern. What are their effects upon the nature and quality of work. Who benefits from new technology? What are the economic factors involved? Are people 're-skilled' or 'de-skilled' in their work?

You should be able to distinguish between the influences of handcrafted design, the developments of robotic or computer-controlled design, and the changes in methods of mass production. You should also be aware of the notion of good and bad effects of technology on design, including the difficulties of clear and rational arguments concerning the value of certain technologies.

'At a keystroke!'

At 8.30 p.m. on Tuesday June 25, 1989, a 15 lb [7 kg] bomb exploded at the Carlton Club in London's West End. Several people were injured at the club, a bastion of the Conservative Party since it was opened 158 years earlier.

In the aftermath, it was neatly demonstrated that technology is only as good as the people who use it: a video camera which would have revealed the bomber's identity had been left switched off.

For journalists on *The Northern Echo*, one of Britain's most successful regional morning newspapers, the bombing was a relatively routine story but to tell it they called upon a range of technological resources which have enabled them and newspapers throughout the world to provide a better service both in terms of content and design.

The computer – what else! – was the catalyst of the revolution that changed the British newspaper industry during the 1970s and 1980s, and at the heart of what British journalists called 'new technology' (though it wasn't new to the rest of the world) was the ability it gave them to directly input their stories from VDUs or portable computers and then transform them into type at the press of a button.

Although computers for typesetting had been in existence for decades in the newspaper industry elsewhere in the world, British publishers had been slow to catch on. This was due to lack of entrepreneurial vision, inadequacies of people management, cost and the stranglehold of trade unions. Until the computers marched out of silicon valley and heralded the invasion of the cheaper and cheaper microcomputer, columns of newspaper type had been produced from hot metal, individual lines of type (called 'slugs') cast by machines that might have excited Heath Robinson.

This was a hopelessly inflexible system and that newspapers could be produced using it was mostly due to the large numbers of people employed to cast and assemble the columns of type. Although the actual material was cheap and economical – the metal could be recycled – the natural rigidity of the type tended to restrict design to columns of standard width. As magazines with their photoset type pushed back the design boundaries, newspapers began to feel increasingly constrained.

But the embracing of the technology to change all this was that of wrestlers rather than lovers, because cheap as the raw material was for hot metal setting, the people were expensive. To the surprise of no one then, given the the self-evident nature of computer technology and the backward-looking stance of the newspaper print trades unions, this was seen as a threat to employment. It was, of course; and had the print unions not countenanced all kinds of 'Spanish customs' – working practices that restricted the service to readers and bled dry proprietors – they might have had some public sympathy. But there was precious little, and in a climate cultivated by the Thatcher government managements were finally persuaded to grasp the nettle of economic production.

So the awakening to the benefits of photocomposition was fuelled, like most things, largely by cost rather than design considerations. Of course, the problems of maintaining traditional typesetting equipment were another factor but newspaper managements could finally resist no longer their Holy Grail – the capture of the computer keystroke which would become the undoing of the labour and cost stranglehold which had inhibited them for so long. Although among regional newspapers it was managements in places like Nottingham and Wolverhampton that first boldly stepped into the fray, it was not until national newspapers embarked on their exodus from Fleet Street that the public generally sat up and took notice. The ensuing bitter struggles and violence at the new dockside sites at Wapping thus became another indelible reminder of the inadequacies of industrial management and relations in Britain.

But how precisely did technology bring about this sea change and usher in a long-awaited revolution? How were newspapers transformed in content, design and approach at a keystroke? What technology enabled *Northern Echo* journalists, for example, to present the Carlton Club bombing story the way they did?

Typesetting by computers unlocked the first swathe of chains. Although large numbers of people were still initially involved in re-keying original editorial and advertising material on computers instead of typesetters, the writing was on the wall. The whole process was uneconomic.

For example, a reporter on *The Northern Echo* would type a story in a district office – the first keystroke – then read it out over the telephone to a typist (the second keystroke). That typed story – or 'copy' as it is known – was passed through the editing process and was typed again by a compositor (the third keystroke). The typeset copy would be checked against the original dictated version for keystroking errors and once these were corrected by further re-keying (the fourth time), the type was handed on for assembly into a page. Every single word potentially typed up to four times!

Photocomposition, which involved change from hot metal casting to output on photographic bromide paper, did not in itself solve the repeat-keying process. But it clearly underlined a now redundant area of production: redundant because here was a technology screaming to be let in that enabled newspapers to capture, hold and manipulate the reporter's original keystrokes. Re-keying was unnecessary – and at a stroke three areas of newspaper production came to an end. The economics of that finally proved irresistible to proprietors.

But this revolution also unleashed a design freedom that many journalists had coveted. With one bound journalists and designers were freed by photocomposition typesetting and from the stultifying practices of demarcation: the only limitations were the capabilities of the equipment and their own imagination and sense of enterprise.

The single-keystroke issue is the most significant aspect of how technology has changed the face of newspapers but the versatility of the computer has extended far beyond this initial area. It has transformed opportunities for better communication from the reporter's original story to the wrapping and labelling of individual copies of the paper: it has given back time to the originators and thus improved the quality of service to the increasingly complex and sophisticated range of newspaper customers. It has also lowered the cost base and made possible the production of publications which would otherwise have been unviable.

The computer has changed every area of newspaper design and production: photographers can use still video cameras which capture the image on a small floppy disk; video grab equipment enables journalists to snatch pictures from live or recorded TV footage; reporters use laptop portable computers then transmit over public telephone lines from locations all over Britain and the rest of the world, into the newspaper's host computer. Or they use VDUs; journalists can search their own or other electronic databases for background information – details, for example, of other mainland bombings; information graphics can be downloaded from national or international news agencies or other newspapers; reports and colour photographs of national and international events are beamed into newspaper offices by satellite or along special high quality phone lines; text is edited and typographically composed on VDUs with WYSIWYG (What You See Is What You Get) facilities; classified advertisements are keyed directly by advertisement staff; display ads are designed and composed on screen; whole pages of editorial and advertisements are assembled on screen with colour and graphic elements included; image plotters output the pages in photographic bromide form or as negatives for press plate-making. Some newspapers are outputting pages direct onto printing plates; pages can be transmitted to remote printing sites by satellite or special terrestrial phone line.

Not an area is untouched: the computer has made it everything with chips. In reporting the Carlton bombing, *The Northern Echo* made use of every aspect of that new technology with the exception of the still video camera which it believed at the time required further refinement. But apart from the flexibility of being able to endlessly manipulate text and pictures, designers on newspapers are being liberated by the kind of graphics and page make-up software that can now be used on computers like the Macintosh. If there is one computer which has opened up newspaper designers' vision, it is the Apple Mac, and the desktop publishers have led the way here.

At the very minimum, Macs are superb creative tools for designing editorial and advertising graphics though some papers were sceptical about their ability to handle the large quantities of file transfers required in full-page make-up on daily newspapers. However, Eddie Shah used them to produce the ill-fated *Post* in 1988 in his second attempt to establish a successful national newspaper, and the *Post's* failure, in the event, was not due to the pioneering use of Mac technology. Indeed, within two years a similar system had been bolted on to the SII front end system of the *London Evening Standard*.

At the time of the Carlton bombing, Macs were being used at *The Northern Echo* for creating information graphics and display advertisements, employing design software like MacDraw and Adobe Illustrator and page make-up programs like the front-runner QuarkXpress. That night, in addition to downloading by telephone a customised colour weather service, the editorial Macs pulled out the information graphic on the bombing prepared by Britain's largest national news agency, the Press Association. By using the same software, individual newspapers can customise the art and the typography, to adapt it to house style. That night, the agency's bomb blast graphic was used unchanged, squirted through a device to convert its format from postscript to bitstream and then into the newspaper's Xenotron page make-up system to be used as black and white art.

Artists and graphic designers can create and re-shape their work at will on Macs and the range of special effects achievable grows more impressive every year. That said, *The Northern Echo's* redesigned paper for the 1990s contained attractive scraperboard logos as well as Mac-generated art because there are some computer techniques that have not yet made redundant the artist's skills.

The principal liberation of Macs for designers is that the computer can almost instantly handle the mechanics of preparing artwork – drawing shapes and rules, applying text, tones etc. – thus providing more time for creativity. Yet if newspaper editors get too greedy for graphic output at the expense of that quality we will not see the improvement in design so desperately needed in British newspaper graphics. Overseas newspapers, especially in the United States, are already years ahead in design quality because they provide not just the technology but the time and human resources too.

Newspaper and magazine graphics development is an area which could stand more attention in art colleges too, especially in terms of mastering computer-created art. Already in Britain, some newspapers have identified the need for a new specialist – not just a journalist, not just an artist, not just a page designer, but one who has the essential qualities of all three.

However, the Mac, outstanding as it may be, is but one way in which technology has affected design. Now that three potential processes of re-keying have been eliminated, journalists have had new challenges thrust upon them. They found there was no hiding place. Immediately exposed were inadequacies in keyboarding skills and spelling and grammar. Previously, mistakes of this kind had been picked up during the editing and composing operations. The lack of 'cover' also exposed inadequacies in journalists' design skills that had been masked by the constraints of old technology. Once journalists were freed by computers to exercise their design skills some fell prey to lack of design imagination and to typographical indiscipline. Computers enabled them to squeeze type or expand it by methods that must set type designers squirming or turning in their graves.

Typographical disciplines – the point size of text and display founts – are about readability, legibility and establishing attention priorities for readers. For example, a headline in 60pt Century Schoolbook Bold was intended to catch the eye before one in 42pt. But lazy journalists who could not write headlines to fit the column widths began to distort type and blur the differences. Pretty soon, they discovered they could make one fit in 53pt and the other in 49pt. Prior to photocomposition and direct input by journalists, *The Northern Echo* banned such practices.

It also posted notice of its opposition to other forms of design distortion made possible by computers. For decades, newspaper journalists all over Britain had edited out 'dead areas' from photographs, for example spaces between people. These were practices known as 'Hammersmith jobs', named after a London hospital and in newspaper terms this simply meant cutting out 'dead' areas of photographs: a scissors and paste operation.

But the newest technology has created opportunities to make the photograph lie in a way undreamed of by the early crude exponents of making reality fit a design shape. Computers attached to image scanners allow newspapers and magazines to turn black to white, to give hair to those who are bald, to make Ol' Blue Eyes Sinatra into Ol' Brown Eyes – or any other one of the 16 million shades it is now possible to create on a computer. Already national newspapers are using this technology to help them fit photographs to design shapes, a practice which they justify on the grounds that the information content of the image has not been changed. Technology and design now conspire to create a truth trap through which many will plunge. In America, sufficient numbers have already distorted reality to provoke calls for legislation to make the media declare such trickery. Gone are the days when you could say the photograph never lies – and newspaper page designers and editors are responsible.

Technology has had its impact too in journalistic and design attitudes. People love the advantages of computers but they hate the unforgiving nature of them: inadvertent clumsy keying, a power blip or inexplicable lock-ups can destroy patient work. The frailties of telecommunications, especially poor-quality British Telecom lines, can be both frustrating and damaging. So newspapermen and women have developed a love-hate relationship with new technology which extends far beyond naive initial worries that Big Brother management would be able to assess individual output more readily. There is, in some areas, a reluctance to be responsible for – not to mention an ineptitude in – the composition skills that were originally those of the printer.

But what many journalists now see clearly is that technology has opened up the gateway to new opportunities in telling the reader what is going on. The ability to tell the matter-of-fact story of a bombing has been enhanced by the microchip revolution and now it is up to journalists to become – and remain – the masters and not the slaves of the computer.

'A paint pot in the public's face'

Art and design products tend to relate to the social, economic and political circumstances of the period in which they are produced. This pertains to the twentieth century as much as to any other time. However, another factor becomes equally important, that of the personal expression of the artist or designer, especially as, on many occasions, the 'shock' of new ideas is not easily assimilated or understood by the rest of society. Artists and designers, be they painters, sculptors, film producers or directors, musicians, poets, playwrights, novelists, fashion designers, graphic designers, architects or product designers, are often held to be the leaders of taste and style.

As far as artists are concerned, has society fully accepted the notion that artists are free to express their own opinions in any format they believe to be 'correct'? As you walk around a modern art exhibition, what are your comments and thoughts? Do you deride some of the modern exhibits because they do not display illusionist images and may appear to be lacking in skilled draughtsmanship, or do you accept that in this modern age, the age of the camera, art must change in format and style from that of the previous centuries?

Falling Rocket by James Abbot McNeill Whistler.

The nineteenth century in France witnessed a progression of artistic styles. Neoclassicism had been opposed by Romanticism, both styles being dismissed by the revolutionary artist Courbet with his loud cry of Realism. The work of the Impressionists was critically condemned in the 1870s, being seen as unfinished sketches not worthy of public display. The four great Post-Impressionist artists, Seurat, Cézanne, Van Gogh and Gauguin, all took a unique artistic path of their own choosing. Following this example, twentieth-century artists produced highly personal, unique statements on their canvases, employing original methods of representation and technical presentation. Many also explored new formal qualities in their work.

In nineteenth-century England art was generally narrative in form and frequently sentimental and moral in its theme: Landseer's *The Old Shepherd's Chief Mourner* (1837), Roberts's *The Empty Sleeve* (1856), Redgrave's *The Sempstress* (1844), being but a few examples produced during this period. The highly prized Victorian ethic of hard work was associated with the production of an artwork and many painters laboured for years over one canvas. Students following the government-prescribed drawing course would be expected to take months over the copying of one of the plaster casts required at the various examination levels.

The great artistic guru of the day was John Ruskin (1819–1900), who loudly advocated hard diligent work. He taught drawing in his own college for working men and was a very influential art critic, producing his own magazine to discuss art as well as being the author of a number of books on art and architecture. He supported the work of the Pre-Raphaelites for they upheld one of his major principles, that artists should 'go to nature in all singleness of heart . . . rejecting nothing, selecting nothing and scorning nothing.' They lavished much hard work on their canvases, each area of the painting being painstakingly executed, one canvas often taking months, and sometimes years, to complete.

James McNeil Whistler (1834–1903) did not attempt to follow the acceptable style of Victorian art; rather, he chose to pursue his own interests on his canvases. Influenced by Japanese art, as many Parisian artists of the period were, he was concerned to depict a particular mood or feeling in his work, rather than the illusionistic representation of objects and a narrative subject matter. Although many of his paintings were portraits, he used them as exercises in tone and colour, leading to the suggestion of a particular mood and giving them such titles as *Symphony in White* or *Nocturne in Black and Grey*. Initially, even Paris did not fully appreciate his work, his *Symphony in White No. 1* being rejected by the Salon in 1863, and then, along with Manet's *Déjeuner sur L'Herbe*, causing a sensation at the Salon des Refusés of that year.

Whistler continued to perfect his style, learning to suggest a form or figure by a few rapidly executed brushmarks, rather than by painstakingly representing every detail. During the 1870s he received favourable comments from some critics, although others remained quite mystified. However, he was able to remain true to his principles and to make a living for himself. In July 1877, when Ruskin wrote a review of the exhibits at the new Grosvenor Gallery and stated, with particular reference to one of the eight Whistler paintings on display, *Nocturne in Blue and Gold: the Falling Rocket*:

> For Mr. Whistler's own sake, no less than for the protection of the purchaser, Sir Coutts Lindsay ought not to have admitted works into the gallery in which the ill educated conceit of the artist so nearly approached the aspect of wilful imposture. I have seen, and heard, much of Cockney impudence

Constructed sculpture from Gabo to Smith: Dween Gallery 1991. In the Tate Gallery, London.

before now, but never expected to hear a coxcomb ask two hundred guineas for flinging a pot of paint in the public's face.

Whistler saw that action was necessary and he sued Ruskin for libel. Both men looked forward to the idea of a showdown case, each believing his concept of art to be correct, however Ruskin was ill and unable to attend the trial and therefore the public was denied the dynamic battle that it had expected. Ruskin had Frith, Burne-Jones and Tom Taylor to speak for him, while Whistler called, as witnesses for his case, William Rossetti and Albert Moore. Ruskin's case centred around the belief that Whistler's painting was not worthy of the high price placed upon it, whereas Whistler's defence was one that could stand for the whole of modern art, that it is the right of the artist to paint in what ever manner he or she wishes.

Under cross-examination, Whistler was asked to define a nocturne – 'an arrangement in form and colour,' he stated – and to explain the *Nocturne in Blue and Gold: the Falling Rocket'*. 'It is a night piece and represents the fireworks at Cremorne.'

'Not a view of Cremorne?'

'If it were a view of Cremorne,' he replied, 'it would certainly bring about nothing but disappointment on the part of the beholders. It is an artistic arrangement.'

This concept of an artistic arrangement is quite acceptable to our ears but in Victorian Britain such an approach to painting had never before been stated. Pictures were seen as faithful copies of the real world, not

Nocturne in blue and gold, Old Battersea Bridge by James Abbot McNeill Whistler.

artistic statements. However, such points were not the issue of this court case, rather the fact that Whistler had asked a price for a piece of work which, in Ruskin's estimation, it did not merit.

Whistler agreed, on cross-examination, that 200 guineas was 'a pretty good price for a painting' and when he was asked how long it took him to paint a nocturne, he replied, 'I knock off one possibly in a couple of days – one to do the work, and another to finish it.'

'And that was the labour for which you asked 200 guineas?'

'No,' replied Whistler, 'it was for the knowledge gained through a lifetime.'

Looking at the painting *Nocturne in Blue and Gold: Old Battersea Bridge*, the judge asked, 'Are those figures on the top of the bridge intended for people?'.

'They are what you like,' Whistler replied.

Again this remark was not taken up at the trial, but Whistler had voiced one of the principles that was to form the basis of twentieth-century modern art – that a painting was not merely concerned with the accurate representation of an object on the canvas, but that a work of art was the outcome of the artist's own experience and the understanding and receptiveness of the spectator.

When Whistler was asked to explain the beauty of *Nocturne in Blue and Gold: the Falling Rocket*, he said, 'It is as impossible for me to explain to you the beauty of that picture as it would be for a musician to explain to you the beauty of harmony in a particular piece of music if you had no ear for music.'

Following the judge's lead, although the jury found in favour of Whistler (that he had been libelled), he was only awarded one farthing ($\frac{1}{4}$ old penny) in damages, the smallest amount possible and without costs, which meant that he had to pay his own expenses. This bankrupted Whistler.

Here, then, was an artist stating that he had the right to paint in the manner he chose; it was up to the public if they wished to pay the price for his work. Regardless of critical opinion, he would paint in the manner he believed was correct. How often are artists still derided for maintaining such a belief? How often does society ridicule a single artistic statement with the remark that a five-year-old could do better, without giving any consideration to the concepts behind the work or the previous study and investigation that lead to that piece?

David Hockney, born in Bradford in 1937, is one of the most famous living English artists. He submitted a painting, free of charge, that was eagerly accepted by British Telecom for the front cover of their Bradford telephone directory. It was not an illusionist work; it did not attempt to be photographically realistic. It was a personal statement by Hockney, attempting to distill the essence of the Bradford area. It created a local outcry, bringing to the fore many of the issues that have continually dogged modern art. A large percentage of the general public appeared to believe that paintings should still be faithful copies of the real world.

Mr Naylor, an inhabitant of Bradford, sent a strongly worded letter to British Telecom, stating that in his opinion the picture 'is pathetic . . . A child could have painted a better picture of Bradford than that. It is monstrous.'

David Hockney's cover for the new Phone Book

Monstrosity!

SIR — Should not the humps of the Loch Ness Monster, in Mr Hockney's cartoon on the front of the new Phone Book, be more rounded than pointed?
He can walk into any primary school in Bradford and will in comparison find masterpieces by five-year-olds on the classroom walls.
Kenneth Wood, Farway, Holme Wood.

We should be proud of Hockney

★ SIR — I feel I must write in defence of the cover of the Bradford telephone directory.
★ What an ungrateful lot you are!
★ I am not insulted by the painting by David Hockney — in fact quite the reverse. I am very proud that a world-famous artist has honoured us with a painting.
★ How many more cities can boast of this? Let's stop the bickering and start being proud of our fellow Bradfordians?
★ I say, well done BT and a very big thank you, David Hockney!
Mrs P Appleyard, Toftshaw Lane, Bradford.

David Hockney . . . world famous

The Hockney controversy.

However, British Telecom were more than pleased with the cover design, which caused such interest, that many art collectors ordered personal copies. Indeed, not all local voices were raised in opposition.

Graham Carey pointed out in a letter to the *Telegraph and Argus*, one of Bradford's local papers, that:

> It is an important achievement for any artist to struggle through the loss of innocent artistic expression that we all once had as children to regain a mature blending of spontaneity and freshness – which child art possesses – with a wider and deeper understanding of reality.

Anne Crowther, British Telecom's area spokeswoman, praised Hockney's design and Martin Wainwright described it as:

> A glowing mix of greens and yellows, ditching the Yorkshire city's smokey, J. B. Priestley image, in favour of the surrounding dales and moors. Wild imagination contrasts with precise detail: the local Cow and Calf rocks are painted bright red, while a bus beetling up one of the hills is the correct shade of Bradford Omnibus blue.

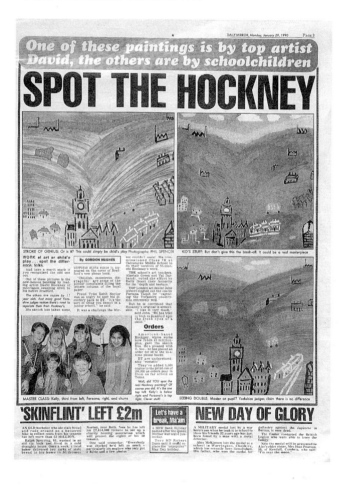

The *Daily Mirror* on Hockney, January 29, 1990.

An example of a case study to work

With particular reference to the Bradford Telephone Directory cover designed by David Hockney, using clear, succinct language and including any other relevant examples to support your argument, present a debate for and against the right of twentieth-century artists to express themselves freely in whatever subject matter, form or technique they wish.

This study was conceived by Jean Stokes, South Tyneside College.

Learning about design from nature

Knowledge of the processes of evolution can assist our understanding of design.

Chinese painting of camels. The characters read: while drinking water, think of its source.

A camel is jokingly said to be a horse designed by a committee. What is the implication of this statement for the capabilities of people when they design? Also, can humans redesign nature for greater usefulness? Could you produce a cartoon based on designing a racing pig? Can we control the natural tendency for things to evolve and change?

The essential scientific information used in the following pages was written by Dr Steve Farrow, Sunderland University.

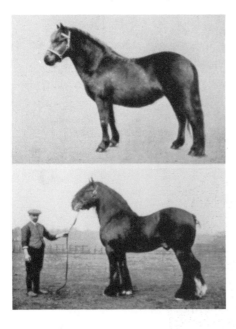

Man redesigns for greater usefulness.

In *The Blind Watchmaker* Richard Dawkins describes the principles and concepts of evolution in a very practical way, especially concerning 'natural selection' and 'living design'.

We may say that a living body or organ is well designed if it has attributes that an intelligent and knowledgeable engineer might have built into it in order to achieve some sensible purpose, such as flying, swimming, seeing, eating, reproducing, or more generally promoting the survival and replication of the organ's genes. It is not necessary to suppose that the design of a body or organ is the best that an engineer could conceive of. Often the best that one engineer can do is, in any case, exceeded by the best that another engineer can do, especially another who lives later in the history of technology. But any engineer can recognise an object that has been designed, even poorly designed, for a purpose, and he can usually work out what that purpose is just by looking at the structure of the object.

The important issue concerning the principle of 'cumulative selection' for a general study of design, is that 'living organisation is the product of cumulative selection' rather than step by step selection. These ideas can only be briefly introduced here; the reader should study the relevant texts in more detail to obtain a fuller appreciation of evolution theories and their relationship to our general notion of design.

Design knowledge, especially the products of design, is generally the accumulation of the best options in a given time, and environmental context. Professor Rechenberg, an engineer at the Technical University of Berlin, sought inspiration from nature for his experiments on flight, using a wind tunnel. He studied the aerodynamics of wings, not by mimicking nature but through evolved generations of the form of a wing.

He 'bred' the ideal wing through cumulative selection based on random mutations. This experiment was conducted in a case where the ideal form was known. For example, a flat plane wing is the best configuration for an aerofoil that has minimal drag. Through a random selection process, based on a mathematical model, Rechenberg evolved the best solution for this known design. If the best solution can be obtained in an easy case, is it possible to obtain solutions to problems for which there are no answers as yet? Many leading German engineering companies are developing such techniques, for example Siemens and Audi.

Consider the following problem, which was demonstrated by Richard Dawkins on the BBC TV *Horizon* programme. Sixteen points on the periphery of a network are to be supplied with gas or liquid from a single supply. This example could be found in a chemical factory, and the aim is to achieve a smooth flow of gas or liquid, with the minimum of back-pressure in the system. Rechenberg used evolution to solve the problem and Dawkins modelled it on a computer.

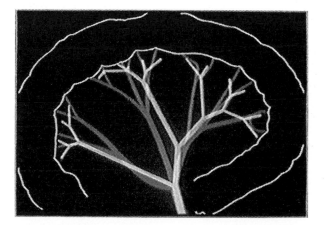

The Blind Watchmaker, an Horizon programme.
A screen image of a 16 point problem.

Nature has also solved this problem. It happens that the supply of blood to tissues in a dog's lung requires a similar branching system to that evolved for the best flow of liquid in the above example. The dog's lung enables the dog's blood system to receive oxygen from the air sacs on the periphery of the animal's lung, and this branching 'design' enables a smooth flow of blood. This solution overcomes the problem of back-pressure in the system.

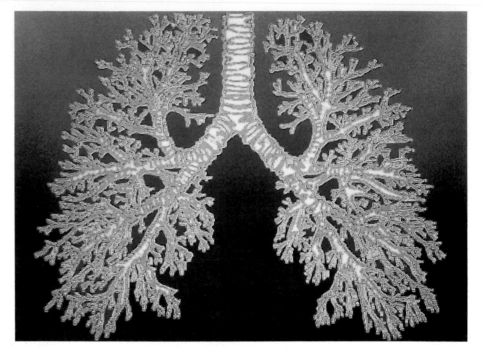

False colour (computer graphics) photograph of a resin cast of the human bronchial tree, the network of airways serving both lungs.

Further, design is concerned with the successful development of ideas and schemes through processes of invention and technology into production. In many ways it complements the analytical aspects of science because it is thought to be equally concerned with discovery. However, science discovers things by controlled experiments and the observation of variables that can be reduced to theories and laws. Scientific methods rely on developing ever-increasing accuracy concerning observation and experimentation. Science aims to be devoid of subjective judgement whereas design thrives on it.

Design is not like science. It is a wide-ranging activity, formed more by the synthesis of ideas to be focused upon, rather than the piecemeal teasing apart of matter or ideas. It is more intuitive, and pragmatic than science because it requires choices of the best options to be made, rather than accurate conclusions to be drawn and left for further investigation. Design success, as with that of technology, relies on value judgements. Thus, design is concerned with decisions of taste, choice and sensitivity.

Are the processes of evolution similar to design processes or are they different? Is it true that nature generates the optimum design of living things according to their adaptation to their surroundings and the cumulative selection of the best survival characteristics? Consider some 'design' examples in nature.

Form and function – the design process of natural selection

For thousands of years, people have made and used an enormous variety of devices which, in some way or other, make life simpler. Such artefacts range from the simple bone needle of neolithic peoples, to the enormously complicated mechanical and electronic devices with which modern keyhole surgery is performed. In similar fashion, people have made use of plants and animals in order to help them to survive in relative comfort.

Neolithic peoples are thought to have been hunter-gatherers, and it is generally believed that the first of the 'metal' cultures, the Bronze Age, marked the beginnings of organised agriculture. The long process of the domestication of plant and animal species of use to mankind has actually been a process of 'artificial selection'. People have chosen particular features of plants and animals that they wish to preserve, and have bred from them in order to produce a particular result. Examples include the production of cereals from wild grasses, and the domestication and refinement of draught and food animals.

However, long before humans appeared on earth, another form of selection was occurring – the 'natural selection' of Darwinian evolutionary theory. Put simply, the theory states that those plants and animals best adapted to any particular environment (in Darwinian terms, the 'fittest') are the ones that will survive. As generation succeeds generation, small characteristics that confer advantage to individuals will accumulate (by heredity) until individuals of a species are adapted to a particular environment. It is important to realise that natural selection is driven by the environment, not the organism. It is not an active process on the part of individual organisms, but a response over time by generations of organisms to the varying conditions imposed by the environment.

Organisms do not live in places because they 'like' them but because they can tolerate the prevailing conditions. The plants that grow on a salt marsh do so because they can tolerate high levels of salt in the environment, and can survive these conditions better than other plants. If the salty conditions were removed, they would soon face competition from other plants.

Natural selection is the selection of those species able to survive in a particular environment as against those that are not. The driving force of natural selection is environmental change, and the survival of a species in the face of such change depends on its genetic capacity. When an environment has remained stable for long periods of time, the populations of organisms that survive are those that are best adapted to that environment – the 'fittest'. Under these conditions, natural selection slows down and eventually stops. If, however, a change occurs in the environment, for example climatic change, flooding or the onset of drought, then renewed selection pressure is immediately placed on those organisms and over many generations those that are best able to survive in the changed environment will emerge as the successful members of the new ecosystem.

So, for millions of years the global ecosystem has been the generator of a constantly evolving 'design process'. As each species copes with changing environmental conditions, the genetic coding in each individual organism enables countless 'new' designs to be produced. These designs are evaluated in the starkest terms. If they are inappropriate and do not confer some advantage, however small, to the individuals concerned, they simply do not survive. The fossil record is strewn with many such designs – plants and animals that not only no longer exist, but are also unlike any forms living today. Clearly such species were adapted to conditions which are no longer found on earth today.

The plants and animals that can and do survive dramatic changes in environmental conditions all exemplify a particular design concept, which is the relationship between form and function. Specific living things look the way they do because they reflect a mode of survival in

103

Ash Single-winged keys carried by wind

Willow-herb Seed carried by wind on hair parachute

Traveller's joy Seed carried on a silky hair

Agrimony Bristly fruit catches on to animals' fur

Cranesbill Pod explodes, shooting out seeds

Water lily Spongy berry floats until saturated

Sea rocket Pod drifts in the water and breaks in two

Sycamore Two-winged seeds carried by the wind

Avens Hooked seed catches on to animals' fur

Seed dispersal mechanisms.

a particular environment. Three examples of the ways in which plants and animals have developed special survival strategies are as follows:

1. Through a variety of responses to the requirements of a major life cycle component.

Essential to the survival of flowering plants is the requirement to disperse seeds as far from the parent plant as possible. This has resulted in a wide variety of forms.

2. Through variations to morphological components.

The feet of different birds, for example raptors, woodpeckers and rails, clearly illustrate adaptation to specific ecological niches.

African Jacana.

Greater spotted woodpecker.

3. Through a combination of features that allow for survival in the face of environmental hostility.

The head and the foot of the rough-legged buzzard.

Xerophytes are plants that are capable of tolerating very low moisture availability. They are sometimes termed 'drought-resistant'. They exhibit a variety of forms, all of which are designed to prevent moisture loss from the plant. Many xerophytic plants have leaves with a minimal surface area, which lessens the effect of transpiration. Examples include the 'spiny' leaves of cactus plants.

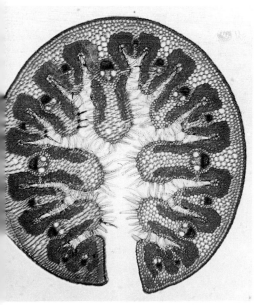

Transverse section of marram grass, *Ammophila arenaria*, showing unrolled leaf with spines.

Dunes being stabilized with planted marram grass, *Ammophila arenaria*, South West France.

From the examples given it should be possible to see that natural selection has driven a process of design, where success is measured in terms of 'fitness' for the function concerned, and that fitness assists a particular species in its struggle for survival in any particular environment. Do these criteria also apply to the things that we design and make?

105

3 Analytical and Critical Studies

ANALYSING AND CRITICISING DESIGN

Practical uses of design awareness

All students of design should be able to talk and write about design, especially what it means to them, and, specifically, for their design studies.

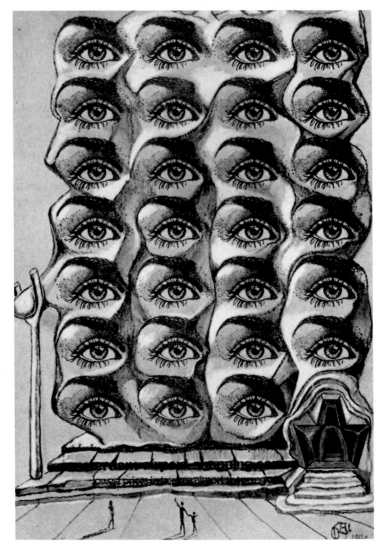

Architecture of Eyes by Salvador Dali. ©
DEMART PRO ARTE BV/DACS 1994.
What can you say about the design of Dali's
image, the paper clip and our need for different
kinds of car? What lies behind the eye and
mind of the artist or designer of these things?

A giant paperclip is released near Oslo to mark the 90th birthday of this Norwegian invention.

The differences in identifying and interpreting what a design is, what the designer intended and what people think of a design are important considerations in a general study of design and designing. Knowing why a designer produced what he or she did is crucial to understanding what lies behind the eye and mind of the designer, and for general understanding of the consequences of design.

Note how successful designs are, as well as how popular and attractive they are for their function and for use by people. Knowing something about why people buy a design, as well as whether or not it is durable and a pleasure to use and own is valuable experience. Good design should be worthy in its own right, but will, to a great extent, be dependent for its success upon people's likes and dislikes, needs and economic means.

Design is also a fundamental component of business and the commercial aspects of design are widespread. Knowledge of design in industry and as used by consumers will always be valuable. But do designers react to our needs or do they perpetuate stereotypical ideas?

Throughout human existence, people have used tools and ideas to protect themselves and their families, by developing clothing, shelters and food production techniques. Survival has depended on ingenuity, including the needs for transport and communication, as well as entertainment and leisure. These things are the substance of our needs and dreams. Work and earning the means to live are the methods by which our lives are controlled. Manufacturing, buying and selling are central for our social wellbeing and development. We no longer need to be technological on a daily basis entirely for our survival, however, we do now use design to bring variety and quality into our lives.

We need cars, televisions, cosmetics and so on for our well-being, rather than for our mere survival. However, we survive in an economic climate of ever-increasing growth, where even design in itself is bought and sold as a commodity. It is used to perpetuate the mass market and mass consumer world. Sometimes it is used to create false needs; it is used to develop and enhance the 'consumer habit' and is

A Lada.

107

the unifying force prompting many deep-seated needs in individuals. We buy things for what they mean to us as much as for their direct functional value. When did you last buy something that made you feel good and what was it?

Design is often used by organisations to encourage individuals to buy things purely for the sake of owning them because of the status they acquire by possessing such a design. For some time electrical goods have been based upon a 'black box' style of design. Is it true that as the 'black box becomes a dominant part of our lives, we need visual clues as to what the product means'? Are manufacturers providing the choices we would like?

> In the case of product design, the metaphor is a visual analogy that enhances the function of design, making both a statement about the product's character and context. Images recall other images that give a point of reference, either to abstract ideas, familiar environmental forms of notations from a historical perspective . . . A stand-out success was the portable video camera, visually referring to the old style movie cameras. 'You know exactly what this equipment is meant to do,' say the designers. The functions were considered to be well executed for easy use.

Thus, the art of 'product semantics' is where the designer designs meaning into products and 'visual metaphors were to be used to achieve the desired social value of the product' (*inForm* magazine, Philips)

Is care in shopping our only need for design awareness? Are you aware of what lies behind the product? Our sense of self, our identity, as well as the pleasure or power that artefacts bring to us are very often derived from their design. Such dreams are catered for through design, and economic pressures are at the heart of our consumerism, as well as forming a particularly powerful aspect of our culture. Shopping fulfills many needs, but can happiness and fulfilment be bought? Should it be designed for?

The commercialism of design is important in the context of effective enterprise and the employment benefits that are derived from design success. Examine the packaging for a Christmas game or Easter egg and establish for yourself the extent to which these items are 'overdesigned'. In this context, too much design eventually means a waste of materials and resources.

Should we 'live simply in order for others to live in the world'? This slogan, which has been employed to raise individuals' consciousness, is a feature of contemporary discussion concerning the exploitation and irrelevant use of certain of the world's resources. How simple should our lives be? If design brings pleasure, why should it be criticised?

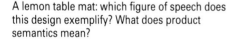

A lemon table mat: which figure of speech does this design exemplify? What does product semantics mean?

Gathering, interpreting and reporting design information

Design study is based on analysing and criticising the possibilities for design action, and knowing about the value and effect of design. Designing itself is the combining of these experiences. The next study is based on examples which highlight understanding personal reactions to designs, the thoughts and feelings of other people, as well as the views and opinions of manufacturers, retailers and expert design evaluators. It will also focus upon what designers do and reveal some of the consequences of design.

Protect the lie

expression. It controls the image in the marketplace – an economic order that is by its very nature unstable and unpredictable. To consolidate this confidence trick, the design world glorifies the consumerist values the market place depends on for survival. Design becomes 'inflated into a way of life, a key to national salvation' (Kinross). It promotes itself as a vital mechanism of the system to its corporate patrons; furthermore, the design world believes itself to be essential to any and every form of communication. Nothing is left naked.

But at what cost? The marketplace has created artificial wealth in the short term, but in doing so it has brought us to the verge of cultural bankruptcy. As we seek to 'look sharp', have we cut off our heads?

'I think the fact that you see our work all over England almost ends up looking like a corporate identity for the country. We never set off with this in mind, but that's the way it seems to have evolved.' – Margaret Calvert, assistant to Jock Kinneir, designers of national signposting systems.

ARRIVALS, Departures, Accident & Emergency, WAIT, SLOW…NO ENTRY. The chaos of modern society requires such commands, categories and regulations: graphic design. Today, this collides with commerce to insist that the only doors you pass through are the entrances to shops. Airports are chockablock with consumption: Sky Shop, Duty Free, Bureau de Change. Hospitals, as they veer increasingly towards private medicine, advertise themselves as hotels where room service comes complete with plastic surgery. In Money Culture, a shop is any service, system or outlet that depends on advertising. Britain is a supermarket. Our leader is a shop assistant. Culture is up for sale. Tourism, after all, saves us from facing up to the real lessons of history. Our past comes gift-wrapped, and it's on special offer!

Britain's signposting system is a model of efficiency, but many of its creators have been unaware of two areas vital to any communication – process and context. Firstly, it is necessary to clarify the motivations and their process, so that design can be a popular rather than an elitist form. Secondly, the willingness of designers to perceive and interact is gone – both with the context of their work, and the effect that it has on everyday life.

It is a question of responsibility, and research. From Top Shop to Virgin, what do the designers of our High Street shops think they are doing when they clutter the environment with appropriated graphics that are obsolete before the signs are even fastened to the wall? They are, of course, 'following the brief', making a fortune, and flooding our eyes with rubbish. The client wanted it.

Where does the brief come from? That's a good question. Does it come from the supermarkets themselves? From television? From the success of 80s 'lifestyle' magazines? Does it come from Rupert Murdoch? Or does it come from the public? Shopping has become a vital means of expression during a time of authoritarianism. We are a long way from 1945. There is no longer any plan – simply a conspiracy of shared interests. On the one hand, greed. on the other, the need for economic survival. Money, the ultimate protection racket. The modern system that facilitates this is signification – the process by which all cultural ideas are reduced to mere codes, and a method that enables design to appear to share the common language of its target market with no more meaning than commercial familiarity.

As Jon Savage put it, 'how did it happen that the current pinnacle of pop culture should be found in adverts?' This is the frame. You are the integral part of the set-up.

The real success of the Design Industry has been its willing to change its skin so often that you rarely, even in The Guardian, get more than a glimpse of the whole picture. This might begin to sound alarmist, but after working at the heart of design culture, we feel it is time to call a halt. The speed and the scale: billboards that increase faster and faster, neon lights flashing faster and faster

Such language problems allow no middle ground, no balance. 'Style Revolution' really means imitation overload – a complete loss of nerve on the part of writers, musicians, editors, designers, when it comes to releasing experience. It's so much easier to act the part than to live the life.

The notion of creativity itself has been colonised by advertising. Never have so many 'creatives' unleashed such destructive forces in their bid for your minds. This language no longer leans towards the opening of possibilities, but to the integration of all forms of expression and identity into plain commercialism. The new 'Silk Cut' ad rips the 'L from LIFE. Integration becomes disintegration.

Cultural expression rests upon the visible plane of an invisible strata. All forms of Media operate on the surface of this strata. During the last decade, its layers have been intensively sucked to the surface and eaten away through the total reliance upon

design world faces an abyss of its own making in the mad denial will eat the Culture is not a bottomless pit that can infinitely ransacked – it needs a purpose present, lived experience with which to nourish its context and vocabulary.

This is now up an impossible. Consider the latest fashion in London, 'Acid House', hybrid of 60s libertarianism and 80s compression… glued together by the insistent bond of the beat. It harbours allusions towards past freedoms (which in the present climate is at least to be welcomed, if not swallowed whole) – freedom of movement, freedom of expression, freedom to take strange chemicals without worrying about the consequences. But even more so than previous subcultures that cross-over, 'Acid House' proclaims itself as a designed invention, matching past form to past form to dance and smile away the present. It's fun, a celebration, but of what?

The main lesson of 'Acid House' has been its speed of assimilation – approximately nine months – from London's scene to prime time Radio One DJs wailing 'acieeed' across the airwaves and onto the front page of The Sun. Bans and moral outrage are par for the course, more so now – for in the present puritanical climate, Fun must be strongly resisted. It should come as no surprise, therefore, that the most radiant smiles of young people, as pictured in the media, can be seen on the faces of those who jive in front of a cashpoint machine.

'Acid' is simply a quest for freedom, a craze that expresses young people's desire for sensory

To hell with Helvetica

(With a little help from Garamond)

Review Guardian, December 3 1988

John Willett

THE PAGE in the Guardian Review by Neville Brody and Jon Wozencroft is vivid illustration, both visually and textually, of the sad situation which it sets out to describe. The alarming slogan "Protect the lie", the baffling arrows pointing at nothing in particular, the strong rightward thrust of the unfortunate **Guard.** all stir the curiosity. What is this about, who is it by, What is this about, who is it by. Answer at the end:

"Do not accept. **THE SETUP**."

I agree, though without seeming much need for that hesitant full stop before deciding just what not to accept (or the final burst into **boldness**). But, but… is not the whole thing a picture of the setup itself?

Only three days earlier readers could have seen John Heartfield's Grosz prospectus of 1917, an ancestor of this kind of design. He had a penchant for arrows around 1920 if I remember right. The propagandist of sans typefaces came from the Bauhaus and the Munich typography school soon after it had originally a special purpose

that, while mainly practising and preaching the former approach they were quite willing to do advertising or exhibition design without beating their breasts. At the Bauhaus, for instance. the word "stylist" was unknown; perhaps consciences were all the clearer for it.

Certainly the strong socio-economic element in design at that time helped spread those common principles which gave the mid-European avant-garde its striking coherence. If you liked Gropius's architecture and Hindemith's music you were also for printing in lower-case sans.

In England today, the arts have been exploiting the formal innovations of 70 or more years without enough sense of the attitudes of mind that brought them into being. This is one factor making for this kind of alienation and disillusionment which designers associate with THE SETUP. Another, which we likewise find unconsciously demonstrated in the Wozencroft/Brody manifesto, is the relatively new economic practice of calling almost any money-making activity an "industry". Newspapers are an industry. advertising and design are industries, so are tourism and pop music and insurance.

There are admittedly still exceptions to this catch-all category – the army, for instance. or prostitution – but there are now surely enough materially unproductive (and at bottom inessential) "industries" to make the apparent industrial successes of the last few years impossible to define except in monetary terms. No wonder many of us have a sense of living in a sham.

True enough, there is a lot in the so-called "real world" of the money culture which isn't nauseating. Britain's postage stamps, for instance, instead of being reliable symbols of our country and its monarchy, have become about as dignified as those of the Cayman Islands. In the post office itself we may be forced to shuffle between ropes at a video screen advertising dispensables, other a flashing sign above the under-

1908, as they proclaim the values of INDEPENDENCE (youth with arms akimbo, seen from below), FREEDOM (shirted, square-chinned girl with arm raised in greeting). FUTURE, (even squarer-chinned youth, saluting) and finally ACTION! (youth and girl gazing into the distance side by side, the youth shouting, maybe at his bank manager). Such disquieting reflections of a bad past are also to be found in post-modern architecture (RHI please watch. And beware of Albert Speer).

It is not so much that there is some vast conspiracy under way to corrupt the arts, killing design by overpromoting it; more that a particularly nasty Zeitgeist has escaped from the bottle and nobody knows quite how to cork it up again. Nobody?

Well, what has happened to the Australian movement of a few years back, started (I believe) by a group of Sydney doctors, to amend the posters advertising drink and tobacco and make their message counter-productive? My favourite was the romantic "Marlborough Country" advertisement where the cowboy is quietly smoking as he and his horse gaze confidently into the sunset. Two balloons were added – Cowboy: "Cough cough". Horse: "Poo, this macho stinks". And the name of the movement Billboard Utilising Graffitists Against Unhealthy Products, or BUGA UP.

The bright Sydney adpersons were not amused, they sued for "vandalism", though iconoclasm would be more like it. And in the Guardian we have a half-page ad by the Home Office, part of their "Crime. Together We'll Crack it" campaign, denouncing graffiti (singular, like media) as a form of Vandalism which is "among the most prevalent and offensive symptoms of crime".

Of what, did you say ? An illustration in painting-by-numbers style shows a wall covered with statements such as "Goths" and "United Rules", an expensive way of revealing the Establishment's fear of the freely-painted word Crack. What was that breaking ? Crime ? Or free expression ?

European Modernism, and the whole concept of "experimental writing" could be brought to new life on a more fruitful plane.

Perhaps this may seem too optimistic. But there are cheering signs of true originality – as against mere self-assertiveness – in various corners of the dreaded media. Television

---

1961 type design for the Westinghouse Electric Corporation. From Paul Rand: A Designer's Art, published by Yale at £16.95.

Guardia igitur

Effective analytical and critical studies rely upon the gathering of information through identifying and interpreting issues followed by reports. Evaluations outline the essential meaning and value of a particular design within its working situation or according to the various constraints that apply to it. Choosing a suitable working context or appropriate audience for a design report, including its mode of presentation, is also important.

One of the first ways to appreciate design is to acknowledge your own personal reactions to design, and then to identify and note them in a systematic way. Interpreting the value and place of a design might then ensue. This should be followed by the presentation of a folder or report to bind together the evaluation of the design in question, and to account for its success or failure.

Criticism of the value and effect of appearance, function and costs in design, as well as the esoteric aspects represented by fashions, trends and cultural influences, can be based upon the following ideas.

Gathering information about designs so as to identify:

- personal reactions to design recorded through notes and sketches, based on feelings, interests and the senses;

- design in objects, actions or ideas and images;

- issues, contexts and constraints that bring about design;

- design processes and activity;

- form and meaning in design, values, likes and dislikes, variety;

- possibilities for designing;
- the value of design awareness and design capability for people, and knowing the differences between them.

Interpreting information about designs:

- knowing how we judge a design, whether or not it is successful, or how it could be improved or modified to be more economical;
- understanding the effects of design in different lifestyles, cultures and industries;
- interpretation of the images of culture;
- interpretation of the effects of technology on design thinking, techniques and methods; applying scientists' reductionist theories, or artists' humanistic concern for the quality of life; knowing its value and function.

Evaluating and reporting issues and findings concerning design:

- through accounting for the effect of a design, the creativity of the designer and its value to people;
- by the representation of information about design to an appropriate audience, based on an effective format, so as to obtain interest in the content of a design report.

Research can be obtained from various sources by studying and using the knowledge of what designers have achieved. This approach will not only inform personal designing – a crucial requirement for any design student – but also forms the basis of relevant criteria for assessing the value and place of designers' work. This will include some of the main issues with which designers are involved.

This chapter synthesises the notions of identification, interpretation and evaluation. These three aspects of design analysis and criticism are the essential research issues required to marshal evidence and source material so as to structure design awareness and enrich design capability. The success of your studies is dependent on your powers of discovery and your ability to discriminate.

Aim to distinguish between artefacts, systems and images in design. Develop your own descriptive models and style for analysing and criticising design. If in doubt, use your common sense and keep it simple.

Design history or criticism?

Understanding design also entails awareness of the differences between 'design history' and 'design criticism', including the value of these activities. This area will inevitably raise philosophical issues concerning 'definitions for design', including the skills, knowledge and values that people often understand design to be.

The term 'design' is a relatively modern phenomenon, and the differences between historical comment and critical judgement about its effect on our lives are problematic. This is essentially because most studies concerning design revolve around contemporary issues, practices and examples, and also because design ideas are generally a reflection of cultural and social thinking, as much as the individuality of talented people. An effective way to study the history of things is to work from the present and then establish their background development. This will include knowledge of what things do and why people have developed and used them.

Overcoming the difficulties of effective description and understanding of design, perhaps through the study of certain stylistic periods, or based upon certain influential figures or organisations, is part of the creative act of promoting design. Sometimes the use of periods or styles is not successful or acceptable, because they can impinge upon the subtleties and complexity of design description. They may place limitations upon the possibilities for design action because there is a tendency for people to copy past techniques.

There are many problems associated with design criticism because we need to be aware of how we look at designs and how our views and tastes are formed. How we actually see, develop our perceptions and form certain concepts, as well as how we comprehend certain aspects of form and techniques involving colour, shape or texture, all relate to design expression and creativity. You will need to employ specialised knowledge for each design example you analyse.

Compare Hamilton's image with Rousseau's, especially with regard to understanding the artist's motives at the time of creation. Hamilton has recently redesigned his famous collage using computer graphics to depict his views of the 1990s. Design your own collage that depicts the same question about today and use this as a design study.

Self portrait, 1890 (My self portrait) by Henri J F Rousseau.

Just what is it that Makes Today's Homes so Different, so Appealing? by Richard Hamilton. © Richard Hamilton 1994 All rights reserved DACS.

Develop your own studies. Look at the design of women's swimming costumes or men's hairstyles in the twentieth century. Say something about what has been designed and how the issues of design history and design criticism can be dealt with? Should you concentrate only on the quality of design relating to fitness for purpose, materials and manufacturing processes, performance, durability, appearance, safety and value for money? What other criteria could you use?

CRITERIA FOR STUDYING DESIGN

General criteria for studying design

This chapter outlines certain general criteria for studying design. It illustrates some of the different ways that we might understand design. The categories used are not meant to be taken as ways that we should appreciate design, but to indicate how people often find themselves reacting to, and thinking about, design.

Aim to study and establish criteria for describing, analysing and criticising your personal reactions to design, the influence of designers, and your understanding of the consequences of design. These criteria can be formed from the following three aspects of design awareness. There are other criteria which can be established, for example those concerning 'expert appraisal' of design. Exemplars are provided throughout this work.

Personal reactions to design

Curiosity is a prime motivator for a designer. Simply being interested in issues and ideas is a very valuable starting point for understanding design, and analysing your personal reactions to design and design issues is also crucial. Thus, making explicit your own feelings by expressing a personal view is the crux of design analysis and criticism. Record your reactions. It is most important that you express your own view, especially your likes and dislikes. Your points of view and your notes, especially sketches, are vital to inform your whole design approach. You should aim to distinguish between your emotional responses and intuitive feelings towards a design, a work of art or an item of technology, and the technical qualities that encompass the example.

> When you have thoroughly learnt perspective, and have fixed in your memory all the various parts and forms of things, you should often amuse yourself when you take a walk for recreation, in watching and taking note of the attitudes and actions of men as they talk and dispute, or laugh or come to blows one with another, both actions and those of the bystanders who either intervene or stand looking on at these things; noting these down with rapid strokes in this way, in a little pocket-book, which you ought always to carry with you. And let this be of tinted paper, so that it may not be rubbed out; but you should change the old for a new one, for these are not things to be rubbed out but preserved with the utmost diligence; for there is such an infinite number of forms and actions of things that the memory is incapable of preserving them, and therefore you should keep those [sketches] as your patterns and teachers. (*Leonardo's notebooks*)

'One day the world's biggest fish came and sniffed at the Kon-Tiki. That was a sight we shall never forget. It was as improbable as the tallest story.'

A page from Leonardo da Vinci's notebook.

'Seeing is believing'

Revealing our direct experience of things aids our initial appreciation of their design. Our common-sense appraisal concerning the personal use of different types of design, as well as information about how other people use these designs, is also very useful in our understanding of things. This appreciation will involve knowing something about expert comment and manufacturers' data.

Collect information that will remind you of the overall purpose of an object or system. For example, if you are going to analyse a washing machine, you should keep foremost in your thoughts the idea that it is designed to wash clothes. Every other item of detail can then be reviewed in relation to the machine's major function.

If people respond to design propositions as though they are real, the item's function and purpose will be communicated to the designer, the public or the technical people involved in its manufacture. Your reactions to design ideas and images are similar to your response to photographs; you see them as the real thing. Naturally, artefacts or images *are* real, and our common-sense understanding and experience of these things can be analysed. Recognising what artefacts and systems do is crucial to our design skills. The best way to acquire information about the function of things is to use them. This is called a 'user trip'.

Ask yourself: What does the design look like? What does it do? Who uses it? How is it made? How are its parts assembled? How does the design work? Why has the design been thought of and/or made at all? Compare your positive responses to your negative ones, and see how what you find helps you to formulate ways or learning about design.

Knowing the common-sense views that are held by other people concerning things is vital to any further development or improvement of a design. Are the designs useful to you or anyone else? Are you aware of your reactions to them and can you explain them? What do other people think of them? Can you compare your findings with the assertions of the manufacturer or retailer? Is an expert opinion available? Did you use the design or just observe it?

Student Matthew Euglefield's hubless wheel. Does this design for the hubless wheel, where the bearing is integrated with the rim, mean that the axel has been 'disinvented'? Does this design bring about exciting and new possibilities? Reprinted from 'D' magazine autumn 1989 © The Design Council.

You should be able to distinguish between facts about a design, and your opinion of its function and use to people. It is too easy to be 'blinded' by technicalities. Aim to study familiar things with a view to seeing them anew. When looking at an idea for a design, why is it important that you see it as though it were real? Why is it also important to establish new knowledge?

The great art of adapting means to ends

Revealing the principles that underlie the nature of objects, actions or ideas, including demonstrating ergonomic criteria concerning comfort, safety, ease of use and/or ease of maintenance, is an essential formal aspect of design analysis especially with regard to a design's functional value.

Comment upon the originality of a design and/or the degree of improvement brought about in the version you are analysing over previous examples. Note the scope of the issues tackled, whether simple or complex, as well as the plausibility and potential of the artefact, system or image created.

Being conscious of some of the problems that technology solves or poses is a facet of design analysis. Aim to find examples of human daily life that demonstrate our reliance on the products of technology. Understanding about technical, mass-produced, hand-crafted or computer-aided design, within the making, buying, selling and consuming patterns of modern living is important in design criticism.

Design is an empirical activity. All forms of knowledge can be brought to bear in designing, as and when appropriate. In order that design should not be seen merely as an activity that produces things, it should also be thought of as part of our social process and culture. A designer does not only create things, but also contributes to our sense of ownership and taste, our economy and general wellbeing. Thus the products of design are not only concerned with the appropriate use of materials and quality of performance, but also with setting trends and meeting needs.

Know how to describe the products of design

You need to know the difference between facts, values and beliefs concerning design. You also need to know which particular issue you are studying, because it is this issue, to a great extent, that determines much of your design action. You will need to know the difference between design as a total experience and the design of constituent components or systems.

Which type of design might the following examples be:

Spectacles case and spectacles
Kidney donor card
Gone with the Wind film poster
Heathrow Terminal 4
HOTOL
Neighbourhood Watch

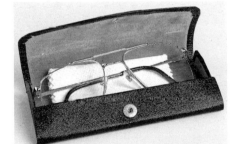

What do we mean by artefacts, systems and images? Define for yourself the various terms for design products by analysing various examples. Are artefacts, systems and images separate issues or interwoven, according to the particular type of design? How can the term 'environment' be used to describe designs?

Artefacts and images are the products of human art and workmanship. They are both two-dimensional images and three-dimensional objects. Images can be seen as things when the term refers to an artificial imitation of the external form of an object, generally as a picture. Imagery has more symbolic meaning, due to notions of iconography and the meaning and value of designs, including how people use them, treasure them or discard them.

Systems are designed; they involve the organisation and control of actions and processes into complex wholes or sets of connected things or parts that work together. Assembling the components of solid things creates something, and the final product may be of use to people. Social inventions like the Open University, Relate (formerly the Marriage Guidance Council) or *Which* magazine are examples of holistic systems design.

Generally, a model can be described as a representation of a proposed idea or thing. It is a simplified representation of something constructed for a specific task. There are three different kinds of model: iconic, analogous and symbolic. Drawing is also a powerful means of modelling and its essential skills are derived from observation in the world.

Iconic models represent the properties of reality, but to a different scale; they look like what they are supposed to represent, for example drawings, photographs and model cars. Both two-dimensional and three-dimensional models are fundamental to designing.

Re-model a well-known advertising slogan as a 3-D object. What design processes will you go through?

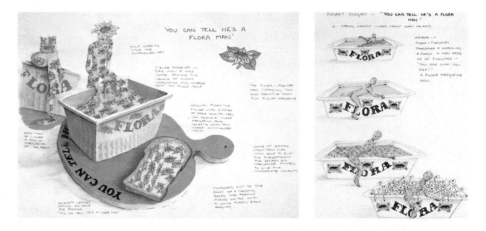

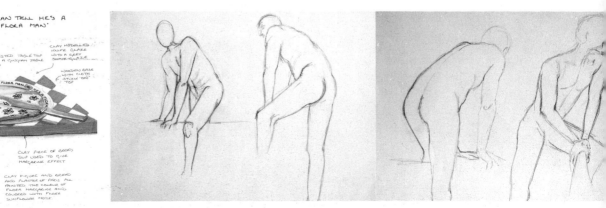

HIV virus model. Which type of model is represented here, how was it formed and for what purpose?

Analogous models use one set of properties to represent an idea or thing; for example the flow of water is analogous to electrical current and contour lines on a map represent different heights of land.

Symbolic models represent the relationship between principles, ideas, variables or information; they are arbitrarily chosen to represent something and should mirror real life. For example, the relationship between distance covered and the time taken is $S = D/T$. This is a mathematical equation which is a symbolic representation of speed.

Try to find out the total effect of what design means and what designing does, as well as to acknowledge the valuable place of components and contributory ideas and skills. Is the whole greater than the sum of its parts?

'Appearances aren't everything'

Identify the association between the form of designs in relationship to their meaning. This can be achieved through basic recognition of aspects of 'appearance', 'function' and 'cost', in designs. This should also inform identification of the interrelationships between what things do, what they look like and how they are valued.

Try to judge and criticise the true value of designs. Look for humour or social comment being used to clarify the creative narrative in a design. How can objects have meaning? Which ideas are associated with the design? Is metaphor being used and is the design a symbol for anything?

Consider the ways in which colour can function in designs, especially with regard to communication through lettering. Colour can be used for 'impact'; to create optical illusions where shapes and forms can appear larger than they really are due to the different ways people perceive different colours; for better legibility; for product identification; and for the general suggestive nature of colour, whereby certain colours are associated with particular symbols, feelings or real things.

If, after looking at the Red Cross emblem, you think that the red represents blood and the white represents a sense of safety, cleanliness and efficiency, then you are linking, in your mind, the colours in the sign with some of their real-life associations.

Yellow is a very strong colour and has been associated with notions of newness and the future; combined with red, this yellow provides a very dynamic feeling. Kodak use yellow to suggest 'golden sands of faraway places waiting to be conquered'. There is even now a colour called Kodak yellow because it is used so much by the company.

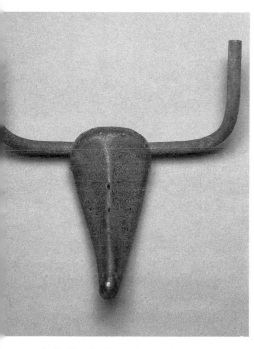

Bull's Head by Pablo Picasso.

Everybody has a soft spot for the Mini.

Figure au bord de la mer by Nicolas de Stael. © ADAGP Paris and DACS, London 1994. From the Kunstsammlung Nordrhein – Westfalen, Düsseldorf.

Hedgehog-flavoured crisps?

Look at an example of abstract art and establish which sensations or emotions it elicits from you. Consider the use of colours; if it contains blue, is it reminiscent of the sky?

Decide which examples of design are good and which are bad; those which represent good taste; those which are elegant, or not. Consider your own views, as well as what others say. Look for the differences between design proposals and realised design, and decide who would be critical of the designs and in which ways. Make a careful note of the difference between how something is made and why it is made. For example, consider why certain materials, techniques or tools are employed in relation to the function and appearance of the design. How much did it all cost economically, as well as in terms of the use of resources and its toll on the environment?

Bring together your ideas about the relationship between form and meaning in design. Can you identify the value of design? Do designers consider how certain materials, skills or ideas will affect what they design? What meanings do they place in their designs, and which meanings do you place on the things that you own and use? Should you see what the designers saw?

'The best truth is fiction'

Being critical of the value of design requires some understanding of how things become successful. Many designs are diffused into our way of life and we accept them as though they are part of the natural scheme of things. The Hoover and the Biro are typical examples of diffusion. Some of these examples can be admired because they are useful or pleasant to own. Your task is to analyse and interpret how successful certain designs are by questioning what it is that makes a design successful or not.

Notions of success can be established by noting popularity, the extent to which a design is bought or sold on a large scale and how elegant, durable or pleasurable a design is to own or use. On the other hand, it may be successful simply because it is the only example available. Consider how designers reflect, stimulate, manipulate or change personal or popular tastes.

FONTAINE'S SELF-MOVER.

The Klondyke balloon railway of 1898 was used as an advertisement for the training agency

Yo Dudes! Check it out!

The motives for design are complex, but to what extent is design used to solve problems for living and to promote the general well-being of people, or does it just support commercialism entirely? Young and Rubicon, an advertising studio in the 1980s, used the ploy of determining certain categories of person when designing their advertising campaigns. They devised classes of people according to whether they were in:

a) The 'mainstream' of society – people who purchase brand-named goods, lead a 'secure' way of life, and seek a sense of belonging;

b) The 'aspirers', who seek status, esteem and material success;

c) The 'succeeders', the affluent managers, who are in 'control';

d) The 'reformers', who wish to take responsible, prudent action in their lives, and who have the well-being of the community at heart, as well as their own self-esteem.

Once such a model is devised, then other ideas spring to mind. There could be a category for 'individuals', those people who take a more eccentric view of life, and so on.

'The best truth is fiction.' Advertisements are said to be the only copies of original ideas or things that do not exist. The trend in the early 1980s was for advertising to highlight the pursuit of individuality; whereas the early 1990s aim to promote a sense of belonging. Advertisers seek the cutting edge of culture in order to create different trends, or tune into the subtle changes of people's interests and values. An effective education, based on a full cultural understanding, should challenge and temper the domination of a commercial advertising culture!

Does 'failure' to own, appreciate or even know about certain designs reveal insensitivity, or does it simply not matter at all? Why do some people think that you are something less than you are if you don't know about certain trends or fashions? Why do people revere owning an expensive car, or wearing a designer label, or *not* wearing a designer label? Devotional feeling about designs can be seen in people who enjoy owning old cars, or special sports shoes; they also identify with the rarity value of things, anything from collecting regimental badges to juke boxes. Why are 'freak' stamps valued so much? Why are some works of art 'priceless'?

We are affected by what we think things are worth more than we perhaps realise. What has engendered this in us? We realise that prices are affected by aspects of 'supply and demand'. What emotions do you feel when looking at a unique painting that has suffered unnecessary damage?

The influence of designers

Awareness of what designers do and how they influence us, including knowing about the types of issues in which they are involved, can inform personal designing capabilities, as can design work requiring co-operative procedures. Knowing how people react to designs, as well as what lies behind other designers' intentions and motivations will help you to make a start on designing. This form of analysis will enable you to structure design ideas and issues and synthesise your own design propositions.

You must always establish appropriate criteria with which to appraise particular examples of designers' working approaches, attitudes and achievements. Investigate the factors that stimulate your own design ideas; list these and compare the results with other students.

'The eye is always charged with thought' (Proust)

Analysing design requires some understanding of what is meant by a design aesthetic, as well as notions about creativity. An aesthetic ideal can be a set of principles that are concerned with how a design 'looks' and 'feels'. Knowing what lies behind the eye and mind of the designer informs our understanding of his or her work; knowing what you look for in design reveals what you value about it, and why you like the design itself. Which aesthetic principles interest you, and are you aware of how your sensitivities have evolved? Do you admire designer creativity?

Portrait head (in progress), Elizabeth Frink, 1982.

Much appreciation of an aesthetic is derived from your perception, as well as your conception, of goodness, truth and beauty. Would an artist and a designer agree about these issues? Look for the aesthetic ideals that motivate and inform designers? How do you react to their designs with regard to your aesthetic sensibilities? Are these realistic ideals?

Developing ways of understanding the different layers of meaning in designs, as well as knowing about the essential techniques that designers employ to communicate their aesthetic sense, is crucial to the

Dizzie Gillespie.
Why did he enjoy playing this trumpet?

development of your imagination and creativity. It is the very stuff of design history and criticism. The semantics of design is concerned with unmasking the hidden messages in things. Some of these layers of meaning are open to personal interpretation, and are often placed on things by their owners, rather than by designers, while some meanings are explicit and intended.

It is important that design students know how to separate the different layers of meanings that are being designed into products. What do things mean to you? Do we live a rather sentimental and sanitised way of life, cluttered by things we don't really need? Are our tastes determined for us? Who or what idea would influence you? Are you aware of innuendo in designs and is this something to be wary of? Study examples of design to see if you can establish their meaning for you and others. Should you always be on the look out for deception?

Note the connections between the subject matter of the design and its meaning and purpose. Find examples where semantics comes into play, or when the user or spectator cannot judge at first hand, what the objects or systems represent. Consider past semantics as well as present semantics, and see how understanding a second layer of experience alters our view of the design, especially the way we react to it. Consider the value of the specialised knowledge required to understand designs.

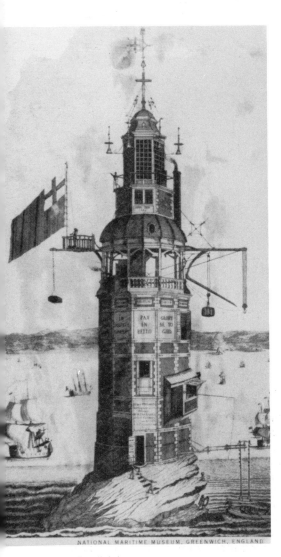

The first lighthouse.

Designs have a basic function or task to perform, but also tend to 'mean' something to people. The study of images and their meanings is called iconography, and the study of products and product systems is called design semantics.

When you see something strange, do you react to it by questioning whether it has been designed at all? We are all affected by the visual appeal of things, but can you say something about the aesthetic appeal of something that contains the ideas of truth, harmony and beauty? If so, how can these qualities be evaluated in design. 'This kind of thing contains the very thing I've been looking for . . .'.

Aim to find out how things present or carry a value, or represent the decision-making that affects people's tastes. Try to reveal the semantic value of designs, whereby objects appear to be capable of meaning more than their function suggests. Look for examples that demonstrate beauty as part of usefulness, including where the relationship between form and meaning is developed.

Can things be created other than by design?

Identification of design processes, including whether or not it is design at all, are the main activities here. Use the notion of revealing your personal reactions to designs to uncover the processes and motives for the derivation of chosen designs. Are you participating in what you see and do, or are you somehow divorced from the situation, as an observer?

The two-crossed emblem, 'Croix de Lorraine', is formed by thirteen unit squares, although other versions exist. It was made famous by Charles de Gaulle during the Second World War. The problem is to draw a straight line through point A, so that the total area on the shaded side of the line equals the area on the other side. This problem involves the golden ratio, which asserts that A is to B as A+B is to A, on any line. How long is BC? Will design help you solve this problem? Is this an example of design?

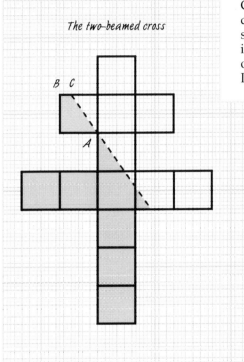

The two-beamed cross

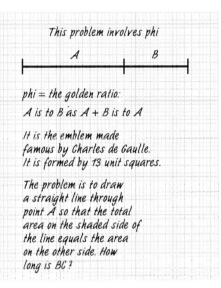

This problem involves phi

A   B

phi = the golden ratio:

A is to B as A + B is to A

It is the emblem made famous by Charles de Gaulle. It is formed by 13 unit squares.

The problem is to draw a straight line through point A so that the total area on the shaded side of the line equals the area on the other side. How long is BC?

When given certain facts and information, always check whether you have enough knowledge or whether you will need to research the topic further. This exercise is intended to make you consider what design is, and how best you can describe what it means to you.

Find examples of what people think designers do. When is something the result of individual work or some form of collaboration? When does it appear to be design but is considered to belong to another field of experience?

The common reed (*phragmites australis*) has been planted on Teesside to 'soak up' pollution. Part of the plant is able to absorb large amounts of the nitrogenous compounds found in sewage, and it is hoped that such use of this plant will have the effect of reducing the level of toxins from sewage in the water system. The moral issue surrounding this experiment hinges on whether or not it actually deals with the problem at source. Is it, instead, dealing with the symptoms rather than the causes of the problem. This last notion is a reminder that no course of action is value-free, and perhaps we should acknowledge that, no less than anyone else, designers who have an impact on the environment need to confront the major issues that are inevitably thrown up by such considerations.

Is the use of common reeds to clear up pollution an example of design? Should a 'technical fix' be the only solution to the problems that pollution poses?

use of its high productivity, the common reed (Phragmites) has been ...ted on the freshwater margins of estuaries, where its rapid growth mops up' large amounts of nitrogenous waste from sewage effluent.

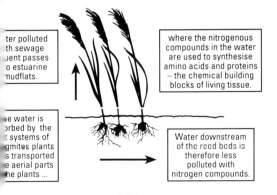

...ter polluted ...th sewage ...uent passes ...o estuarine ...udflats.

where the nitrogenous compounds in the water are used to synthesise amino acids and proteins – the chemical building blocks of living tissue.

...e water is ...orbed by the ... systems of ...gmites plants ...s transported ...e aerial parts ...he plants ...

Water downstream of the reed beds is therefore less polluted with nitrogen compounds.

Phragmites capabilities.

The Lensman microscope designed by Richard Dickinson. Powerful pocket-sized, nine-element, folded optical system, suitable for tripod lighting arc for reflected, dark-ground and transmission lighting. It has the facility to access a wide range of microfilmed colour reference material in the field.

The prepared mind

There are occasions when specialised knowledge is required to understand what a design or work of art is and why it came about. Yet, how prepared are you for new ideas? Where do design or designer ideas come from? The aim here is to consider the value of developing a repertoire of experiences which may inform fresh design needs or concepts. Knowing about past, as well as contemporary, design is crucial to the overall effectiveness of every designer's work.

The Lensman Microscope is an example of a modern artefact that requires specialised knowledge in the user. It is an important example of the radical transformation of a traditional object. The 'old' microscope has been designed and made anew. It is portable, functions to a high technical specification in the field and can easily incorporate a 35 mm camera. It is an example of good design, and its merits are based upon how it successfully solved the physical problem of carrying light across a shape in a microscope.

Often knowledge about what things are and what they do is lost in time because their use is no longer required. Indeed, it is often the case that we do not know very much about contemporary artefacts or systems. Knowing about present techniques used in design can be just as mystifying. Aim to discover not only specialised techniques or skills but also the origin of ideas and motivations for designers and artists.

Find your own examples of past and present designs that require specialised knowledge to understand their use and value. Will the notion of 'the designer lifestyle', a contemporary trend, be understood in the future, and is it widely understood today?

Try to establish specialised knowledge to aid your critique of issues concerning past and present paintings. Many devices and techniques are no longer used in art. This is especially true of symbols once used in painting, as well as the interests, ethics, morals, guiding principles and religious ideals from the past, which are now forgotten. Look for the aesthetic ideal in the design of things.

Initially, you might react to Hunt's painting on a personal level. Many students become dismayed at the vehemence that certain

The Awakening Conscience by William Holman Hunt.

'informed' people exhibit when attesting their opinions of the qualities of works of art. Make up your own mind about this example of Pre-Raphaelite art, especially as there are many differing, strong feelings and opinions concerning this style and period.

Knowledge about the artist's intentions and aesthetic motives are very important for a special understanding of a work of art.

William Holman Hunt characteristically based his conception of realism and painterly symbolism upon his religious belief. . . . He believed that without faith, art becomes materialistic, empty, literal, and dead, because such unspiritualized art can only present facts for their own sake. This dread of meaningless fact explains how Hunt, who painted in such a supposedly realistic style, could emphasize in *Pre-Raphaelite and the Pre-Raphaelite Brotherhood* that he and Millais always thought art had to express feelings and thus could never be 'the icy double of facts themselves'. He emphasizes 'we were never realists', for he and Millais – much less Rossetti – were never

125

interested in making 'a representation, elaborate or unelaborate, of a fact in nature' for its own sake, because to do so would destroy the imagination, that 'faculty' which makes man 'like a God'. According to Hunt, 'a mere imitator', who does not make use of his imagination, necessarily 'comes to see nature claylike and finite, as it seems when illness brings a cloud before the eyes'. (*W. H. Hunt and Typological Symbolism*, G. P. Landow)

The Awakening Conscience was designed to parallel Hunt's directly religious statement in *The Light of the World*. It was devised to explore the dilemmas and problems in actual 'material' life and to 'show how the still small voice speaks to a human soul in the turmoil of life'. The painting was not fully understood in its own time. Its subject-matter, of a lover and a kept woman, was disapproved of in Victorian times. Prostitution was a social problem in cities, and a great deal of literature and art dealt with the notion of 'the fallen woman'. Notice how Hunt emphasises the impropriety of the relationship by not giving the woman a wedding ring, and also dressing her in her 'under dress'. The lover's soiled glove thrown on the floor symbolises the likelihood of the woman being cast aside by the man.

Edward Lear wrote to Hunt on 12 October 1853, saying, 'I think with you that it is an artificial lie that a woman should so suffer and lose all, while he who led her to do so encounters no share of evil from his acts'.

The man in the painting has been characterised as, to use a modern term, 'nasty'. Notice how his forehead and eyes are formed, reflecting a Victorian interest in phrenology and also physiognomy, a very widely used theory for discovering, from the structure of the head and body, as well as from facial expressions and gestures, the 'true' character of a person. This idea even extended to animals. For Victorians, the man's countenance would suggest moral weakness.

On the positive side, the message of the work is that redemption is possible.

. . . the cat is a straightforward type of the seducer, but the bird it has been tormenting has escaped. The web in which the girl is entrapped is symbolised by the convolvulus in the vase on the piano and the tangled embroidery threads on the carpet. The title of the engraving above the piano, *Cross Purposes*, is appropriate in the light, of the lover being 'the unconscious utterer of a divine message'. (The Tate Gallery Exhibition Book, 1969)

The seemingly endless proliferation of detail was best defended in Ruskin's letter to *The Times* of 25 May 1854:

Nothing is more notable than the way in which even the most trivial objects force themselves upon the attention of the mind which has been fevered by violent and distressful excitement'. Most critics attacked the sensational appearance of the painting and ignored its underlying spiritual message.

The mirror on the wall behind the couple was much misunderstood, and no one commented on its crucial role in the composition: nature, seen through the French windows, is presented as a mirror image; it represents the woman's lost innocence, from which she has divorced herself by her present way of life. The ray of light in the right foreground suggests, however, that redemption is possible.

Hunt thus uses many iconographical devices to portray the title idea. The picture's frame also contains a message in its design. What do marigolds, bells and the star at the top symbolise? There are many more images, all of which require some specialised knowledge of Victorian life and art to interpret.

Dürer's image is a likely source of inspiration for Hunt, according to Landow. '. . . not only is the disposition of the two figures much closer,

Young Woman Attacked by Death, by Albrecht Dürer.

but the main theme of *The Awakening of Conscience* appears in Dürer's engraving, for in Hunt's view the seducer is an embodiment of death from whose arms she must struggle to reach Christ and new life.'

How original is Hunt's painting and how did he prepare himself to paint *The Awakening of Conscience*?

From this you should be able to see the value of specialised knowledge in the analysis of design, even if it is difficult to find and very subjective. Knowing where to begin looking is important. The above example derived its information from personal observation, the opinion of someone else, an authoritative book and a recent exhibition catalogue. How important would it be to see the actual painting?

Knowing about designs, past and present, can inform our immediate needs, as well as bring credibility to our knowledge of culture. Much effective design is done by designers who are prepared for all manner of opportunities. Building a repertoire of exemplars and experiences is part of good design.

Specialised knowledge is required at many levels in design. It is needed to decipher the icons of the past as well as to inform fresh possibilities. Acquiring and using particular experience is crucial in the development of a cultured and prepared mind, technically and aesthetically.

A contemporary satirical cartoon satirising Newton's theories of gravitation. Notice the pun on 'levity'. Why were these ideas satirised? Was it because they were so new and required genuine understanding?

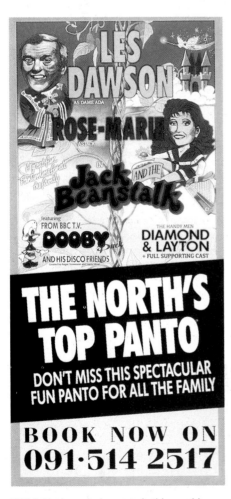

Which 'design rules' operate in this graphic design?

When an apple fell on Sir Isaac Newton's head, he did not suddenly realise the laws of gravitation and motion. However, his mind was prepared to make an imaginative leap to an insight about a clearer interpretation of nature. An artist's vision may well be brought about in the same way. A designer needs to be prepared to bring about a synthesis of knowledge and experience. Practically, this may mean that a designer might reflect upon aspects of existing designs that could benefit from redesign or modification, in addition to creating entirely new concepts.

Forget all the rules about design

Interpretation of the ways in which designers develop and celebrate their skills is invaluable information for design criticism. Do certain designers stick to certain rules? In fact, are there any rules for design? Why are certain designers influential?

Understanding the creative force behind the designer's 'eye', can affect our understanding of his or her work. This will involve seeing the creative narrative of the work. You might identify with a designer's technique and revere him or her as a master of the essential skills required for successful designing. Do not lose sight of your own abilities to contribute to design. There are no rules, only the ones that work for you.

When studying design there is often a tendency to copy styles and techniques that established designers use. Admiring skill and ingenuity is important in design development. In this regard many people take pleasure in owning 'influential' examples. This tends to happen when design students identify with the particular ideal or aesthetic value that recognised designers hold. Which design messages interest you? Study examples of designs that celebrate skills and techniques.

Do you have a feeling for design? Which design skills do you have, and are you confident in using them? How did you acquire these skills? How long did it take you to acquire them? Can you, through

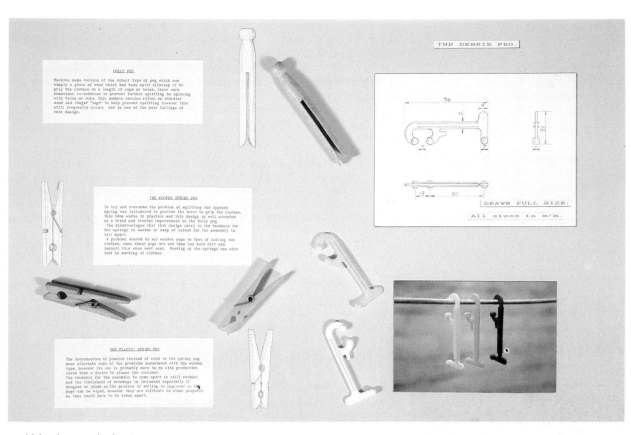

Pegs by Ray Ross: which rules were broken to develop different peg designs?

How bold is this design?

your own force of personality, interest other people in your work? How do other people regard your design skills? Can you turn this information to good use in real situations? How do you find what is valuable, useful and challenging? Would you pass on your design knowledge?

Bob Gill, an American designer, wrote a book entitled *Forget all the rules about graphic design. Including the ones in this book.* In it he said that 'boring words need interesting graphics, and . . . interesting words need boring graphics . . .'. How true are these 'rules'? He goes on to explore the notion that 'the problem is the problem: . . . if I could express the uniqueness of what the problem was trying to communicate with an image which was valid only for that problem, then I would have invented a unique image. In other words, defining a unique problem would inspire a unique solution.'

Is it true to say that a powerful message requires understanding through basic lettering as a feature of its graphic design? How can you apply Gill's approach to graphic design to the examples on these pages?

'Good art is not always good advertising art.' This advice was given in a book entitled *Drawing for Advertising* (1938), where it is argued that

. . . it may please you to make your sketches decorative, informative, real, impressive. It will not please your client unless, in addition, you have made them persuasive. The advertiser does not commission your work because he wants to improve the appearance of the hoardings, the shop windows or the newspaper pages; but because he wants to sell more of his goods . . . Let your work combine all the attributes of a sound business proposition with a touch of personal talent and you can look forward to a happy and prosperous career.

How much has this attitude determined the quality of our lifestyles today? Have we improved our use of design? Are these the unwritten rules?

Design itself can be bought. It is a service that many companies develop and exploit. Consider the following design approach by a leading design agency, Fitch & Company, in their approach to utilising corporate identity for various companies. This design tactic has a long-established tradition in industry and commerce, and was a key commercial feature of company promotion in the 1970s and 1980s.

Fitch state that corporate identity can be established through design.

Our approach to corporate identity is that, what an organisation believes itself to be or indeed actually is, is far less important than how it is perceived by its various audiences of customers, employees, suppliers, etc.

People's perceptions can directly influence an organisation's success and, therefore, careful control should be effected over all elements of an organisation which may influence perceptions. These may include: people, products, environment, advertising, public relations, corporate visual identity, packaging, etc.

The corporate visual identity of the organisation is often one of the first elements an outsider sees. In creating a major corporate visual identity, there are two elements to be considered: first, the establishment of the most appropriate projected (as opposed to operational) structure, and second, the actual design deemed appropriate to this structural definition.

How valuable are these procedures?

The consequences of design

Being part of a sustainable environment and being aware of our influence upon natural life are important issues towards which designers should always aim to be sensitive. There is a growing need for the stable development of consumer articles, and for designers to be mindful of costs, resources and ecology. Your study of design is essentially concerned with developing your understanding of how and why certain designs come about. Aim to reveal the motives for commercial design as much as possible and to analyse the consequences of different designs for yourself and other people. 'It is better to light a candle than curse the darkness.'

Do we make independent choices about the things we need and buy? Are we able to design and make all the things we need or are we dependent on a complex social and cultural infrastructure of deliberate or continual change in things. This could be in the hands of people with vested interests in making our choices for us, or simply part of cultural evolution generally.

The squirrel toy: what can be added to or taken from this design to make it better?

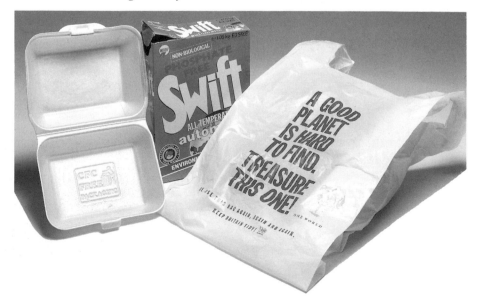

'Environmentally friendly' packaging.

'If there are two ways of action, always choose a third'. (De Bono)

Another factor in your general analysis of design is the identification of your reactions to variety in design, including noting the specific design issue at hand. Aim to be appreciative of the processes that the designer considered, concerning how he or she identified and developed the issues, or tackled the problems and the ways proposals were generated, including the variety of ideas that were pursued.

In design criticism too much emphasis is often placed on the appreciation of design techniques. Craft techniques employed by artists or designers tend to be the most scrutinised aspect of general design appreciation, especially when viewing the product. As with most things, a sense of balance is required and such techniques should be considered alongside the designer's motives and the significance of the work. It is important to know about and appreciate painting techniques and to know something of skilful work.

Try to learn about different techniques and experiment with your own style. Be prepared to be open to suggestion but also have conviction in your own design. Consider differing ideas for contrast, and keep your ideas straightforward, because an appreciation of simplicity is important, as is your continual development of a variety of techniques and ways of presenting your work.

Why is there such a variety of designs? Make notes and sketches that will help you to describe which example does its job best, as well as which design appears the best in your view. Distinguish between alternative designs, different possibilities for design solutions and the way in which you might choose a design from a variety of examples. Are designs different because they have developed, one from the other, to do a better job, or are they varied because people require or choose different designs? Should all cars have the same standards of durability as a Rolls-Royce?

Variety in design is crucial to the development of alternative solutions to specific design problems and to give choice in the marketplace. It is a basic issue in design because we thrive upon seeking alternative versions of commonplace things. We need to make choices according to our individual tastes and requirements. So far we have considered personal taste concerning design. It is also vital that we know something about how market forces are determined by different designs for similar products.

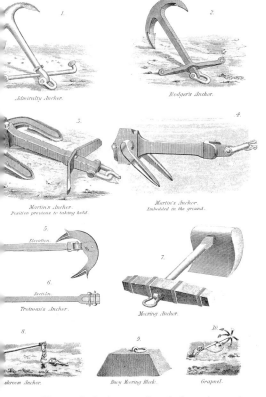

How and why have anchor designs changed or remained the same over the centuries?

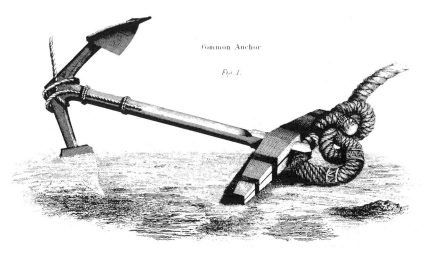

A photograph from 'This is Britain', a publication from the 1940s which explores the British way of life, for example, village cricket at Wombourn in Staffordshire.

Vive la différence!

Designers can change people's habits or perceptions; they can preserve the social order or challenge it. Interpretation of the effects of different lifestyles and cultures on design is part of the development of a wider appreciation of the influence of designers. Can you see how different ways of life are reflected in designed objects? Can you see your own culture in things? Conversely, can you see how different designers or design styles influence everyday life?

Your task is to reflect and present a different culture or set of values and beliefs through your criticism of a chosen design. Being functional and basic is not the only purpose of design analysis. Consider where a common item like a knife originated from, and how many versions there are of it. When is a chopstick a knife? You are asked to decide how and why different designs reflect different cultures and what it is that creates the differences.

Examples of different advertisements. Look at the four images advertising Lux and discuss why they are slightly different.

Different examples of artwork using the subject of horses. Which example depicts the true nature of the horse and why are such works used in public places?

Is there something universal about design? Do all humans design in the same way? Your argument will depend upon your explanation and interpretation of valid examples of design from different cultures.

How do we acknowledge the design of different cultures? Anthropology can be studied in museums, where the artefacts of the past are used as crucial primary evidence of the technologies of past societies. There is a need for a systematic way of recording design achievements in historical terms as well as considering contemporary work as a resource for designers.

The adoption of different stylistic periods and a historical approach to design criticism can be very useful ways to present design. Primary evidence for various designs can be established based on official documents, trade brochures, and so on. Patents and records of previous work can inform fresh work and determine its direction. How designs are graded and catalogued is also influential, because the terminology used very often indicates the value of the items. Terms like 'significant', 'new', 'daring', 'reactionary' are often used to describe designs and artwork. Museums like the Victoria and Albert provide this service to artists and designers.

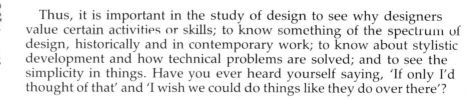

Thus, it is important in the study of design to see why designers value certain activities or skills; to know something of the spectrum of design, historically and in contemporary work; to know about stylistic development and how technical problems are solved; and to see the simplicity in things. Have you ever heard yourself saying, 'If only I'd thought of that' and 'I wish we could do things like they do over there'?

Reading the images of culture

Learn to see the images and the semantics of three-dimensional design that occur in our own culture, as well as that of others. This is an important design task, which requires effective research techniques. This activity focuses on the capacity of images and semantics to alter our ways of thinking, and to shape our way of life.

Study advertisements for video or book clubs. How much are these images part of our way of life?

Black and white photographs tend to evoke nostalgia and are felt to be credible documentary statements about the recent past, especially in such images as poor children in the streets. Why should poverty be used as an artistic status symbol in glossy coffee table books? Why is this style of presenting the past so powerful, and what does it tell you about people's values in photographic art?

'Working the lines', Cromarty, c. 1900. Who would be nostalgic about this image?

Images lull us to sleep and at the same time shape our values. They tell us who is masculine and what is feminine, how problems are solved and what it takes to get ahead ... these images divert our attention away from the critical questions of our culture and fill our minds with fluff. (E. Eisner)

Find and review the ideas, things and images that are often used to present our way of life. Which commercial images are you influenced by? Some years ago the image of the Marlborough man astride a horse under a bright blue Montana sky was intended to become part of a smoker's unconscious self-image about smoking. The advertisement presented the notion of the healthy, manly freedom of smoking. Has this view been altered, or does it persist?

Culture is concerned with taste, manners and an urbane approach to life, including artistic and intellectual developments, especially with regard to the performing arts. It is also a way of describing the habits and interests of a clearly distinguished and complex form of human behaviour. It is associated with the artistic and intellectual activities of one particular culture as distinguished from other cultures and it is simply a pattern of the typical behaviour of a specified group of people. What is it that marks out your culture; can you see its effects, in the designs you know about?

Sunday Times Magazine images of sixth form style, 30 July 1989. Photos by Iain McKell. These students all attended Solihull VIth Form College, West Midlands.
Do different generations establish their own styles and fashions or are these brought about by some other means?

There is a capacity for the images of culture to change our minds. It is vital that we are not hoodwinked by commercial design interests and mass media techniques. If we do not know how to recognise and judge the images that pervade our lives, then we are impoverished and vulnerable. Being uncritical adds to our dilemma. Culture has the potential to expand our thinking and enrich our lives; we must

A chalk drawing of Charlotte Bronte by George Richmond. Is this your image of a Victorian woman?

Why was Jean Shrimpton representative of 'the changing face of the 1960s'?

'Biggest surprise of the International Motorcycle Show was the Kawasaki ZXR400 making its simultaneous (with Paris) world debut, being helped into the limelight here by a suitably impressed robot! Many works racer type features have been incorporated in this superbly crafted machine, that will retail at around £4,700 next spring.' (A Kawasaki press release) What has a robot got to do with a motor cycle? Why did Kawasaki use this image?

endeavour to know about the power of design and enjoy all manner of differences and possibilities for change and renewal. This should not detract from a respect for past achievements, although reverence for them without understanding can be limiting. Should a 'great' designer be a heroic figure?

Assume the position by David Mach, as seen at the Gateshead Garden Festival. 'I believe the piece goes further than three very contemporary caryatids treating their knight in shining armour as something of a joke, although I like this idea too'. (Festival Landmarks '90)

African family.

What do you see in the picture of the African family? If you react to the family in a room, with a window, gathered around a man seated on a chair, you have used an industrial culture, based on experience of rooms with right-angled corners, and drawings that represent windows. If you saw a young girl with a can on her head and the family gathered around a tree, then you saw the scene from an African point of view, where people carrying things on their heads is a commonplace experience. The double image is deliberate, and is exploited to indicate how a cultural perspective determines what we see. Problems of pictorial recognition often occur as people from different cultural backgrounds place different interpretations upon some of the 'cultural cues' within certain images.

The notion of style is also an important design issue which can enable you to reveal something about the influence of design.

"How is it that so many things from a particular era seem to have something in common – the style of the period? The cars, buildings, dresses and factories of the 1920s all seem to cohere in a subtle but unmistakable manner. Is this because people become used to the things of a certain period in conjunction; or is it that there is, truly, a 'zeitgeist' which influences designs across a range of things? What is style?" (*Theories of Vision Perception* Ian E Gordon).

Dead salmon – downstream from Sunderland sewerage works.

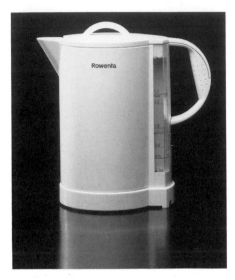

Powerspeed kettle in polypropylene.

Hotpoint washing machine.

'Nature is victimised by the triumphant march of industry'

'Save Lake Baikal' is splashed across a poster at the Baikalsk bus station. The threat of pollution has prompted a long campaign on the lake's behalf.

Should it remain a feasible proposition that consumerism and a material life should continue at all costs? Does continual design for consumption deplete the world's natural resources and materials at an unacceptable rate? Is there a rational answer to this type of problem which design can help to give? Will supermarkets instigate reusable packages and bottling? Will things become more durable rather than ephemeral? Will materials used in design be used more sparingly and thoughtfully, or is this the case already?

To what extent does industrialisation improve the standard of living for different peoples, and provide the products people need? Design is certainly a major influence on business and, without it, there would be little or no commerce and trade. Design does have an effect on the economies of industrial societies.

The relationship between these issues should be analysed so as to establish their true worth and value. Consider the following statement made by the Design Council at an exhibition in April 1990 which explored issues of design and the economy, and where comment concerning domestic electrical appliances was highlighted for public attention.

Bucking the Trend!

Applying design: Italy dominated Europe as the leading producer and net exporter of white goods. Last year (1989) the Italians accounted for more than one third of Europe's production, but less than 15% of consumption: Zanussi, the country's biggest manufacturer (but owned by Sweden's Electrolux), exported over 70% of its 4.3 million unit output. Against such mighty competition, British products can only hope to gain advantage through excellence of design, performance and reliability.

But severe overproduction of domestic appliances throughout Europe has brought the market near to saturation point, with little promise of more than minimal growth in the foreseeable future. The prospect of vanishing profit margins has led all manufacturers to make design a priority.

With US suppliers now looking to Europe as sales drop in their own home market, and the Japanese – with quality and technology as their selling points – eyeing the market too, the climate in Europe looks set to become even more fiercely competitive in the 1990s.

LINKING CRITICAL STUDIES TO EXAMINATION WORK

Good design or good taste?

[Leonardo] wished to pillory the type of scholar who relied on authority rather than on critical reason. (Martin Kemp,'Leonardo Then and Now' in *Leonardo da Vinci* Hayward Gallery Catalogue)

The words and phrases listed opposite are often associated with a whole variety of activities across many design-related areas, from intuitive approaches to art and design at one end of the spectrum to very tightly structured approaches to technological design at the other. Some appreciation of the contribution they make to these areas may give us a clearer understanding of the significance of our own work as well as that of others.

This chapter tries to clarify many of the elements underpinning design capability and design awareness. However, it is not possible, or perhaps even desirable, to offer a checklist to enable you to appraise the work of others, or a guide to support your own work. It is easy to become both pompous and academic about art and design and, indeed, a considerable body of philosophical and practical research has already been undertaken to clarify specific areas such as aesthetics and creativity. There is also the danger of assuming that a greater understanding of this complex subject will automatically result in work of a higher quality, and of course this does not automatically follow.

With these points in mind, there does appear to be an imbalance in our design activities, between the energy devoted to making and doing (design capability) at the expense of critical appraisal of the outcome of design activities (design awareness).

The Design Museum in London has been established to inform and make us aware of the way design influences our lifestyles.

The Acropolis in Athens, 480-30 BC.

The Byzantine and Russian influences can clearly be seen in St Basil's the Blessed in Moscow, 1550-1650.

Throughout the ages, different civilisations and cultures have given their artefacts a distinctive form and appearance. The ancient Greeks found the solution to the well-proportioned rectangle mathematical formulae. One of their most common proportions is 5:8, generally known as the golden ratio. During the Renaissance, the Latin word *'ars'* covered a host of activities including fine arts, sculpture and carpentry. Leonardo da Vinci's world included the word *'arte'* which meant skill, and *'scientia'*, which meant knowledge. Any attempt to separate art from the social, moral or religious function it served or to elevate it on account of the skill displayed by the artist would have been incomprehensible. However, this schism gradually emerged, and is summarised by Hildred Redfern in her book *Questions in Aesthetic Education*.

This conception of artwork as a thing of beauty reached its peak with the 'art for art's sake' movement which flourished during the latter part of the nineteenth century, especially in the fields of literature and the visual arts. Whatever further interest a work might have, it was held irrelevant to its status as art. In its most extreme form this doctrine of aestheticism demanded that art not only need not, but must not, have any concern other than beauty. Such a view thus goes beyond the claim that aesthetic interest is a necessary feature of artistic interest. Furthermore the movement was typically associated with a special attitude to life as a whole, also known as aestheticism: art and beauty were regarded as supreme values, even to the point of all others being despised.

This notion of art as something to be valued in its own terms, and enjoyed for its own sake, was in the main unfamiliar to classical antiquity, the Middle Ages and the Renaissance.

Central to the development of our capability and awareness in design is our ability to make informed judgements about the work we are engaged upon. Our perceptions of this work are not merely limited to our visual or auditory impressions, but also involve considerable interpretation, where many other influences will temper our judgement. These influences may include the limited experiences of our own cultural background, the ever-changing trends of fashion, the influence of advertising and marketing, motives of profit, concern for the environment, or the emotional pull of nostalgia. With such a complex cocktail of inputs and interpretations, it is not difficult to appreciate that your summative viewpoint may find you agreeing with one set of individuals while disagreeing, perhaps violently, with others.

The Victorians are often criticised for their excessive use of applied decoration and heavy use of materials and for allowing their design decisions to be dominated by the machines of the day. However, it must also be recognised that the best of Victorian design can be both imaginative and appropriate. The concern is that we develop a generalised view and opinion without any individual or balanced appraisal of the artefact under scrutiny. There is always the danger that individual preferences and prejudices will be passed on by educators, authors, the media and other individuals in positions of authority or influence, without the recipient questioning the validity of the viewpoint.

In his speech at the Corporation of London Planning Committee dinner on 1 December 1987, Prince Charles made the following observations about post-war architectural development in the city.

> You have, ladies and gentlemen, to give this much to the Luftwaffe. When it knocked down our buildings it did not replace them with anything more offensive than rubble. We did that! Clausewitz called war the continuation of diplomacy by other means; around St Paul's planning turned out to be the continuation of war by other means . . .

Strong sentiments, yet how do we establish their justification? How can we avoid indoctrination, or at best an unwitting transmission of group or personal preferences or prejudices.

Should not individuals in a democratic society feel free to express thoughtful opinions about architecture, planning, the environment or any other aspect of the made world. Many educators and philosophers, including Roger Scruton, have discussed the need for individuals to be aware of 'an aesthetic of everyday life'.

At this point it is necessary to explore in more detail our understanding of the term 'aesthetic'. The word was first penned by the philosopher Baumgarten in 1830, derived from the Greek *aesthenai*, meaning to perceive. In its original context, the term was used to describe an all-embracing mode of experience, both emotionally, visually, audibly or through our other sensory functions. This is different to the much narrower interpretation often associated with aesthetics today, i.e. a visual experience. The more we explore this latter viewpoint, the more we can recognise its limitations. For example, if we view a country landscape, we may find it comprises functional elements such as farms, fields containing crops, dry-stone walls, etc. It will also include colours, shades, materials, forms,

The Menai Bridge, 1819-26 (span 177m/579ft). Although an enthusiast of cast iron, Telford did as much as anyone to prove the suspension principles with his use of wrought iron.

textures, moods, smells and sensations of heat or cold. Our receptiveness to this situation will include an assessment of all these elements in an additive sense. In a similar way, the more information we have about the artefacts we are appraising, the clearer, and perhaps more objective, will our impression become.

For design awareness judgements to be justified, students must be in a position to understand what is involved. Prior contextual identification must be made before artefacts can be explained or evaluated. Part of this process may also require some sense of historical perspective. In this situation, it is inappropriate to think in terms of a set of predefined criteria that can be specified in advance of any particular case. General or specific criteria can only be selected in relation to a particular artefact or range of items. Philips Industries employ design as a corporate strategy and use the following general criteria to judge the success of their electrical product design:

- Is the product ergonomically designed to satisfy human factors; is it intelligible?

- Does it not only meet minimum safety standards but extend to anticipate potentially dangerous situations?

- Does the product successfully solve a consumer need, not only in itself but as an element of the environment in which it is being used?

- Is the product designed to utilise materials, production processes and energy in the most efficient way?

- Are the aesthetic elements such as form, colour and texture, as well as graphic information, integrated in an appropriate manner?

Do you feel there are any significant omissions to the general criteria listed above which you, either as a

1. Designer for Philips, *or*

2. A consumer of Philips products
   would wish to consider.

Later in this book you will be asked to use these criteria as a means of evaluating products.

As a further illustration, the following article by Anna Somers Cocks outlines her particular views relating to some specific and general examples of design. Read the article carefully and then discuss the issues raised by the questions that follow.

Anna Somers Cocks and the sculptured
fountain discussed in her article.

142

Anna Somers Cocks registers a protest at the Bond Street fountain and at the rising tide of watery design

I used to be an assistant keeper at the Victoria and Albert Museum before it started getting into the news. The first thing I was taught was how to describe an object minutely. This produces numbingly boring prose, but that doesn't matter, because no one is seriously expected to read it. It's a training exercise, a discipline, like the naming the parts of the Lee-Enfield rifle.

After you have taken note of all the bits and discovered what their names are, you are nine-tenths on your way to understanding how the thing works. In the case of a designed object, whether it falls into the category of a work of art or not, you are going over the same mental steps as its creator.

This way of looking at things has become a habit, and I find myself doing it automatically, whether I'm looking at a telephone or a gothic sculpture.

A few months ago I was walking down Bond Street, and I was unpleasantly surprised by a new fountain someone had erected there. I say unpleasantly because, not only is it feeble and ugly in design, but it doesn't even work properly - the base is too small for its height, so the water piddles all over the pavement and runs down into the gutter; come winter it will cause the odd fractured elbow. As the Romans would have said, it is neither useful nor beautiful.

Here it is, in a shortened museum-style description: "From a tripartite, lobate, carved base of stone in the Art Nouveau manner, rises an erect bronze column of spiralling lily pads, encircled at the crown by three flying ducks and dominated by three bull rushes from which issues water."

In this case the insight into its creator's mental processes is rather cloudy.

Is it a joke? An ironical side swipe at bourgeois values: the three plaster ducks of the suburban lounge converted into 3-D. On the whole, I think not, as there is nothing else remotely humourous about the piece, and it sits there stolidly in all its expensive traditionalism - stone and bronze, the usual materials of grand sculpture.

What is clear is that the sculptor is fumbling about in a language he doesn't understand. The swelling, sinuous lines of real Art Nouveau have become tight and rigid in his design and the phallic column of lily pads, bull rushes, ducks etc (a daft idea anyway), which goes back ultimately to 19th century Japanese naturalism, lacks, on the one hand, the minute precision of the original, and on the other, any compensating movement or textual interest.

We have never been much good at fountains, if you leave aside the occasional splendid cascade like the one at Chatsworth. London is remarkable for its shortage of waterworks and the dullness and meanness of the ones that do exist. Occasionally, a benefactor tries to do something about this, but no one seems to care very much. Lord McAlpine presented the city with a Naum Gabo fountain, and after much humming and hawing, the authorities stuck it away in the courtyard of St Thomas's Hospital. Bond Street, on the other hand, got flying ducks. How on earth did something so awful come to be designed?

I think it's because we in Britian have been addicted to an often inappropriate naturalism in design for as long as anyone can remember. One hundred and forty years ago the founding fathers of the Victoria and Albert Museum, already trying to raise the standard of English design thought that it was our worst sin, and it remains true today. They had a kind of Chamber of Horrors in their museum illustrating "False Principles in Design," where they showed carpets heaving with 3-D roses, and cluttered chintzes - very much the kinds of things that you see in the decorating magazines now, that have percolated down from Colefax and Fowler to Marks and Spencer, getting more and more diluted in the process.

We have an unthinking way with flowers - we stick them on toasters; on saucepans; on tiles, in a haze of pink, beige or grey; we print them all over sheets in pastel colours, we spoil high quality bone-china plates from honourable old Staffordshire factories by enamelling them with weedy, asymmetric pseudo-modern floral patterns.

I recently asked the manager of one of these famous factories why they didn't produce a clean elegant modern shape and leave it in the white to which the answer was, "We are not in the fashion business" - which is why you have to buy German or French, if that is what you want at a reasonable price.

It has all got so much worse recently with the loosening up of the straitjacket of modernism. Ornament is back in fashion, but it's a forgotten language, so we get gobbledegook when people try to use it: misunderstood rococo in its umpteenth revival; misunderstood japonisme; misunderstood architectural classicism. We are a nation of visual illiterates who need to be drilled in the naming of parts so that we might at least *notice* what we are buying (that being the first step toward looking at it critically).

If the V & A is serious about being the "National Museum of Art and Design", as it has recently taken to calling itself, it might take up the cause of explaining ornament and design rather more vigorously than it does at present, instead of just leaving the objects to speak for themselves. But I'm afraid that the Museum intends to go a-whoring after cultural history, which is much more fashionable in academic circles, but a waste if you have the world's finest collection of decorative art from which to teach. Some people don't know when they're lucky.

Another reason why we get flying ducks is because of our traditionally very luke-warm attitude towards modern art. It's not without its followers, but they tend to be isolated in pockets, rather that spread evenly throughout society.

Your average duke and your average bus driver tend to agree about Carl Andre's Bricks. And yet modern art is not dispensable, because it is inextricably linked with creative modern design, the vigour that goes into one indirectly giving life to the other.

What is I M Pei, architect of the pyramid of the Louvre, and of the beautiful extension to the National Gallery in Washington , but a Minimalist sculptor writ large?

Whatever you may think about the placing of the pyramid in the 19th century courtyard, there is no doubt that Pei has demonstrated that most elegant mastery of geometric form, surrounding the glass building with shimmering triangular mirrors of water and two abundant jets d'eau to bring sound and life to the space.

Now *that* is the kind of fountain we need in London. We wait for Mrs Thatcher's *grand geste*.

- Do you agree with the writer's view that 'We in Britain have been addicted to an often inappropriate naturalism in design'. Can you give examples of artefacts that support your views.

- Do you believe that 'Modern art is inextricably linked with creative modern design'? Give examples to support your viewpoint.

- The late 1980s saw a strong interest in reviving old styles and the retrospective application of design features in many aspects of architecture, furniture and interior design. What do you think were the reasons for these trends?

- Do you think that any one particular style will dominate design trends in the 1990s, and where might it emerge from, or will a more pluralist approach to design evolve?

- Do you think that Anna Somers Cocks relies on authority or critical reason when presenting her argument in the article quoted here? How else might you present an appraisal of the fountain?

Product analysis through critical appraisal

Product analysis can be employed in a number of different situations. It can be used as a way of gathering background information on a range of products prior to starting a design project, for example the lighting project on page 171. As the initial investigation in a major project of your own choice, you may find it useful to analyse existing products and see how the user interacts with them as a basis upon which to launch your own designs. You may also critically appraise a number of similar products in order to identify 'the best design', depending upon which criteria you use to arrive at your conclusion.

At this point it is important to define the term 'product', as used in this context, to include artefacts, systems and environments where these are the result of purposeful human design. Consequently, an isolated valley in the Lake District, which contains no evidence of human settlement, would not come into this category, whereas an out-of-town retail development would. It is important to develop your critical awareness of products for two reasons.

1. As a designer, you will contribute to the continuous evolution of products by the refining and synthesising of new developments that will technically improve upon what already exists. In order to identify the contribution that new developments can make to a product, it is first necessary to be critical of that product, observe its limitations and identify any scope for further improvement, for example the introduction of lean-burn engines, i.e. engines that can use lead-free petrol, goes some way towards making motor vehicles more 'environmentally friendly'.

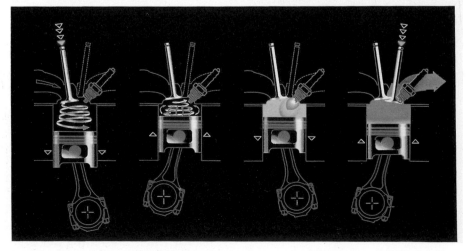

3. WHAT DOES LEAN BURN DO FOR YOU?

Lean burn engines offer you two principal advantages over a conventional power unit:

● they use less fuel to achieve the same power output and levels of performance;

● they give off cleaner exhaust.

Ford was the first manufacturer to introduce the concept of lean burn to production car engines. That was in 1983, and the range of models available with lean burn power units is still expanding.

It is all the result of intensive research into methods of running an engine on leaner mixtures over a wider operating range without affecting driving characteristics or your driving pleasure.

When the load on the engine is light – cruising at moderate speeds in high gear, for instance – it is relatively easy to run on a lean mixture. The combustion process is not so sensitive when only low power is required. Control of the mixture becomes much more critical, however, when you drive at high speed, accelerate or look for more power to maintain your speed uphill.

In a conventional engine, sudden changes in the speed at which air is drawn in can have a detrimental effect on performance. When you accelerate suddenly, for example, to overtake, tiny droplets of vapourised fuel tend to get left behind on the walls of the exhaust manifold, or are carried unburned into the exhaust system. It's wasteful of fuel and interferes with engine efficiency.

These are some of the problems which Ford engineers have tackled – and are solving with the new lean burn technology. For you, as the driver, lean burn is good news all round. You get more miles to the litre of fuel – and cleaner exhaust.

Lean burn engines.

2. As a consumer, it is an important part of your general education that you should be able to make rational judgements about consumer durables and able to marshal evidence in a systematic way to enable you to arrive at an informed decision.

Criticism of the design of a product is an important stage in its evolution and helps to provide fresh impetus to its development and refinement. Indeed, although we often see the term 'evaluation' listed at the end of some linear models of 'the design process', the activity of evaluation is often the starting point of the launch of new design proposals. 'Design by comparison' is an accepted way of improving upon existing designs and generating technically superior products that supersede their predecessors.

Identify stages in the development of new products when the skills of evaluation should be employed?

In order to develop skills of critical appraisal, it is necessary to become familiar with, and employ, methodologies that will help you to arrive at objective forms of evaluation. One of the first questions you need to ask is what form of judgement, or test, can you use to assess the worth of the product being evaluated? The difficulty here is that different products need to be evaluated using different yardsticks or criteria. A criterion is defined as a 'standard of judgement' that is applicable to whatever is being assessed. It is necessary to distinguish between those criteria that might be applied to a number of products, for example value for money, safe in use, environmentally friendly – i.e. **general design criteria** – and those that might only be applicable to certain products, for example road handling, all-round visibility, kilometres per litre, would be examples of **specific design criteria** applied to motor cars.

It can be seen, therefore, that there is no simple answer to the question of whether a product is an example of 'good' or 'bad' design, as both of these terms are relative. Very rarely are products totally bad, although they may be so unsafe as to put the user at risk, whereupon the Trading Standards Department may try to withdraw them from sale to the consumer.

You may have access to the following products:
personal stereo   small personal computer/word processor
alarm clock radio   pocket calculator

Make a list of general design criteria that you might be able to apply to all the products, as well as a list of specific design criteria that you might use to assess two or more products of a similar type.

The major problem to be faced when evaluating products similar to those listed above, is that our knowledge of a particular product may be limited to experiences of that particular product as a user. We may not understand the technical superiority of one type of personal stereo compared to another; we may not be experts in this area. Therefore, in order to build up an accurate assessment of any one product, we may need to employ a variety of evaluation strategies to produce an objective appraisal. It can be misleading to focus purely on the ergonomic or anthropometric aspects of a design, or to be purely concerned with ease of manufacture, appropriate use of materials or visual appeal. Good design is concerned with optimising all factors that will lead to success without compromise. Conflicts and tensions may well be generated between a number of design features, however it is the need to resolve these conflicts ingeniously that makes the task demanding and exciting.

Listed below is a number of 'specialist' or 'expert' sources of information that will help you to develop greater awareness about specific aspects of product development.

BSI (British Standards Institute)
The Consumer Association – *Which*? magazine
Ergonomic texts and anthropometric data (e.g. Humanscale, designed by Henry Dreyfuss Associates)
Furniture Industry Research Association

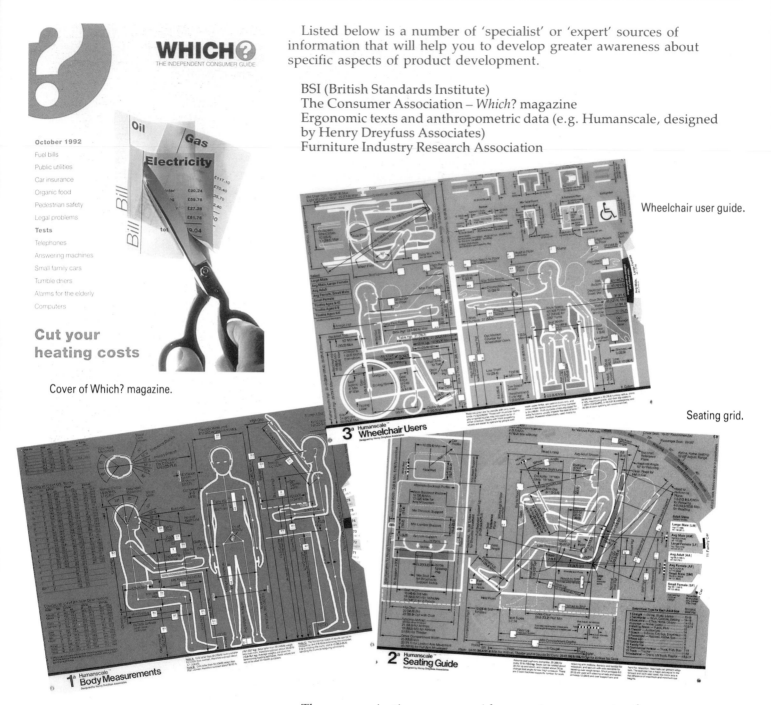

Cover of Which? magazine.

Wheelchair user guide.

Seating grid.

These organisations can provide expert assessments of many products because they usually have the appropriate facilities and individuals who can devote a great deal of time and technical expertise to the testing of products. Included in this analysis will be performance tests, where the use of the product will be simulated by a controlled test which may be repeated many times in laboratory conditions in order to obtain accurate data which can then be used to assess the product. This is very useful for long, repetitive or dangerous tests, for example the testing of flame-retardant foams for use in furniture or the impact resistance of motor-cycle crash helmets. Many of these results are published, or the information obtained may be used as a basis for setting standards or to help frame consumer legislation.

Examples of product testing at the BS/FIRA test centre.

Static load test on tables and desks (BS 4875 Part 5).

Test for interval bond on medium-density fibreboard (BS 1142).

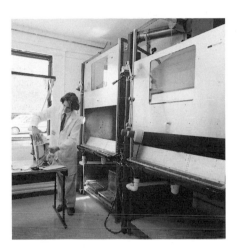

Testing cabinets for flammability, match and cigarette test (BS 5852).

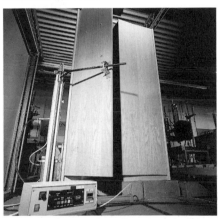

Door operation test (BS 4875 Part 7), right.

Fore and aft safety test for pedestal chairs (BS 5459 Part 2).

Gathering your own information

As a consumer or 'user' you are in an ideal position to make judgements about products, and you may do this by employing a number of recognised forms of investigation.

User trips

This involves you in simply using the product and recording your observations about the way you interact with it. What difficulties did you experience using the product, and why? What design features do you like about the product and why? Is the product 'user friendly'? You may also need to organise more than one 'trip' to take into account different environmental factors, for example the control panel of a hi-fi system may be perfectly easy to read in daylight, and yet may suffer from glare under artificial lighting. Think of all the different environmental factors that may influence your assessment of a motor car, i.e. driving in bright sunshine, fog, snow and ice and windy conditions. Each of these conditions may give you a totally different reaction to the vehicle. Regardless of the number of user trips you make, it is essential to record your observations as soon as they occur. You could use a tape recorder and speak directly into it, or write down your observations as soon as you can after the event.

It is also important that any criticisms that you make are justified, for example if you find something is uncomfortable, can you explain why and then find out how it could be improved. If you believe that a particular material that has been used in manufacture is inappropriate, can you suggest why, and then recommend an alternative. However, you must remember that user trips can be subjective; other people's reactions to the product may be totally different from yours.

User observation

To balance out the subjectivity associated with user trips, you could also gather information by watching other users and recording their interactions with the products. However, you will need to be thoughtful about whom you really think of as 'the user' in this context. An analysis of toys at a preschool play group may prove to be more informative if you obtain the views of parents and nursery staff as well as observing the children at play. In this example, and in many others, the user may be found in more than one interest group. In a public transport system, is the user the passenger, the maintenance engineer or the operator?

Product testing is not new. This photograph was taken in 1936 and shows the test track for Fiat cars and other vehicles on the roof of the Fiat Lingotto workshops in Turin, Italy.

Once again it is very important to record your findings and present them in an informative way. Plan your visits carefully, and work out the questions you want to ask the users, as well as the specific points you wish to observe. Experience shows that informal questions posed to users can produce a more honest response than detailed and more formal questionnaires, although, ideally, you could employ both techniques. Remember to include background information about your users, for example age, sex and whether they are experienced users of the product or not. It is also useful to photograph examples of user participation for inclusion in your report, to help illustrate specific points about your research and conclusions.

A product analysis study

Illustrated here are sample sheets that formed part of a product analysis study undertaken by Richard Webster, an A-level student following the Oxford design course. The subject of the study was the comparison of two swivel-head torches marketed under the names of 'Rotalight' and 'Durabeam'.

Richard explained his reasons for choosing this topic in his opening paragraph.

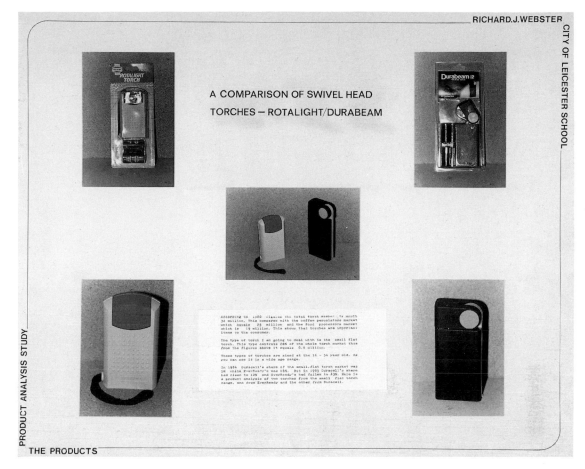

Comparison of two torches.

According to recent statistics the total torch market is worth £32m. This compares with the coffee percolators market which is worth £25m, and the food-processor market which equals £19m. This shows that torches are important consumer purchases.

The type of torch I am going to deal with is the small flat torch. This type controls 20% of the whole torch market and thus from the figures above it represents £6.4m. These types of torches are aimed at the 16-54 age group.

In 1984 Duracell's share of the small, flat torch market was 5%, whilst EverReady's was 48%. But in 1985 Duracell's share had risen to 12% and EverReady's had fallen to 43%.

Richard then proceeded to establish a set of criteria under which he made assessments and judgements about each particular product. The criteria he selected were:

- Packaging and presentation of the product to the consumer.

- The efficiency of the on/off mechanism.

- Access to the battery compartment, including the ease with which the batteries could be replaced.

- The design and efficiency of the bulb compartment.

- The ergonomics of the torch, with specific reference to the grip.

- Safety aspects of the torch.

- An assessment of the appropriate use of materials.

> • The cost of the product to the consumer in terms of 'value for money'.

Are there different criteria which you might use to assess the worth of the two torches? To what extent do you agree with Richard's list?

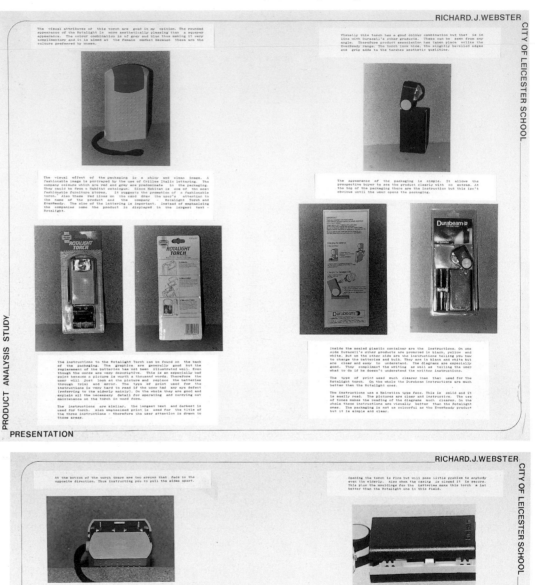

Packaging and presentation.

An analysis of the battery compartment.

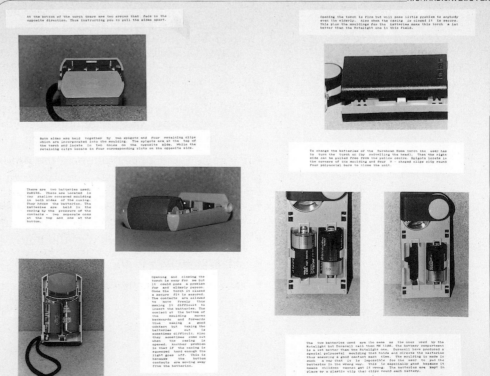

Design evaluation

Redesigning a guitar

Brief

Produce and present a folder that assesses the design and technological significance and value of an item in everyday use or in use by you, so that you can indicate ideas for its improvement and/or its redesign, wholly or in part.

Examples: a child's game or puzzle, a washing machine, a musical instrument, a juke-box or an item approved by your tutor.

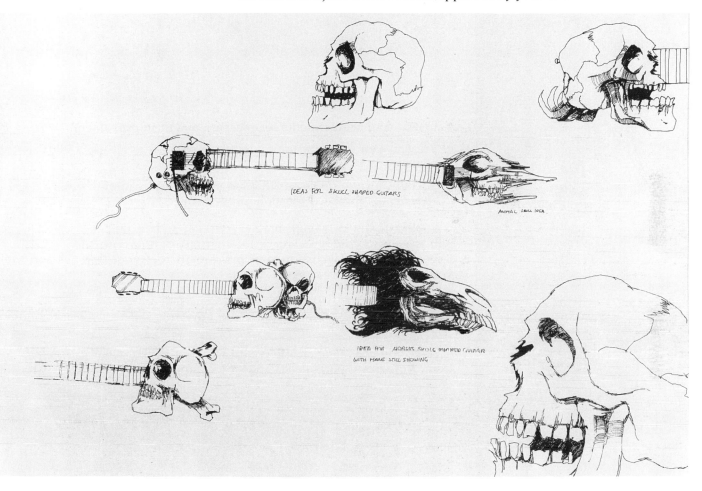

IDEAS FOR SKULL SHAPED GUITARS

ANIMAL SKULL IDEA.

IDEA FOR HORSES SKULL SHAPED GUITAR WITH MANE STILL SHOWING

Your task is to carry out and report on your evaluation of an object in terms of how well it is designed for use by people. The purpose of this evaluation is to identify which features of the object would benefit from redesigning, and to create an idea for something new or find something that can be improved upon concerning the object, and to develop and communicate your ideas.

Your folder will be judged using the following criteria, which will establish how well you:

- Describe your chosen item, through a combination of words and drawings.

- Explain the procedures and techniques you use in your evaluation.

151

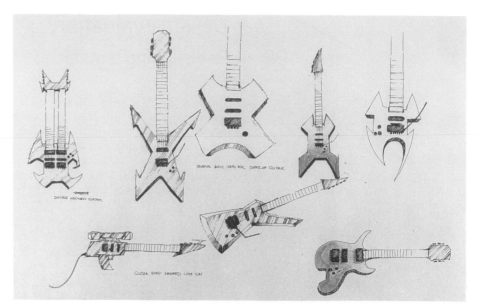

- Justify your requirements for redesign and/or improvement.

- Present your ideas for improving your selected item, especially visually.

- Account for the processes that led you to the creation of your redesign or the need for its improvement.

It is important that your work is coherent and systematic, especially with regard to your selection of relevant ideas and information. These issues are also invaluable in your interpretation of your findings and to your presentation of a cogent design evaluation.

Assessment of this activity will employ the following criteria:

- Description of chosen item, especially through a combination of words and pictures.

Have you conveyed clearly what the object is like, what it is made from, how many parts it has and, most important, what it does? Are

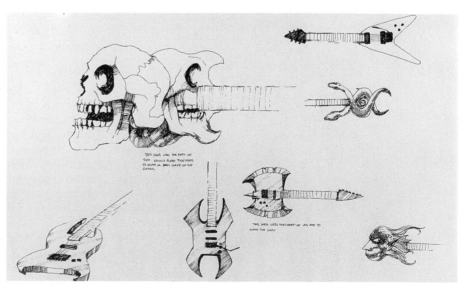

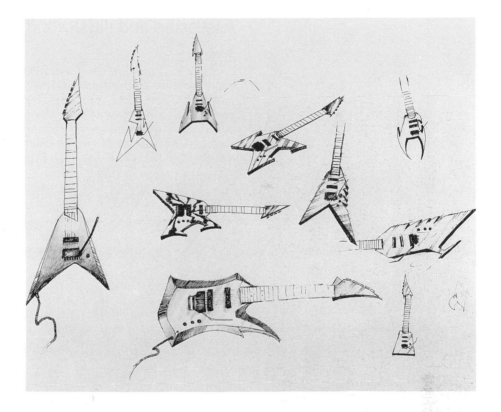

the notes coherent and do they complement the drawings or are there any repetitions, gaps or inconsistencies?

- Explain the procedures and techniques used in the evaluation.

Have you tackled the evaluation systematically by acknowledging your own use of the design, its use by other people, and expert appraisal where possible?
Have you described its 'fitness for purpose', how well it is made and from which materials, as well as whether or not it is value for money, durable, safe to use, its appearance and so on?

- Justify your requirements for redesign and/or improvement. Do your ideas for redesign come out of your evaluation findings? What is the scope of your design ideas?

Do you discuss the limitations and reliability of your findings? For example, do you mention the limited usefulness of evaluation data derived from your own study?

- Presentation of ideas for improving your selected item, especially visually.

Are the drawings effective and geometrically correct? Have, you considered a variety of related ideas?

- Account for the processes that led you to the creation of your redesign or need for its improvement.

Did you work intuitively or according to chosen design criteria? For example, have you considered any of the following criteria, ergonomics, economics, technical, aesthetic, cultural merit and so on?

Assessing and illustrating a household product

Brief

Produce and present an illustration, in full colour, of any contemporary household product, for example a coffee-making machine, a computer, a hair dryer, a television set, a compact disc, a dust-pan and brush. Present your drawings on an A2 format accompanied by preparatory sketches on separate sheets. Use this illustration alongside a critique of the product, based upon the following information from Philips which is given on page 142.

Student examples by Steve Brunger.

Criteria for assessing a design illustration evaluation can be based on:

- The production and presentation, in full colour, of an illustration of a household product, which is formed through preparatory sketches, research notes, consideration of the quality of drawing and illustration techniques employed, the presentation of the illustration and a statement outlining a working context for the illustration.

- A description of the chosen item, especially through a combination of words and pictures, which demonstrates that you have conveyed clearly what the object is like, what it is made from, how many parts it has and, most important, what it does. It is important that your notes are coherent and that they complement the drawings and avoid repetitions and inconsistencies.

- An explanation of the procedures and techniques used in the evaluation, to show that you have tackled the evaluation systematically by acknowledging your own use of the design, its use by other people and expert appraisal where possible. It is here that you should describe the design's 'fitness for purpose', how well it is made and from which materials, as well as whether or not it is value for money, durable, safe to use, its appearance and so on.

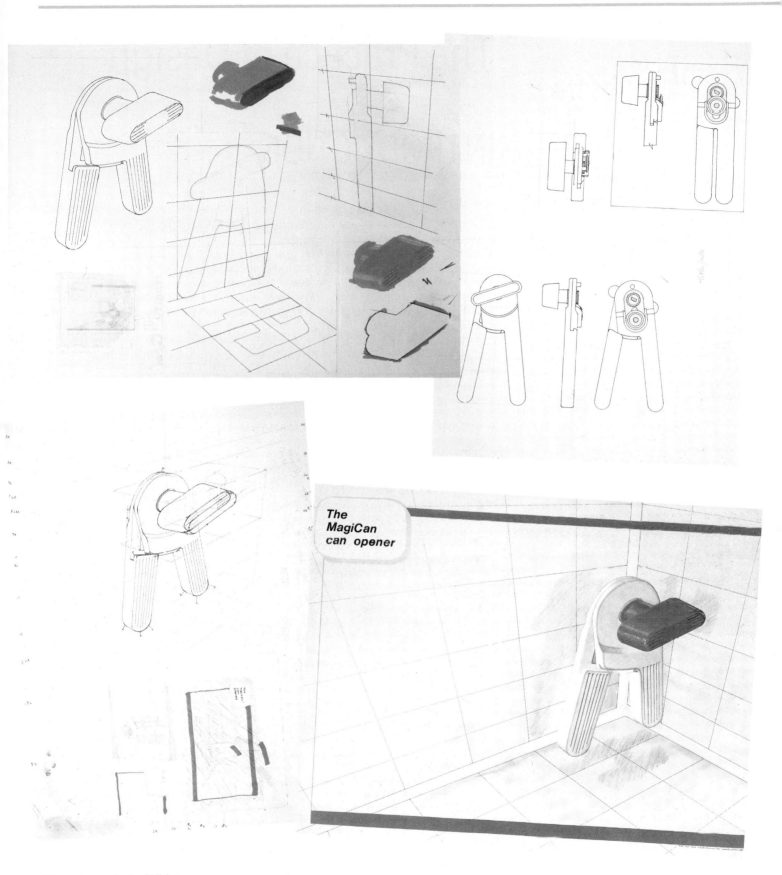

The
MagiCan
can opener

Student examples by Cliff Colman.

4 The Practice of Design

INTRODUCTION

There are some general techniques that most designers use, but courage and boldness are also important characteristics of design endeavour. As a designer, you should be concerned with ideas based on your own creative thoughts, and you should develop the techniques required to draw or model your ideas. Sometimes you will also make and test your schemes or systems.

Your general tasks so far have been intended to develop your own awareness of design, to give you experience of the work of other designers and to enable you to say something about it. Your design capability is dependent upon your design awareness and your willingness to experiment with your own design ideas. But where do you start work when designing? Study the following ideas, professional examples and the work of your fellow students and make designing work for you.

A summary of the processes of designing

Design concepts or processes may be based on an inspirational insight, a modification of a working idea, or form the basis for some instrumental action or motive concerning resources or technical qualities. Designing can be 'idea-led', 'technology-led', 'market-led', 'demand-led' and even 'design-led'. Designs may be derived from within us, or be given to us in the form of a specification or brief.

A designer draws, notes, models and analyses a design idea and simulates a possible outcome. These ideas are made available only to the designer, through drawings and research, or to anyone else working with the designer. At the end of the designer's thinking, a proposal is formed specifying what is to be done. Designing is exploring, testing and hypothesising. While the designer might end up making the design, other people are often involved in this stage.

Designing strategies are a combination of remembering, recalling and evaluating information, thinking about what is to be done and how ideas will be achieved. The design issues and subject-matter for a design can be found in many areas of knowledge and experience.

A designer thinks about a future object, action or idea. A designer imagines what a design will be like when it is completed. A designer ostensibly produces a design, not a real thing, although sometimes designers are involved in actually realising their ideas, as products or product systems. Designers synthesise all manner of information to these ends.

Designers have many skills associated with ways of depicting ideas and realising them. In addition, they are also involved in producing processes in themselves, as they indicate and promote trends and fashions, or as they conceive holistic plans for systems or procedures,

DESIGN ROUTES

ORIGINATION OF DESIGN SPECIFICATIONS AND CONSTRAINTS	
Starting points which are given to designers	Ideas which designers originate

Real world influence of demands from the market, enterprises or businesses; seeing opportunities based on social necessity, playing a part in the community	Briefs, from contexts, peer influence & interests, based on issues, including functional and decorative necessity of things & activities within specified setting	Feelings, interests motivated by one-offs & exhibitions; personal necessity, self-expression

Developed and synthesised through

DESIGNER MOTIVES, CURIOSITY SITUATIONS & SOURCES OF INSPIRATION
& supported by

THE ORGANISATION OF IDEAS	THE APPLICATION OF EXPERIENCE

TECHNICAL & MATERIAL Response to materials, media, techniques and skills, tools and resources	FUNCTION & COSTS Response to principles, theories, economics, 'form & meaning' and affordances, 'what's it for'

SOCIO-CULTURAL & HISTORICAL Response to past techniques, images and developments	'EUREKA'/PREPARED MIND Response due to 'I had this idea!' Being cultured, and having a prepared mind	TRENDS & FASHIONS Response to present market, images of a past period or style and future trends and tastes

PERSONAL RESEARCH Response to interests, obsessions and developments	AESTHETIC IDEALS Response to imaginative and aesthetic ideals & new knowledge & experience

Resulting in

INNOVATION Response to need for modification and improvement of existing ideas or products; to bring about new possibilities; more than adaption, product of effective experiences which inspire experiment	INVENTION Response to the unknown; resulting in creative action based on technical insight and imagination; sometimes derived from vague intentions, hunches or intuition, as well being experimental

with the interconnection of components or operational requirements, for example cars in relation to traffic flow and roads.

Design routes

The willingness to develop a prepared mind, so as to be able to bring together connecting or contrasting principles or ideas, as well as using knowledge and experience to produce specifications, and to plan and organise things through to completion are all human attributes that fuel design capability.

Designed products and product systems are in themselves the result of a combination of many different people's experiences in their use of things, especially everyday items. The process of change is driven by necessity as well as commercial pressures to succeed, and underpinned by the evolutionary processes of human design. In studying design it is worth noting when and how new developments came about and relating what you find to aspects of theoretical knowledge and fundamental technological concepts.

Some designers produce ideas as if by accident and some bring about new or modified products through careful thought. The 'eureka' factor has its place in design mythology. However, it seems far more likely that new inspirations occur to minds that are prepared for fresh eventualities, rather than relying upon blinding inspiration to occur as if from nothing.

Design can be individualistic and originate from the raw talents and convictions of designers. However, since design is a blending of information towards certain ends, designing is a process that is reliant upon designers knowing how to receive, as well as to pass on, information about design possibilities. This is particularly significant when theories and practical studies about how people use things are employed, for example ergonomics or market research.

Designing involves bringing together issues concerning form, function and the value of products, images and product systems. A willingness to co-operate and to seek advice will always be important in design work.

The 'design routes' diagram outlines possible ways of originating designs for actual projects. These examples can be especially useful when structuring activities that link awareness to capability. There are many possible combinations for design examples, experiences and experiments. It is quite likely that many of these will overlap, which is proof that design is a synthesis of many ideas.

Consider your own design experiences, as well as those presented here, and determine which design routes you have used, or will use.

Design examples to work

Consider the starting points and routes through design in the following examples. Consider variations to this approach, especially those that utilise your own special design skills and approaches and develop your own designs.

- Design a package system for mass-produced Christmas tree lights which are sold in large stores. The design solution should have a fresh concept in graphics. The package should be of a novel construction, so that the bulbs are safe, protected, easy to store and will give appropriate information to customers and retailers concerning the various types of bulbs and their power ratings. Indicate the type of market this new product will be aimed at.

- Design a method of controlling paper coming off a computer printer.

- Design a mechanical burglar alarm, rather than one using microtechnology.

- For its main entrance County Hall requires a range of vases and containers that will display flowers and foliage. Design a range of containers for this purpose. In addition to fulfilling their function, these articles should be decorative and interesting in their own right. However, their form should not conflict with the possible arrangements and types of flowers.

- Revamp a recognised product of your choice. For example, consider generating a major change to toaster design. Review the styling possibilities and its appearance, including colours; consider also the technical qualities it can have with regard to its operations. For example, what size and shape of bread can it cope with, how many slots will it have? Aim to create a unique item that will sell realistically. Produce drawings and models that explore the external appearance of the toaster. Present a full-size, realistic mock-up and engineering prototype. Try the same approach on a more mundane example like a dustpan and brush.

- Produce a series of drawings (no more than five) that demonstrate the gradual metamorphosis of one unrelated thing into another for example, change a car into a tortoise. Avoid hackneyed and conventional ideas and use this exercise for a purpose.

- The National Garden Festival organisation has acquired a large number of plain mugs for which they require a surface pattern to reflect the forthcoming festival. Design and develop a set of four co-ordinated surface-pattern designs to celebrate the festival's theme; use onglaze enamel, four colours and an easily applied decoration. Present a prototype set through drawings and worked examples.

- A pet food company requires a new range of animal feeding dishes. Design and make a suitable item for this market.

- From your own imagination and skill, design and make an object for exhibition.

- Design and make an ice-cream cone holder which can be given away at an ice-cream van to someone buying more than four ice-creams

- An exhibition requires work which demonstrates the theme of gentleness and delicate things; design and make a series of ceramic items that can be displayed in this exhibition. Do not make anything bigger than 100 mm in any direction.

- You have received a request through personal contacts for a 'one-off' item. Design a sports trophy for a volley ball club, and submit a prototype or maquette for the club to approve.

- Design a system to dispense the correct daily dose of tablets and pills. Many people need to take several varieties of pills each day, and some do not remember whether or not they have taken their pills consistently. Find out who might benefit from this design. Study the different combinations of pills, their shapes and sizes, as well as the order of prescription.

- Design and make a paper windmill that can be given away to advertise a zoo. If you have personal objections to the idea of a zoo, would you carry out this work? Can professional designers pick and choose their projects?

- Design a set of graphics for a new putty container. Devise a brand name, colour scheme and letter style for this mundane item.

- 'In the future everybody will be world famous for fifteen minutes' (Andy Warhol). Draw a self-portrait and then paint a famous and interesting person whom you admire.

- Design a cartoon based on the following idea: 'If you want a friend in life, get a dog'.

- Design a visual information item that describes the possible effects of 'global warming' on the coastline of the British Isles. Increased carbon dioxide levels in the upper atmosphere are being caused by the cutting down of the rainforests and the predominance of fossil fuels in the production of electricity. This carbon dioxide is causing an increase in mean global temperatures, and is predicted to melt the polar ice caps. The melting ice caps are estimated to increase average sea levels by 5 m. How reliable is this information? What is 'the greenhouse effect'?

  Use Ordnance Survey maps, in conjunction with a pantograph designed specifically for this task, to produce a model of your revised coastline. This activity could also be modelled through a computer.

- Write a brief or specification for a design project which inspires you, no matter how fantastic or mundane.

In designing the context and issues at hand are of paramount importance to a designer. Your capability to design comes from your understanding for the topic which is being explored, as much as the way in which you actually work. Consider the examples in this section and work as a designer.

Coursework Examples

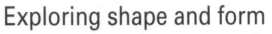

Exploring shape and form

An early part of any design experience should be familiarisation with, and awareness of, the importance played by shape and form in three-dimensional design. For the purpose of this exercise, 'shape' will be defined as two-dimensional, i.e. the outline of a square, circle or triangle, whereas 'form' relates to a three-dimensional object, that added dimension being one of depth. Hence spheres, cubes and pyramids are examples of common forms.

Designers rarely have the opportunity to create forms in total isolation to the function of the product they are designing. Indeed, the 'modernists' held the firm belief that 'form follows function', and when we start to explore design proposals we often work from what we know about the way a product should function in our pursuit to reveal its final form. This exercise requires you to try to put these experiences to the back of your mind and simply explore the visual relationships of shape and form and their interaction with one another. This activity is about investigation and exploration, and as such the only person you are trying to please is yourself. You must decide which of the shapes and forms you have designed you prefer, and you must also try to explain your choices by identifying why you have particular preferences; you may find it difficult to express this reasoning and justification in words, and you may need to familiarise yourself with some of the vocabulary that can be used to describe your observations and feelings.

Exploring shape

- Prepare ten squares of thin black card or sugar paper, each measuring 40×40 mm.

- Using a sharp craft knife or pair of scissors, make one straight cut to break one square into two pieces. Be thoughtful about where you make the cut and try to choose a division of the square that, in your opinion, produces pleasing proportions.

- Repeat this process on each of your squares, making your cuts in different places each time.

- Once you have done this, place the squares on a piece of white paper and separate the two pieces of each square with a parallel gap. For each of the test pieces, choose the size of gap that, in your opinion, visually suits the two sections of the squares.

- Glue the pieces to the white background.

- Make your choice as to which you believe are the two most visually interesting designs and the two least visually interesting designs. Explain your reasons for the choices you have made (250 words).

You could also explore other shapes, such as circles and triangles, in a similar way and make curved cuts as well as straight ones.

Exploring form

When you feel confident and relaxed about handling and generating different shapes, begin to develop your ideas about form.

- Through design sketches, produce a range of proposals for a single modular unit that will be made in wood, metal, plastic or another resistant material.

- The units must be capable of being easily produced to enable you to work with at least ten identical modules. They should be capable of being attached to one another, although this may be done through gluing, soldering or welding, and you do not have to make an integral mechanical joint as part of your design.

- Select one of your modules and manufacture it in an appropriate material of your choice.

- When you have manufactured all of the identical modules, experiment by arranging them into a number of visually interesting forms.

- These different forms can be recorded in photographs.

- Select the form that you find most exciting and secure the modules to one another.

- Discuss your work and justify the design choices you have made throughout the exercise (500 words).

Timber modular design.

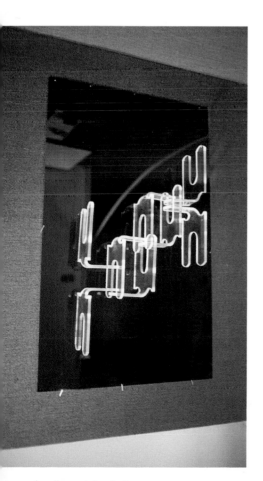

Acrylic modular design.

The exploratory nature of these tasks should also transfer to other more functional three-dimensional work. What is required is an open mind which will help you to generate a much broader range of ideas. In his book *The Dynamics of Visual Form*, Sausmarez explains this journey.

Lettering and typography

The function of the letters of our alphabet when they are combined into words is to convey meaning of one kind or another. They are able to fulfil this function in two ways; firstly, and perhaps most obviously, by virtue of their symbolic content (i.e. their linguistic meaning); secondly by virtue of their graphic content (i.e. their form). Letters are primarily used to express speech sounds that combine to make words with culturally endowed meanings. These meanings are separate from the forms of the words to the extent that it is quite possible for a word to convey one meaning symbolically (linguistically) and something quite different graphically. Take for example the form of the words below.

In a graphic design exercise concerned with lettering it will often be the task of the designer to ensure that the form enhances the symbolic (linguistic) meaning. In order to achieve this the designer will have to make decisions about the following:

- The letter forms themselves, including their shape, size and style.

- Their placement and arrangement, including their spacing, in relation to one another, as well as their location and layout in relation to the overall design.

- The colour, texture and decoration of the letter surfaces.

Students involved in lettering design should begin to develop some of the concepts and skills involved in making appropriate decisions about these facets of typographical design, and the following activities will give you the opportunity to explore and practise certain aspects of this learning.

The relations between symbolic (linguistic) content and graphic content (form)

- Compose at least six words in materials denoted by their symbolic (linguistic) contents. For example, if you were to choose the word 'string', you would form it by using actual string. In this example, as with other materials, it may be necessary to fix them to an appropriate base to assist your observation and representation of the material.

- Make careful and detailed drawings of your chosen words, paying particular attention to those features of the materials you wish to represent (for example, their forms, textures and colours).

In this project you are required to compose your chosen words in the actual material or what might be termed the 'substance' of their symbolic meaning, prior to making detailed drawings of them. There are two reasons for making this requirement:

- Literally forming the words helps you to become more aware of the relationship between the symbolic meaning and the graphic content of the words.

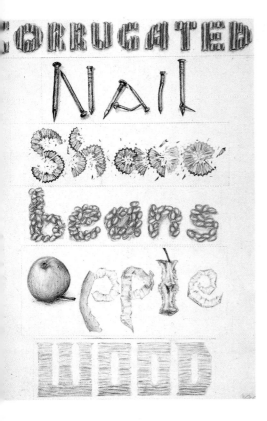

- When you draw the word 'beans' from a word made up of actual beans, for example, this will provide you with a greater opportunity to observe and therefore more accurately represent the characteristic features and specific details of form, texture and colour than could be obtained by drawing from memory.

The potential of placement, size and decoration

- Using a suitable typeface that is already available, select an appropriate word and, by manipulating the placement, i.e. arrangement, spacing and location of the letters

and/or by varying their size but not altering their shapes,

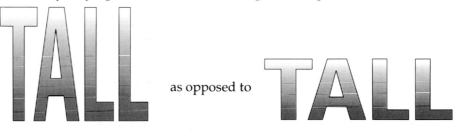

as opposed to

and/or by decorating any of their surfaces,

seek to provide a form for that word which enhances its symbolic meaning.

For example:

In this activity you are requested not to alter the shapes of the letters, which therefore requires you to focus your attention entirely on their placement, size and decoration, so enhancing your understanding of the potential of these particular variables in helping to communicate the meanings of words.

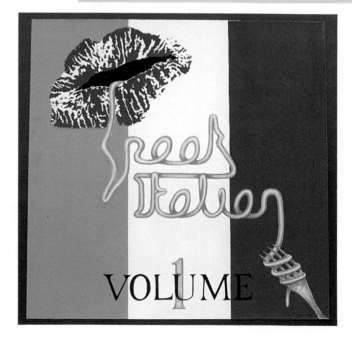

Product design-modelling

An important part of any design activity is the exploration and development of ideas that will eventually lead to your chosen design. This decision-forming process can be assisted through drawing, mathematical calculations, computer-aided design, prototypes and the use of three-dimensional models, either full-size or to scale. This analysis of design proposals is often referred to as 'modelling' and can include a variety of different sorts of models created for different purposes. These may vary from those models that are aimed at proving the feasibility of designs under consideration to those which are used by people who are concerned with selling a new product to a particular market.

One of Fox-Talbot's early cameras against a background made from the earliest negative in existence and taken by him in 1835. This is an excellent example of a model that was being used to prove the feasibility of a concept.

The original Daguerrotype whole plate camera of 1839. Note the use of traditional materials, such as wood and brass, in its construction, and how its form is influenced by the expertise of traditional cabinet-making techniques.

Many forms of modelling are also important because they can assist in communicating your proposals to a wider audience. Architects and planners often use scale models of their schemes to canvass public opinion. Motor car manufacturers will use full-size models, incorporating their latest design features, as a market research exercise to assess public opinion before including them in their latest product range.

This project asks you to develop a product to meet a particular market need, and to employ a variety of techniques that will eventually require you to produce a full-size three-dimensional model of your chosen design.

The design brief

Sunpol is an international photographic company specialising in the manufacture of 35 mm cameras and associated equipment. They have recently established a new design and manufacturing plant in the UK. Following extensive market research they are planning to launch a new 35 mm auto-focus compact camera aimed specifically at the 18–35 age range. The general design concept associated with the product must ensure that the camera is:

- Equally attractive to both males and females.

- The styling concept associated with the product should incorporate and reflect contemporary images, which might include concepts such as 'sporty', 'fun', 'comic', 'designer', 'leisure', 'holidays' or other themes that you might identify as appropriate.

- The camera should sell for less than £100, and the price range you choose should be reflected in the specification and features to be found in your competitors' products at a similar price.

Your first task will be to analyse critically the existing range of 35 mm auto-focus compact cameras on the market for sale at less than £100. From this research you should be able to identify the main technical features and specifications that should be incorporated into your design. You may do this through trying out and assessing similar cameras in this segment of the market (an activity often referred to as a user trip) and collecting expert comment from camera magazines and other specialist publications, as well as the views of your friends.

Your final submission should include

- A market review of 35 mm auto-focus compact cameras. Establish your own set of criteria for this review, and critically appraise the competition.

- A range of design drawings and proposals illustrating your own ideas for the camera. These drawings may use freehand perspective or orthographic drawings.

- Comments about your designs from the target group involved, together with a rationale outlining the reasons for the choice of your final design, and what factors influenced this decision-making.

35mm cameras.

- A full-size model of your final design.

You may also extend this project to include the design of:

- Packaging and 'point of sale' promotional material for the camera.
- An instruction sheet to explain the operation of the camera.
- An advertisement to appear in a magazine promoting your design.

Model-making

A variety of different materials can be used for making your camera model, such as wood, foamed plastics, card, plaster or clay. One timber that is particularly easy to work with is jelutong.

This hardwood tree, found throughout Malaysia and parts of Borneo, is mainly used for the tapping of latex, which, among other things, is the basis of chewing gum. The wood is white or straw-coloured but may be discoloured by staining caused by fungal attack. The timber works equally well by hand and machine tools and has little dulling effect on the cutting edges of tools. Good results can be obtained quickly on the woodworking lathe, which is an advantage when model-making. The end grain of the timber is closely packed and quite dense while remaining easy to work. These characteristics facilitate easy shaping of complex forms as well as easy finishing of the end grain and the avoidance of unsightly grain patterns after painting. Despite being classified as a 'hardwood', jelutong is quite soft and can be easily bruised or dented if harshly treated or dropped. It is a good idea to keep your work wrapped up in soft cloths during transit and storage between manufacturing operations.

Samples of jelutong.

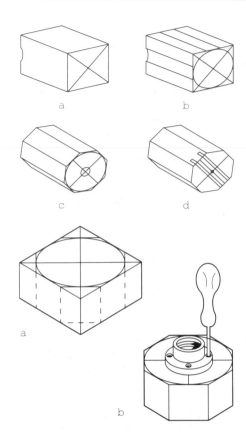

Shaping the wood

A variety of tools and processes may be used to shape and model the form of your camera. These may include bandsaws, planes, sanding machines, spokeshaves, rasps, files and many more. In particular, you will find a woodworking lathe invaluable in the production of precise forms of circular cross-section.

Beginners may find it helpful to carry out some practice work before tackling the precise components they wish to make. To do this, select a piece of jelutong about 200 mm long and 40–50 mm in diameter. Draw diagonals at each end to find the centre (A), then, using a pair of dividers, draw a circle (B). Using a jack plane, take off the corners (C), then drill a small hole, 4 mm in diameter and approximately 6 mm deep, in the centre of each end. When turning between centres, use a tenon saw to cut two grooves at one end of the piece of wood to receive the fork centre (D).

To prepare wood for turning on the faceplate, once again take a piece of jelutong, this time approximately 100 mm square and 50 mm thick. Plane one face flat and draw diagonals on this face to find the centre. Using dividers, mark a circle within the square, draw the tangents across the corners (E), and saw off the waste. Place a suitably sized faceplate centrally on the block and use a bradawl to locate the positions of the screws (F). Select some short, stout screws to secure the wood firmly to the faceplate.

A 'fork' centre.

A 'dead' centre.

Turning between centres.

Turning on a faceplate.

Painting

With the exception of some foamed plastics, almost all small models can be painted most efficiently by using the cellulose-based spray cans that are sold as car touch-up paint. The use of the spray should give you a good finish providing you follow some simple points and do not rush this stage of the project.

If you intend to use cellulose spray finishes, read the manufacturer's instructions carefully and work in a safe environment, extracting the fumes, wearing the appropriate safety mask and taking into account the fire risks associated with cellulose finishes.

- To ensure that the surface finish of your model is as smooth as possible, rub it down with very fine glasspaper or silicon carbide (wet and dry) paper to a perfect finish.

- Apply a cellulose-based-primer to the surface of the model. This can be done using a can of spray primer specifically produced for this purpose and usually available in grey, white or red oxide. Choose the colour that will give the best base for your final top coat. However, you can also use cellulose-based sanding sealer, which can be applied by brush. This will cut down on the cost of spray cans, and three or four coats, rubbed down between applications, should give a good enough base for you to apply the final colour. Always allow these primers to dry until the finish has hardened off before you attempt to rub down any blemishes that might have developed during spraying or brushing. For the best results, remember to spray at a distance of 200–300 mm from the model, and apply a number of thin coats rather than building up one or two thick coats, which will encourage the paint to run and cause drips to form. Always practise on an offcut of the material you are spraying and make your mistakes on this rather than on your model.

Typical spray paints.

- Your final colour should be sprayed onto the primer, and slowly built up with a number of applications, once again, if necessary, rubbing down between coats when the paint has hardened, to achieve a perfectly smooth finish.

- You can also use pieces of packaging or other odds and ends to simulate switches, lenses (a marble set into the body of the model), handgrips, etc. These can all add realism to your finished model.

Examples of completed design drawing research sheets and model cameras.

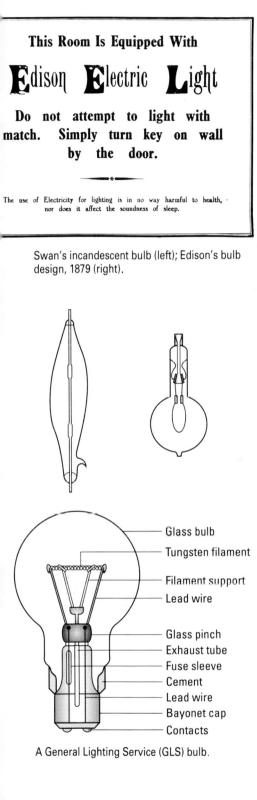

Swan's incandescent bulb (left); Edison's bulb design, 1879 (right).

Glass bulb
Tungsten filament
Filament support
Lead wire
Glass pinch
Exhaust tube
Fuse sleeve
Cement
Lead wire
Bayonet cap
Contacts

A General Lighting Service (GLS) bulb.

Domestic lighting design

For many centuries the only forms of artificial lighting were torches, bonfires, candles, oil lamps and gas lamps. Today, lighting is probably the one form of electrical engineering that is most taken for granted. Early pioneering work by Sir Humphrey Davy and his pupil Michael Faraday led, in 1850, to the introduction of arc lamps and, in 1862, to the first permanent electric lamp installation at the Dungeness Lighthouse. In order to exploit the full potential of these nineteenth-century technologies, considerable development work had to be undertaken to produce a reliable light source that could be used for both commercial and domestic applications. In 1878, Sir Joseph Wilson Swan developed the first incandescent light bulb, and one year later Thomas Edison developed his version. These early bulbs had carbon filaments and, due to the limitations of carbon as a material for filaments, the bulbs only burned for approximately 40 hours. By 1911 the more suitable tungsten filament had been successfully developed and the GLS (General Lighting Service) bulb, more or less as we know it today, came into existence.

Early incandescent electric lamp by Swan and Edison.

Light fittings, often referred to by the trade as luminaires, can be functional, both in terms of the general illumination of areas (ambient lighting), or direct lighting for specific purposes (task lighting), as well as lighting used to create atmosphere and mood.

The aim of this project is to involve you in the design and manufacture of a light fitting of your choice, and an example of a typical design brief is listed below. You may modify this brief if you wish.

Design brief

Design and make a light fitting of your choice from one of the areas listed below.

Battery-operated lighting.
A directional lighting source for a specific task.
A general lighting source for a room of your choice.
Lighting for visual appeal or novelty.
Outdoor lighting for either security or atmosphere.

The power of light. How lighting has been used to create three different moods in the same room. Here you can see how pools of subdued light bring a warm and intimate quality to a spacious room with a pastel colour scheme. Note also how light has been used to define different areas.

Research

Before you start designing, you will need to understand more about both the functional and aesthetic aspects of lighting. You will need to consider electrical safety, the economic implications of using different light sources and the ergonomic requirements of different lighting levels, as well as the selection of appropriate materials and processes that will enable you to make your fitting.

AN ENLIGHTENED INVESTMENT PROPOSITION.

We all know that, if you want to save, you have first to invest. So let's suppose that your firm has two hundred 60 W light bulbs that burn for about 15 hours a day. Here's the proposition: you replace all these bulbs by investing in the new OSRAM DULUX EL.

The average life of an OSRAM DULUX EL is 8000 hours, or, in this case, approximately 24 months. But instead of 60 W, it only burns 11 W of power to give you the same amount of light. So with electricity costing you £0.07 per kWh, your investment has already saved you £5,488. And there's more.

During your 24 months you would have to change a normal light bulb 7 times, on average. With the cost of the bulbs (£480) and the man to fit them at a labour cost of say £2 each, you're talking about £3,280

OSRAM DULUX EL
THE ELECTRONIC ENERGY SAVING LAMP

replacement costs for your firm.

Now, if you take away the extra cost of switching to OSRAM DULUX EL, you'll find you've saved around £6,218 all told. Or £3,109 per year.

If you need any more persuading, you should know that an OSRAM DULUX EL emits a bright, warm light, similar to a conventional incandescent light bulb, and lights up without any flash or flicker as soon as it's switched on.

That's because it's one of the first electronic lamps.

And it's worth mentioning that the electricity your firm is saving also reduces the emission of the 'greenhouse gas' carbon dioxide from electricity generation. So your investment in OSRAM DULUX EL is helping you to save in more ways than one.

The design of a luminaire should provide adequate illumination for the activities associated with the environment in which it is being used; it should also avoid glare, and visually enhance the area in which it is being used.

Product analysis

To help you to familiarise yourself with current fashion styles and developments in domestic lighting, it is a good idea to visit a variety of lighting stores and also to write to manufacturers requesting catalogues of their products. This will heighten your awareness of the topic and help you to develop some informed opinions.

Collect examples of light fittings/luminaires currently on sale and critically compare and contrast your chosen selection using appropriate criteria. Present your findings by setting out your illustrations and comments as research sheets.

What criteria might you use to assess and compare different light fittings/luminaires?

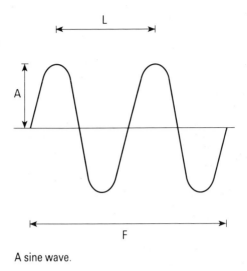

A sine wave.

The ergonomics of lighting

Our understanding of what goes on around us is partially obtained through our two main senses of sight and hearing, although additional information can be interpreted through touch, smell, taste and sensations of heat and cold. The two primary senses of sight and sound are dependent on the transmission of waves of information from our surroundings. The waves that give a sensation of light are a small part of the electromagnetic spectrum. The human eye operates on wavelengths extending from 380 nm at the violet end of the visible spectrum to 780 nm at the red end of the spectrum. When a wave is transmitted from a source it is known as a **sine wave**, whose projection on a plane surface against time is often described as a **sinusoidal curve**. On such a projection the wave has two symmetrical peaks, one above and one below a mid-line, and this complete movement is described as the length of the wave. The wave is defined by the following variables;

Length – distance from crest to crest.

Amplitude – this determines the intensity of the light and is identified by the displacement above and below the mid-line.

Frequency – this determines the colour of the light and relates to the number of waves that are completed in unit time, usually one second.

Recommended values of standard service illuminance

Standard service	Characteristics of the activity/interior	Representative activities/interiors
50	Interiors visited rarely with visual tasks confined to movement and casual seeing without perception of detail	Walkways, cable tunnels
100	Interiors visited occasionally with visual tasks confined to movement and casual seeing calling for only limited perception of detail	Bulk stores, corridors
150	Interiors visited occasionally with visual tasks requiring some perception of detail	Churches
	Interiors visited occasionally but involving some risk to people, plant or product	Loading bays
200	Continuously occupied interiors, visual tasks not requiring any perception of detail	Monitoring automatic processes in manufacture, turbine halls
300	Continuously occupied interiors, visual tasks moderately easy, i.e. details to be seen are large and/or of high contrast	Lecture theatres, packing goods, rough sawing
500	Visual tasks moderately difficult, i.e. details to be seen are of moderate size and may be of low contrast. Also colour judgement may be required	General offices, kitchens, laboratories
750	Visual tasks difficult, i.e. details to be seen are small and of low contrast. Also good colour judgement may be required	Drawing offices, ceramic decoration
1000	Visual tasks very difficult, i.e. details to be seen are very small and may be of very low contrast. Also accurate colour judgements may be required	Electronic component assembly, gauge and and tool rooms, retouching paintwork
1500	Visual tasks extremely difficult, i.e. details to be seen extremely small and of low contrast. Visual aids may be of advantage	Inspection of graphic reproduction, hand tailoring
2000	Visual tasks exceptionally difficult, i.e. details to be seen exceptionally small and of very low constrast. Visual aids will be of advantage	Assembly of minute mechanisms, finished fabric inspection

From BS 8206: Part 1

We are not usually so interested in the light intensity emitted by a source (luminous intensity) for, except when looking directly at a light source, we are more concerned with the amount of light that falls upon the object in view (illuminance). For this reason, when considering the amount of light required in relation to a task being undertaken, it is the brightness of the object that is of importance. The luminance of an object is the quantity of light reflected from its surface and its photometric unit is lux (lx). Different surfaces will have different reflectance values, as some surfaces absorb and transmit different types and amounts of light. To illustrate this, use a simple photometer to take different illuminance readings from a variety of surfaces placed in identical lighting conditions.

BS 8206 recommends values of standard service illuminance.

Different lighting tasks require different levels of illuminance.

Recent developments in lamp technology

Since the development of the GLS lamp, the lighting industry, coupled with consumer familiarity, has been slow to utilise more efficient and, in design terms, more flexible light sources. The old incandescent lamps transformed 90 per cent of their energy into heat, not light. However, in recent years a wider choice of lamps has become available with the introduction of compact fluorescent lamps and low-voltage tungsten-halogen lighting. As part of your lighting design, you will need to know about the advantages of these alternative light sources and their implications for your designs.

In recent years new developments in lamp technology have meant that the accepted deficiencies of the incandescent lamp, i.e. its short life, bulk and inefficiency, have been overcome.

Compact fluorescent lamps

Since their development in the early 1980s the use of compact lamps has been aimed at meeting the increasing cost of electricity, the need to reduce maintenance costs in public buildings and the greater flexibility they allow to luminaire design.

ailable in four wattages:

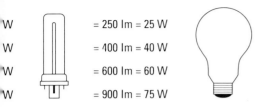

W   = 250 lm = 25 W

W   = 400 lm = 40 W

W   = 600 lm = 60 W

W   = 900 lm = 75 W

Compact fluorescent.   Tungsten filament.

These lamps are now manufactured by a number of companies in a variety of different forms, and some have an integral starter. The Osram DULUXEL is slightly longer than an incandescent lamp, but slimmer by one third. It is therefore ideally suited for smaller luminaires and shallow recessed downlights. The starter is integral in the plug-in base. Against comparable incandescent lamps, most compact fluorescents need only 20–25 per cent of the energy but have a life five times as long. The Thorn 2.D. lamp is ideal for flatter design applications replacing GLS lamps and long fluorescent tubes. A 16-watt version of the Thorn 2.D. lamp replaces 100-watt incandescent lamps and is available in seven vibrant hues, ideally suited for display and visual effects.

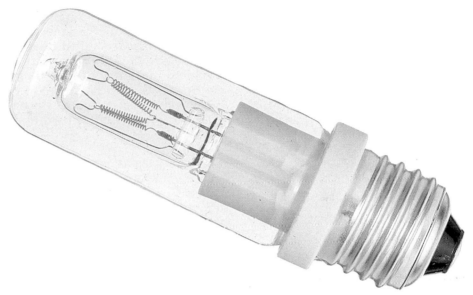

The Osram 'Halolux'.

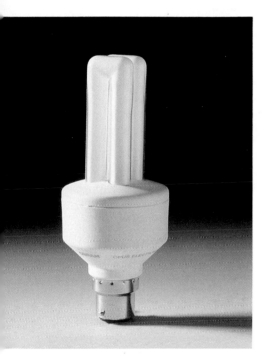

Electronic energy saving lamp.

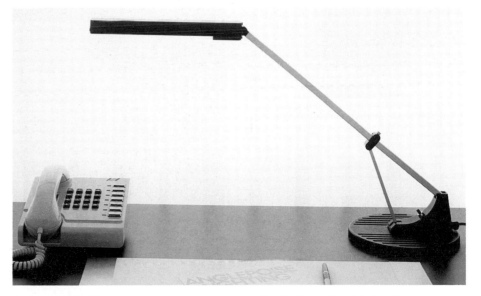

Anglepoise 4.33pP.L. employs an 11W Dulux P.L. lamp. Fitted with 240V 50Hz ballast in plug. Working illumination 700-300 lux across 800mm desk width. Available in matt black/satin silver.

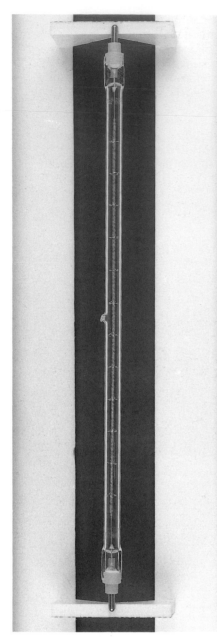

Osram 'Haloline': a tungsten halogen tube.

Low-voltage tungsten-halogen lamps

The low-voltage versions (6V, 12V, 24V) of tungsten-halogen lamps are connected to the supply via a transformer. The fact that they are very small allows them to be incorporated in smaller spaces, opening up a wider range of design possibilities. Tungsten-halogen can be focused into a narrow beam suitable for spotlight applications as well as being able to flood wide areas, as in task lighting. Most of these lamps also have the capacity to be controlled by dimmer switches, unlike fluorescent lamps. The lifespan of some lamps is now as much as 4,000 hours, saving time and money in replacing lamps.

How a fluorescent lamp works

A fluorescent tube is a low-pressure gas-discharge light source. Each tube contains mercury vapour at low pressure, with a small amount of inert gas to start it. The inner walls of the glass are coated with fluorescent powders called phosphors. At each end of the tube is a sealed electrode. When the correct voltage is applied, an arc is produced by current flowing through the mercury vapour between the electrodes. This discharge produces some visible radiation of light, but mostly ultraviolet radiation, which excites the phosphors to emit light. Specialist phosphors are used to obtain different coloured light emissions.

How a tungsten-halogen lamp works

In a traditional incandescent lamp, as the tungsten filament vaporises it forms on the inside of the glass. Over a period of time this cuts down the light output. By adding halogens to the filling gas, the vaporised tungsten is intercepted before it reaches the glass. This compound is then swept back to the filament where, at high temperatures, it breaks down, the halogen returning to the gas and the tungsten to the filament. Although the perfect balance is not possible, the life and brightness of the lamp are significantly extended.

The Osram 'Decostar'.

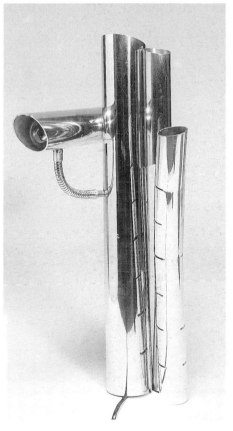

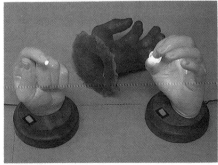

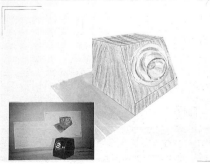

Student's design drawings and completed projects.

179

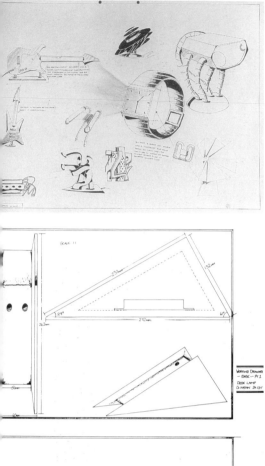

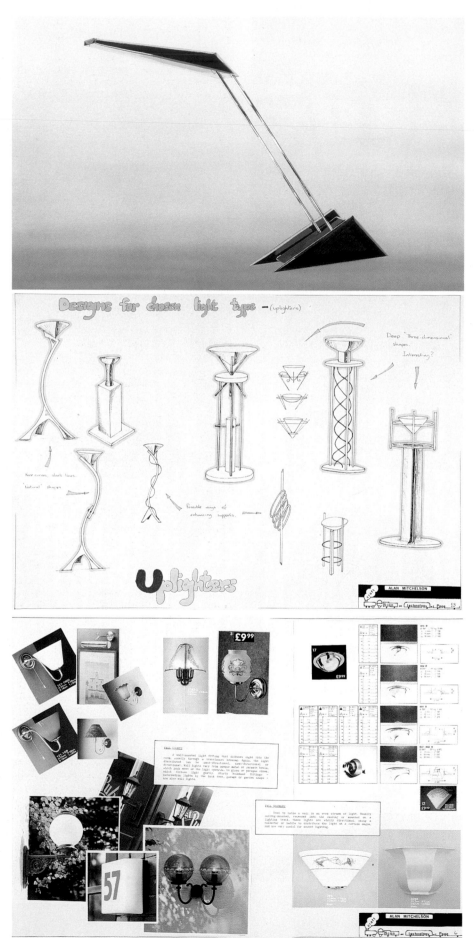

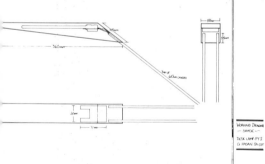

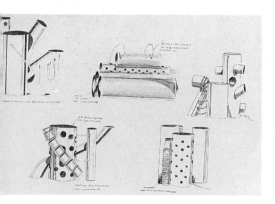

Falling in love with a machine

A Wurlitzer 800, a possible example to illustrate.

. . . the single most loved – and sometimes hated – symbol of its era. Once a feature of thousands of bars and diners throughout the United States, its familiarity made it a friend, while the magic of individual styling ensured that it always retained its mystery. . . for roughly a quarter of a century, commercially designed and mass produced objects, some beautiful, some ugly, some zany, sometimes masterpieces of engineering and sometimes not, found a place in people's hearts and minds and imaginations. ('Vintage Jukeboxes' *The Hall of Fame*, C. Pearce)

Design brief

Produce an illustration in full colour of any jukebox from the period between 1935–48. You should precisely specify any relevant background details concerning the designer, manufacturer, technical or sales information, trade name and qualities as a jukebox.

Your folder should explore the essential processes in an awareness and capability activity, based on your own creative visual narrative for your chosen design. It is important that you choose a working context for your illustration, for example, to describe how a jukebox works, how people use it or as an example in the history of music machines. These examples should be designed for a book, a poster or an suitable working situation where an illustration is used.

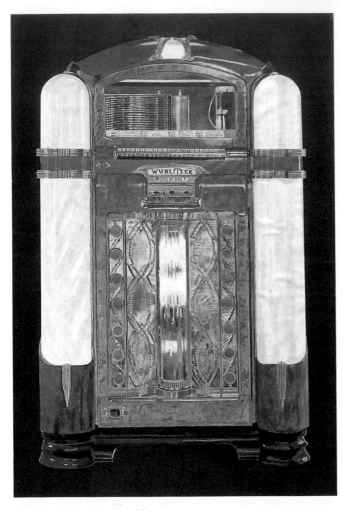

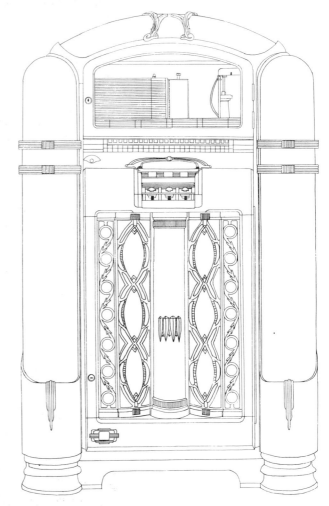

Student examples by Allan Muse.

This activity is devised to produce a bold, colourful illustration, based upon your own research. It will support your use of observational drawing and photographic material and generally promote drawing skills that are useful in design.

Which aspect of jukeboxes will you illustrate? Where will you use your illustration? Who will use it? Establish the context for your work fairly soon; however, if this is not considered to be important, then prove to yourself how your illustration can stand in its own right.

Naturally, this type of design work may be derived from a specification, brief or commission. Write your own design brief and consider how precise it should be for its working context. Write it for someone else.

The research for this design work requires some thought and organisation. During your investigation of source material about jukeboxes will you need to see a real jukebox? Where will you find your information? Would you have the courage to sketch a jukebox in a crowded bar? You will need clear information, and understanding how a jukebox is used may help you to see it clearly. Will you also need to research the technology of these machines?

The actual illustration techniques will also need to be based on a judgement about media and format. Which media technique will you practise? When will you employ freehand drawing and when mechanical drawing? Will you need to explore the surface appearance of your chosen machine? Which view of the jukebox will you select? Should you work from photographs? How will you use and present your research? What part does design play at this stage?

Through a series of sketches, you should present for discussion your proposition for your illustration. Which is the best view of the jukebox? Which is the best view for your chosen aspect of the machine? Are you merely depicting the appearance of the jukebox?

Once you have decided to realise your idea of a jukebox, you should recall all your drawing and illustration skills, based on your view of it. How will you form the drawing and the illustration? Which underlay techniques will you use? Which media will you use, for example gouache?

Evaluation of your illustration can be found by asking why your illustration is successful? What could you do to it to make it better? Does it work in its setting? What can you say about the quality of your work? Does your illustration fulfil your brief?

Any references should be acknowledged, for example:

i) Tsuruta, K. (photographer), (1987) 'Jukebox Calendar 1988', Berkeley, California, Zephyr Press, P.O. Box 3066, (415) 763-3627, Berkeley, CA 94703, USA.
ii) Hiller, B. (1983), *The Style of the Century 1900–1980*, The Herbert Press, London.

Background information about jukeboxes

The term 'juke' originates from the dialect of black people living in the south-eastern USA. It means wicked or disorderly, and was probably derived from an African word. A 'juke joint' is a venue with a jukebox.

Jukeboxes were first produced in the early 1930s in the USA. They are derived from a variety of automatic musical instruments, starting with musical boxes in the eighteenth century and continuing on to the more complex automata of the nineteenth century and the later 'nickelodeons' in America. Jukeboxes did not become popular in Britain until the 1940s.

> A report in *The Times* (4 January 1958), entitled 'Juke Box Boom', outlined the high profits (up to £12 per week from a £300 investment) to be made by speculators, and estimated that there were already 3,000 in Britain and that the total was increasing at the rate of 260 a month. (*The Style of the Century 1900-1980*, B. Hiller)

Jukeboxes are individual machines because of the number of selections made available to a customer. Up to 300 records can be played on some machines. They work as an automated record player, operated by inserting coins, and only play 78-rpm records with a steel stylus. There are two types of record-selecting mechanisms. The first type, made by Seeburg, and called 'Selectomatic', has records standing vertically in a row, and a selector travels up and down the row. This design was used a great deal for home record players. The other type of mechanism, used by Wurlitzer and others, contains records in a magazine which revolves around a selecting device.

Jukeboxes can offer several numbers of record plays. When a coin is put into the machine the mechanism senses, by the weight of the coin, the number of plays to select. This is known as a credit cycle. The selection mechanism requires detailed description, and is worthy of study. Research how these machines work and analyse their modern equivalents, from both a technical and commercial point of view.

> For collectors and cognoscenti, jukebox history is divided into three periods: the radio age, with machines in big wooden cabinets, the golden age from 1935 to 1948 and the silver age from 1950 to 1961. The £16,000 that Sotheby's got for Elton John's jukebox (a Wurlitzer 750 made in 1942) . . . may seem a lot of money, but very special collectors' items such as a rare and beautiful 950 can fetch in excess of £20,000. However, most restored 40s and 50s models are worth between £3,000 and £8,000. (Adrienne Connors, in the *Radio Times*, 11–17 March 1989)

The television programme *Arena* celebrated the fact that 'Jukeboxes are still thriving and jiving in loving homes across the land. For nothing comes between a true fan and his mighty music machine'. Many people explained their fascination with jukeboxes. Towards the end of the programme, Lesley, a true fan with a really good one, a good thumper, exclaimed, 'She's beautiful, isn't she', when talking about her machine. 'She's very round, she's very sensual, very, very sexy . . . I'm probably going to get laughed at for saying this, but there's something kind of fertility symbolish about her. The sort of nice big round part . . . she's very cuddly and sexy. She's not a particularly classy machine. You can find classier ones, but she is analogous with a woman: not particularly classy, but a great female.'

The interviewer then asked if some machines were 'boys'. 'Some are – Seeburgs are boys, I've never wanted to cuddle a Seeburg.'

The sensual and physical fulfilment obtained from owning a jukebox is rather touching. Why should people identify so strongly with a machine? Understanding this notion may be at the heart of successful product design?

Mechanical and electronic devices

Specification of design activity

Essentially this is a product design activity requiring you to design and make a prototype product that exploits some form of movement as an essential feature of its function. The activity is also an opportunity for you to form your own design specification for a chosen product and to evaluate the commercial value of your ideas. What information about mechanisms will you need to research and what role will modelling play in the development of your design?

Thus, you are invited to design, develop and market a novelty product that will serve as a prototype of a mechanical or electronic toy. Your study should include evidence of how initial investigations and research were used by you to justify your chosen market, target age group and design concept. A detailed design specification should be presented, which clearly highlights specific constraints, costs, materials and other relevant information. A full range of drawings and models is required to support a completed, operational prototype of your final design. Evidence of testing and promotion should form the main elements of an evaluation of your ideas, which may be complemented by packaging and advertising concepts.

How to Live No. 17: Spaghetti by Paul Spooner, part of the collection of contemporary automata at the Cabaret mechanical Theatre, Covent Garden, London.

Study the folders of work presented here as typical examples of this form of design study. Notice the value of research, especially the influence of existing examples in this field of design. It is very useful to study professional examples to gain an idea of the breadth, humour and simplicity of mechanical toys. The technical considerations concerning how various movements can be achieved are many and varied and it is left to you to combine whichever possibility suits your needs, based upon mechanisms, gears, levers, linkages, materials, electronic components and so on.

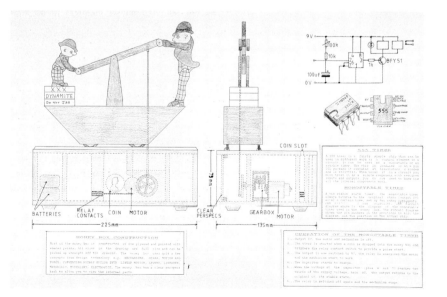

Student examples by Alan Card.

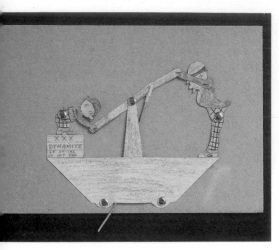

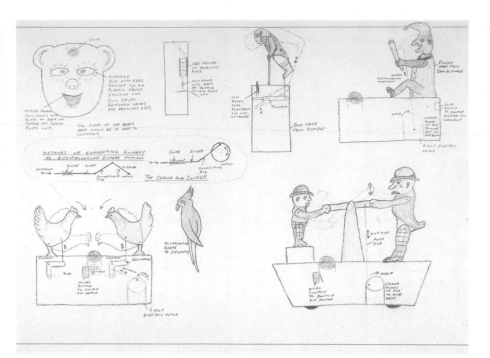

Student examples by Ken Herne.

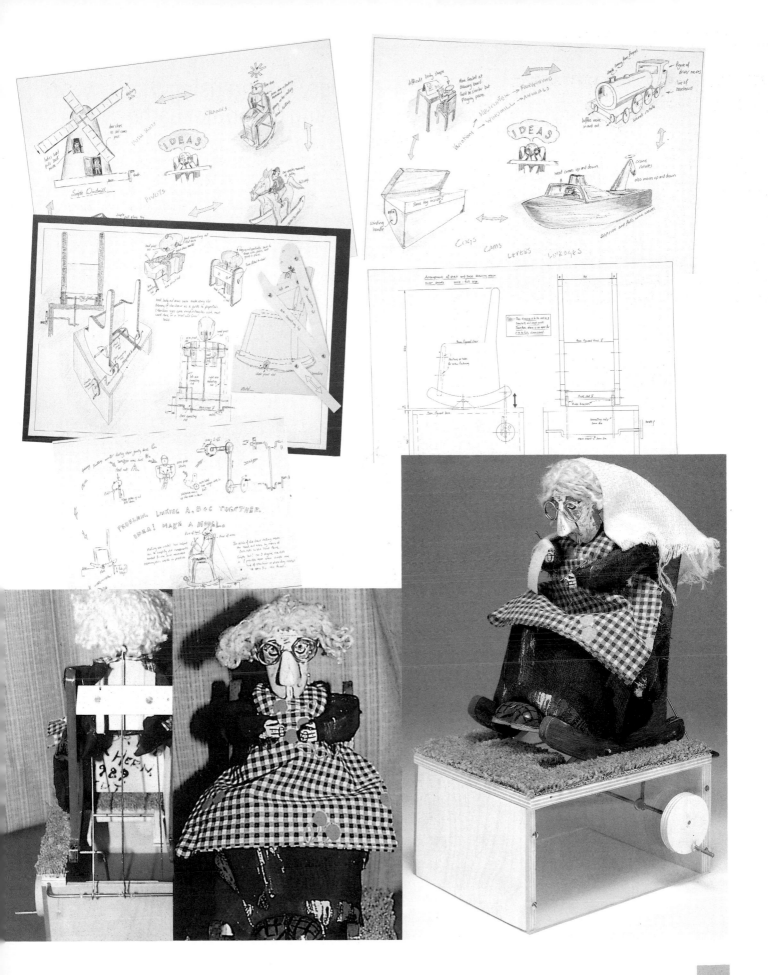

CAD/CAM jewellery design using the Boxford 125 Training Computer Lathe

Background information

The numerical control of machines was developed in response to the aerospace industry's need for machining techniques that could produce complicated components for planes and spacecraft more accurately, faster and cheaper than was possible using more traditional machining processes. Numerical control was developed as a way of automatically controlling machines by using numbers that are translated into electronic impulses. These impulses then control the operation of the machine, where the use of handwheels by the machine operator is replaced by very precise motors that perform the functions of the skilled operator. Before the introduction of computers as the means of programming these machines, punched cards, punched tape and magnetic tape were all used as the input media to convey this information from the drawing to the machine, instead of via a human operator.

At this point it is worth looking at some of the advantages and disadvantages of CNC (computer numerically controlled) machines.

Engineering components manufactured by CNC machines.

Advantages

CNC has been applied to a variety of machines and has gained wide acceptance by industry. Machine tools such as lathes, milling machines, turret drills, boring and grinding machines can benefit from its application for certain jobs.

- The reliability of the system generates higher machine productivity at lower cost with closer product tolerances.

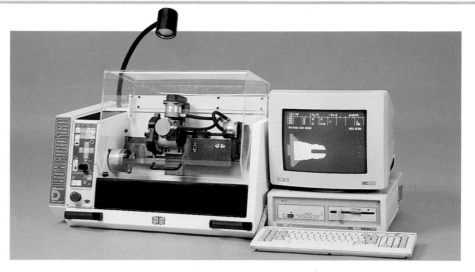

CNC machines in operation.

- Scrap loss is reduced due to the system eliminating the human error associated with manual operation.
- Once the program has been written and the machine set up there should be a 25–35 per cent increase in productivity over existing advanced machine processes.
- Special jigs, usually required for positioning, are not required as the machine can locate positions easily and accurately.
- The machine has greater flexibility, as one machine can often act as a drill, mill and turret lathe.
- The program can be quickly edited to enable components to be modified.
- Complex machining operations can be performed with ease and continued accuracy.
- Inspection costs are reduced due to the reliability of the system.
- Once the program has been test run successfully, the equipment does not require the use of a highly skilled operator, and one person may supervise several machines at the same time.

Disadvantages
- The initial cost of CNC machines is higher than that of conventional machines.
- Maintenance technicians trained in electronics are required to service the machines.
- Personnel must be trained in the programming and operation of the equipment.
- Small production runs of certain components may not prove to be economically viable.

This project is centred around the Boxford 125 TCL, and is intended to develop a design approach when using training computer lathes, employing CNC (computer numerically controlled) codes, featuring ISO format machine tool programming. A variety of CNC lathes are used in schools and colleges, and while the general principles of use remain very much the same, they all possess individual characteristics of operation.

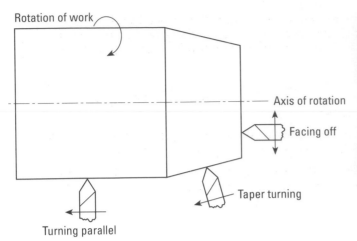

Rotation of work

Axis of rotation

Facing off

Taper turning

Turning parallel

Recommended speeds (rpm) for turning with tungsten carbide tooling

MATERIAL	< ø10	ø12 – ø14	ø16 – ø20	ø22 – ø25	ø26 – ø32	ø35 – ø40
MILD STEEL	3200	2800	2400	2000	1600 *	1200 *
BRASS	3200	3200	3200	3000	2800	2500
ALUMINIUM ALLOY	3200	3000	2800	2600	2400	2000
ENGINEERING PLASTICS	3200	3000	2600	2500	2000	1600 *

* = change of speed range

Maximum depth of cut – turning and boring

FREECUTTING MILD STEEL	2.0 mm on diameter
BRASS AND ALUMINIUM ALLOY	3.0 mm on diameter
ENGINEERING PLASTICS	4.0 mm on diameter

Recommended feeds (mm/min) for turning and boring using tungsten carbide tooling

	metals	plastics
ROUGH MACHINING – general removal of material	80	125
FINISH MACHING – final cuts	70	100
PARTING OFF (Speed 3200 rpm for ALL materials	70	100
BORING	60	90

Recommended speeds (rpm) for drilling with high speed tooling – all materials

CENTRE DRILLING		2800
DRILLING	up to ø5	2000
	up to ø8, after pilot drilling	1200 *
	up to ø10, after pilot drilling	800 *

* = change of speed range

Information to assist the selection of the correct speeds, feeds and depths of cut.

Recommended feeds (mm/min) for all drilling | 50 |

It is essential that students understand the principles of using a manually operated centre lathe before embarking on this project. In particular, students should be familiar with the following processes and operations:

- The selection of correct tools, speeds and feeds when carrying out the following operations: facing off, turning parallel, taper turning, parting-off and drilling.

- How the use of different materials, for example aluminium, brass, mild steel or engineering plastics, will influence this selection.

- Practice gained using the manually operated centre lathe will prove invaluable when it comes to plotting tool paths and cutting operations during programming.

Design brief

Design a piece of jewellery, for example a pendant, brooch, bracelet, necklace, etc., consisting of a minimum of six identical modular units. The modules will be manufactured on the Boxford 125 TCL and you will have to write and test run a part program for your chosen design. You may like to manufacture your modules in brass, which will then allow you to join them together with silver solder and to silverplate them if you wish.

You should tackle this project in four stages:

1. Generate design ideas and final drawing.

2. Write the program to machine the module.

3. Test run the program and edit if necessary.

4. Execute the program and machine the module.

Submission

The work you submit for this project should include the following:

- Initial design drawings illustrating a variety of ideas, and the development of your final design for the piece of jewellery.

- Your completed piece of jewellery.

- An evaluation report, which should also contain a program listing and a printout of your design module.

1. Generate design ideas and final drawing

Here you will find some examples of design proposals developed by students in response to this brief. Your design ideas will be restricted by the fact that the lathe can produce cylindrical, flat and conical surfaces quite easily, as well as holes drilled or bored down the centre of the piece. More complex curved surfaces can be machined by employing more advanced programming techniques. In addition, your module may be modified, if you wish, by using only a segment of the cylindrical cross-section in your final piece.

When you have decided upon your chosen design module, produce a side elevational drawing of the module at five times its full size on a piece of graph paper. The use of this type of paper is appropriate to this project as it allows you to plot the XZ datum point as well as the X and Z coordinates. It is the plotting of these coordinates that enables the cutting tool to take up a relevant position in relation to the material being machined. This concept will now be explained in more detail in the next stage.

Students' design sheets.

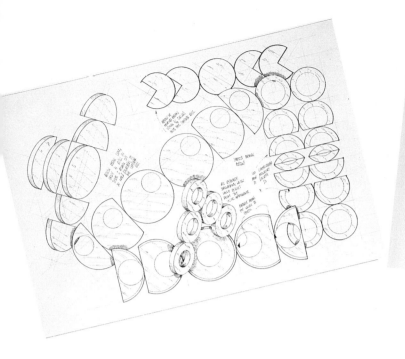

19

A copy of the program used to produce the module illustrated.

TITLE:- GIBSON			O.Dia 12		I.Dia 0		Length 20	
LINE	G	M	X	Z	I	K	F	S
N10	90							
N20	71							
N30			30	10	1	1		1R
N40		04	8	1				3200
N50	01		14	-2			80	
N60			14	-3				
N70	01		6	1			80	
N80			3	1				
N90	01		16	-4			80	
N100	01		0	1			60	
N110			30	10				
N120		05						
N130		06	30	10	7	8		1R
N140		06	30	10	5	6		1R
N150		03	0	4				2800
N160	01		0	-1			50	
N170			0	4				
N180		05	30	10				
N190		06			7	8		1R
N200			0	4				
N210		05						
N220		06	0	4	7	8		1R
N230		03						1200
N240	01		0	-6			50	
N250			0	10				
N260			30	10				
N270		05						
N280		06			11	7		1R
N290		04	16	-5				3200
N300	01		0	-5			70	
N310		05	30	10				
N320		30						

TOOLS USED

TOOL	Xoffset	Zoffset
1	0.00	0.00
7	0.00	20.00
5	0.00	20.00
11	-4.38	-1.96

2. Write the program to machine the module

Positioning of the tool for CNC machining

It is possible to define the location of a point in space with reference to another point by considering three mutually perpendicular axes, commonly called X, Y and Z. The Z axes represent the vertical movement of the cutting tool. When writing a program to manufacture a part (part program), there are two accepted methods of informing the machine as to the position of the tool. These are known as **absolute** programming and **incremental** programming. The difference between the two is that in **absolute** programming each machining location is given in relation to a zero datum or origin, whereas with incremental programming each positioning movement is programmed from the last position. When writing your program, one of the first pieces of information the computer needs to know is whether you are selecting absolute code G90, or incremental code G91 programming. For the purpose of this project absolute programming will be used throughout, along with metric units, code G71, as opposed to imperial units, code G70. Once again, this is an essential piece of early information.

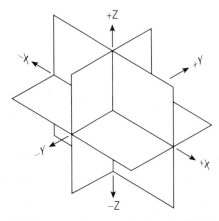

The three mutually perpendicular axes. The X and Y axes represent horizontal movement of the tool or table. The Z axis represents vertical movement of the tool.

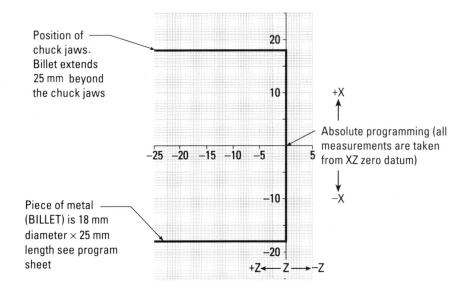

Position of chuck jaws. Billet extends 25 mm beyond the chuck jaws

Absolute programming (all measurements are taken from XZ zero datum)

Piece of metal (BILLET) is 18 mm diameter × 25 mm length see program sheet

To help you write your program; it is useful to draw on your graph paper the actual size of the piece of metal (billet) you are working on as well as the position of the chuck jaws and the XZ datum point. The latter is usually situated at the mid-point and end of the billet.

Onto this background, draw the module to the same scale as your graph paper.

Once you have done this you are ready to complete your program listings sheet line by line. On this sheet you will need to identify every single machine action and the code that denotes this, including selection of incremental or absolute programming, the use of metric or imperial measurements, starting the spindle in forward or reverse, stopping the spindle, instructions for cutting operations including speeds and feeds, rapid movement for positioning the tool (not cutting), ending the program and many more. It is essential that this information is fed into the program in the correct column and in the correct sequence. The sheet illustrated on p196 identifies the main programming codes and functions used on the Boxford 125 TCL. A more detailed analysis and tutorial package are available in the training manual and software package presented with the machine.

The following example traces the writing of a program to manufacture the module illustrated above.

PROGRAMMING SHEET									
DRG. NO.			TITLE		PROG. BY				
NOTES	SEQUENCE NUMBER N	PREP. FUNCTION G	MISC. FUNCTION M	CO-ORDINATES				FEED RATE F	SPINDLE SPEED S
				X	Z	I	K		
G90 Absolute Programming Selected	10	90							
G71 All measurements in metric units	20	71							
No. 1 tool is selected in column I and the number 1 in column K indicates that it is located in no. 1 position in the turret (if fitted). Then rapid movement G00, tool park position X=30 Z=10	30	00		30	10	1	1		
Rapid movement G00 to stand-off point 22, 0. Spindle turns on M04 and attains a speed of 3200 rpm.	40	00	04	22	0				3200
Facing cut at a feed of 60. Cut ends at 0, -1	50	01		-1	0			60	
Tool moves away from final cut ready to move to the next position	60	00		-1	+1				
	70								
	80								
	300								
Rapid movement of tool to tool park position 30, 10. Spindle turns off M05	310	00	05	30	10				
End of program, ready to repeat the process for multiple units -- M30.	320		30						

How to start and end the program. (NB: in the computer printout of the program G.00 codes and the first 1R codes do not appear. However, they must be written into the program.

N	G	M	X	Z	I	K	F	S
Line Number	Preparatory codes	Miscellaneous codes	Co-ordinate of cutting point from centre of lathe	Co-ordinate of cutting point from free end of billet	Additional information as needed	Additional information as needed	Feed rate (mm/min)	Spindle speed (rev/min)

Column N — Line Number:
N 10
N 20
N 30
N 40
N 50
N 60
etc.

Column G — Preparatory codes:
G00 Rapid movement (not cutting)
G01 Linear movement
G02 Clockwise circular interpolation
G03 C/clockwise circular interpolation
G81 0. Diameter turning cycle
G82 Facing or grooving cycle
G83 Peck drilling cycle
G84 Screw thread cutting cycle
G70 Imperial units
G71 Metric units
G90 Absolute programming
G91 Incremental programming
Note: G70, 71, 90, 91 are modal, and remain in operation until they are cancelled. The other codes only operate for one line of the program.

Column M — Miscellaneous codes:
M02 End of program
M03 Start spindle 'forward.' Drill only
M04 Start spindle 'reverse.' Turning and boring
M05 Stop spindle
M06 Tool change
M99 Continuation temporary end of program
M30 End of program if part is to be repeated

Column X — Co-ordinate of cutting point from centre of lathe:
Indicates the position of the cutting point of the tool measured diametrically from the centre line of the lathe

+ X value means the cutting tool is on the correct side of the lathe centre line

− X value means the cutting tool is positioned beyond the centre of the work

Column Z — Co-ordinate of cutting point from free end of billet:
Indicates the position of the cutting point relative to the free end of the billet

+ Z values means the cutting tool is moving away from the workpiece

− Z values means the cutting tool is moving towards the chuck jaws

Column I — Additional information as needed:
e.g.
(i) Number of cutting tool (N30) or when M06 is listed

(ii) Dimension of centre of arc relative to the start of the cut measured radially and incrementally along the X axis during G02 and G03. Circular interpolation

(iii) Indicates the number of cuts during G81. O.D. turning cycle

(iv) Indicates the number of cuts in G82. Facing and grooving cycle

(v) Indicates drill diameter in G83 peck drilling

(vi) Indicates the diametral depth of thread of thread in G84. Screw thread cutting cycle

Column K — Additional information as needed:
e.g.
(i) Dim of centre of arc relative to the start of cut measured incrementally along Z axis during G02, G03. Circular interpolation

(ii) Indicates the reduction of the drill feed during G83 peck drilling cycle

(iii) Indicates the number of cuts during G84 screw thread cutting cycle

Column F — Feed rate (mm/min):
(i) Indicates the feed rate or rate of travel of the tool as it cuts e.g. (Metals)
80 = rough machining
70 = parting
60 = finish (tipped tools)

(ii) Pitch of the screw thread in the G84 screw thread cutting cycle

Column S — Spindle speed (rev/min):
(i) Select the speed range on the line when a new cutting tool is chosen
1R = 320 − 3200
2R = 160 − 1600
3R = 80 − 800
4R = 40 − 400

Select the spindle speed on the line when the spindle

(ii) motor is started

e.g.
Brass
ø 10 − 14 = 3200
ø 22 − 25 = 3000

Aluminium alloy
ø 10 − 14 = 3000
ø 16 − 20 = 2800

Mild steel
ø 12 − 14 = 2800
ø 16 − 20 = 2400
(Tipped tooling)

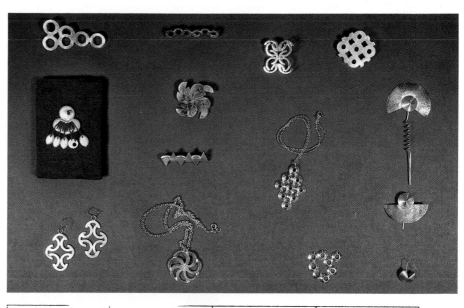

Completed examples of jewellery manufactured on the Boxford lathe and silver soldered together.

TOOL No.1	TOOL No.2	TOOL No.3	TOOL No.4
55 LH Copy	55 RH Copy	Neutral Copy	EXT.Thread
Tools 1/3 EN1A M04 BRASS/ALUM. PLASTIC	Speed(S)2000/3200.Feed(F)50/150mm/min MAX Depth of Cut 2mm on DIA. Speed(S)2500/3200.Feed(F)50/175mm/min MAX Depth of Cut 3mm on DIA. Speed(S)2800/3200.Feed(F)75/200mm/min MAX Depth of Cut 4mm on DIA.		G84 Canned Cycle Z- LH Z+ RH CHECK TOOL/TIP MIN No. Passes 10 M04 Speed Range R4 Speed(S) 300/400
TOOL No.5	TOOL No.6	TOOL No.7	TOOL No.8
Centre Drill	5mm Drill	7mm Drill	10mm Drill
ALL MATERIALS M03 Speed(S)2000rpm Feed(F)50mm/min USE THIS TOOL PRIOR TO DRILLING	G83 Canned Cycle (peck drilling) M03 Speed(S) 1750rpm Feed(F)50mm/min USE THIS TOOL PRIOR TO TOOL No.8		USE TOOL No.6 PRIOR TO THIS DRILL
TOOL No.9	TOOL No.10	TOOL No.11	TOOL No.12
Boring Bar (min.bore 14mm dia) SEE TOOLS 1/3 FOR CUTTING DATA	INT.Thread AS TOOL No.4	Parting Tool (from REAR) M04 QC/ROTARY ALL MATERIALS Speed(S) 2500/3000rpm	Parting Tool (from FRONT) M03 GANG TOOL ONLY Feed(F) 50/75mm/min

Details of Boxford tooling.

Imaginative work in two dimensions

Art and design education

'Would you tell me, please, which way I ought to walk from here?'
'That depends a good deal on where you want to get to,' said the cat.
'I don't much care where,' said Alice.
'Then it doesn't matter which way you go,' said the Cat.
(*Alice's Adventures in Wonderland*, Lewis Carroll)

Art and design activities involve creative thinking, but what part does design play in art? Art and design are concerned with observation, analysis and awareness of forms and structures in nature, as well as in human environments and artefacts. Your objectives for imaginative art and design work are to develop your own individual visual language and style, through the exploitation of the basic skills involving point, line, shape, tone, form, texture, colour, pattern, space and composition. A technical understanding of the nature of materials, processes and practical skills, as well as the exploration of values and judgements, based upon research and problem solving, are also

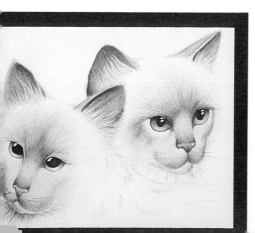

important facets of this study. Working a project, from conception to realisation and evaluation, including using graphic skills to convey freshly explored information, requires the essential processes and building blocks of much of art and design.

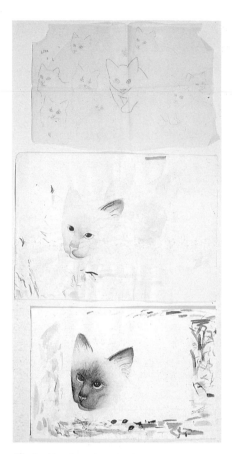

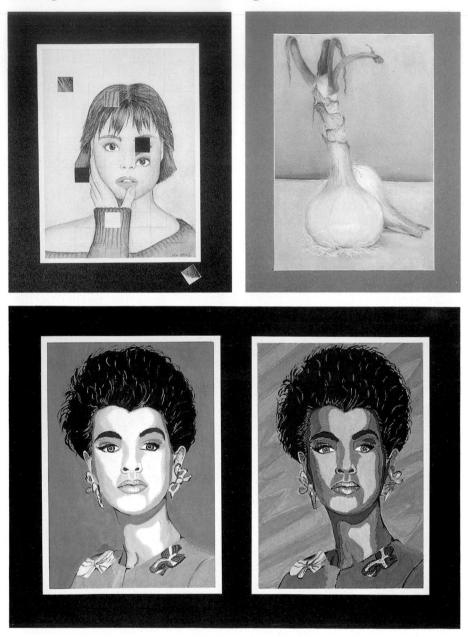

Cats by Lisa Amos.

Girl with Square Missing by Lisa Amos.

Onion by Kathryn Melia.

Twins by Joanna Hughes.

Life drawings by Kathryn Melia.

Ceramic Shoe and drawings by Rachael Brennan.

Through your studies you should become aware of the commonalty of creative experiences shared with many fields of knowledge. This may help to integrate different subject areas and processes in your work, especially those experiences concerned with design skills and thoughts.

You will most likely study projects formed upon design briefs that are devised to provide typical experiences in:

- Drawing and painting from direct observation and imagination, using natural and synthetic forms and the local environment.

- Image-making in two and three dimensions.

- Experience of graphic design problems.
- And possibly the development of some craft skills, for example, ceramics or printmaking.

Throughout your course you should aim to visit galleries, museums and particular design sources. It is vital that you keep records of such visits, as this aspect of art and design is an integral part of courses at this level. The processes of designing and forming and evolving ideas are essential. Use your sketchbook, so that you can present evidence of preparatory and exploratory work. Success can depend on this aspect of your work. You will also need to develop drawing and painting skills, as well as to know the formal requirements of your examination.

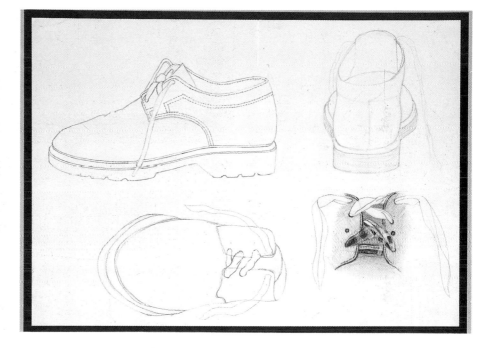

Examples of art and design studies

The examples given here have been taken from Oxford A-level 'Art with Art History – Imaginative Work in Two-dimensional Media' course. They are based on studies extracted from notes given to students involved in this course and are derived from selected themes. All of the following artwork is from students who studied art and design at St Joseph's Comprehensive School, Hebburn, Tyne and Wear.

Notes given to students in order to work on an imaginative composition based upon a set theme

You are required to develop a creative piece of work based on your interpretation of ONE of the starting points listed below. Research and preparatory work are vital to this project. All research, sketches and preparatory studies must be submitted with the final finished work for assessment.

You must note that photographs and other reproductions may be used for reference purposes only and must not be copied except in very special circumstances, for example when including a well-known person or building, which must be instantly recognisable as an essential part of your theme. When direct copying has been used it

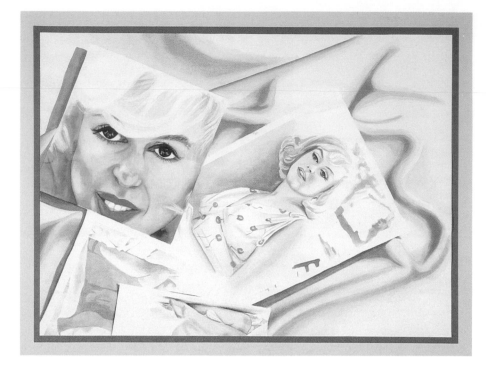

Marilyn Monroe by Mark Diamond.

must be acknowledged by a note on the back of your work, indicating the source.

No precise limitations are imposed on materials or the size of your work, but it is suggested that you work to approximately A2 size. You must read this brief carefully and work within its confines, which include the completion of the project within the set time.

Themes and examples worked by students

1. Use appropriate colours and forms to produce a creative piece of work which explores one of the themes of 'fastenings', 'graceful movements' and or 'worn by time'.

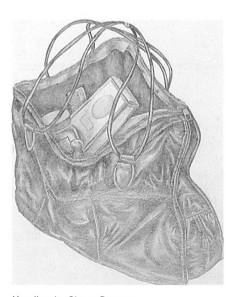

Handbag by Simon Bartrom.
Old Woman by Simon Bartrom.

Bathers and supporting notes by Lisa Amos.

Girl Sitting by a Stream by Kathryn Melia.

2. 'Bathers', 'People at work' and 'Athletes' have often been used as a subjects by artists. These themes offer the opportunity to combine dramatic form, light and shade and the subtle use of colour. Explore one of the themes and produce a creative piece of work supported by preparatory drawings and notes.

3. The disturbing effects of extreme emotions have often been a source of inspiration for artists throughout history. It offers opportunities for the the artist to integrate figures, still life objects, and the environment in a multitude of ways: from figurative to the abstract, from outdoors to intimate interiors. Produce a creative piece of work that is your own interpretation of the emotion of 'fear'!

Self portrait at a football match with the theme of violence by Simon Bartrom.

4. The artist as the subject of a picture – artists have often used themselves as the subject of their work. Their works show not only how they look, but also reveal something of their personality. Produce a self-portrait which is not only concerned with how you look but also tries to express something of your character and background. Include a description of your work with your painting.

Self portrait by Sean Conroy.

Self portrait by Andrew Helme.

Mother and child by Rachel Brennan.

Sean Conroy's self portrait:

For the composition the figure on the right of the self portrait is drawn from observation. The figures show the two biggest contrasts in my life – my school and my social life. The fox was drawn from direct observation of a stuffed model. This represents the devious side to my nature. For the background a drawing of the local coke ovens was made, . . . The train represents my youth while the party ticket indicates my present life style.

Andrew Helme's self portrait:

My composition shows my life style, background and interests. The self portrait was drawn from direct observation as were the artist's paints, palette and brushes. Several studies were made from direct observation of the Tyne bridge, a local landmark. The owl which was drawn from a stuffed model, indicates the wise and knowledgeable side of my character. The records show an interest in music and the NME is my favourite magazine. The McEwans lager beer mat indicates my social life.

5. Artists sometimes use man-made objects as the subject of their work. Such work can show not only the appearance of things, but also reveal their function. Explore the theme of 'synthetic' and produce a creative piece of work which expresses something of the character and function of your chosen object(s).

Rachael Brennan's mother and child picture:

'The Building Site' immediately conjured up in my mind children's building blocks. The setting I decided upon was a children's play area. The wooden blocks and toys were set up in a group on sand and painted from direct observation. Preparatory sketches were made of the fence. Sketches and photographs of relatives helped with the figure painting.

Fashion design

There are many courses in art and design for post-GCSE study from which students can choose. This section on fashion design study is based on work produced by BTEC National Diploma in Design first and second year students from South Tyneside College. The aim of presenting this work is to demonstrate student achievements on courses that operate in a similar way to A-level study.

BTEC courses are specialised and biased towards vocational education. Successful students, on completion of their National Diploma, can apply for places on Higher National Diploma or degree courses to further their specialisation, as can A-level students. Naturally, not all students want to progress to higher courses and many students seek employment directly after finishing their diploma courses.

First-year project: shop report

Brief

Choose a high street retail outlet on which to base your project research. You should find out as much as you can about the following areas: customer profile, typical fabrics, colours and details used, and company policy information. Produce a thorough story board of your findings, either like a collage or to suit your style of presentation for background research.

Design a range of garments suitable for your chosen shop. Your designs must conform to your chosen company's house style and format. Design within these company constraints, but feel free to explore new areas that the organisation could develop as a result of your research.

Produce a finished range plan which presents garment details, including front and back views, colour, fabric and print information. You are also required to promote your range of clothing with a general package that includes swing tickets, carrier bags, label ideas and point of sale information.

Presentation must be of the highest professional standard and it is vital that you demonstrate clear continuity between each piece of design work. Use computers where you can as well as all your graphic skills.

The two fully worked projects are by Chris Hogg who chose the Next project and Nicola J. Shears who worked on a Laura Ashley project. Both students studied at South Shields College. Their work contains sketchbook notes, ideas sheets, storyboards, promotional packages and finished design range plans.

The Laura Ashley Collection.

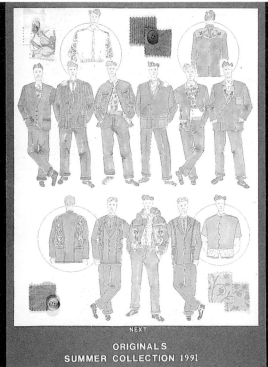

The Next Collection.

An example of an illustration project

Brief

You are commissioned by a well-known designer to illustrate a typical outfit that exemplifies his or her latest collection. The illustrations should be designed as a promotional package which can be sent to prospective buyers or retailers. Your artwork can be in the form of promotional posters, postcards or any suitable format for this task.

You must research the background of the designer's work in order to choose the most distinctive designs. Your work must be instantly recognisable as being in the manner of the designer's style.

You should also illustrate chosen garments in a suitable medium, paying particular attention to precise interpretations of the colours and fabrics used by the designer. All the graphic elements of your work should be to a professional standard of design and finish and it is becoming increasing valuable to design students to use computer graphics in work of this nature. Lettering styles should suit your package idea and image, and complement the total presentation of your folder. Preliminary studies and sketches should accompany your finished illustration.

Major project

Second-year fashion major project

This fashion design activity requires students to present well-researched designs, manufacture garments for a range of outfits and to promote, exhibit and show a specified collection. This project represents the culmination of students' fashion studies over their course. The following design brief represents a typical project and is supported by the fashion studies of two successful students, both of whom will pursue their studies at a higher level. The folders are presented so as to give an indication of the commitment and endeavour of fashion students.

Brief

Choose one of the titles given below or develop one of your own themes for a major collection. Your final collection should be thorough, informative and based upon your design of a range of fully co-ordinated outfits which demonstrate your use of colour, fabric and garment manufacture.

Minimalism and purity in the 1990s
History in the making
1992 – European influence on British fashion
Your own theme.

It is vital that your work is supported by original and creative design ideas that are derived from your research. You are required to design a range of garments by producing a series of working drawings that show their design, manufacture and presentation, including

information about how they will be worn, various fastenings and the overall function of the clothing. Details of fabric, colour, different views of the outfits and any other relevant details should also be clearly developed and presented.

Sketches should be quick, exciting and packed full of information and backed up by clear notes and technical detail. Choose ten outfits from these sketches which can be drawn up on a chosen presentation format, for example A4 or A3 sheets. Each of these sheets should develop the details of one outfit. From these design sheets, your final collection of garments will be selected and they should be made up in good time for an exhibition and fashion show.

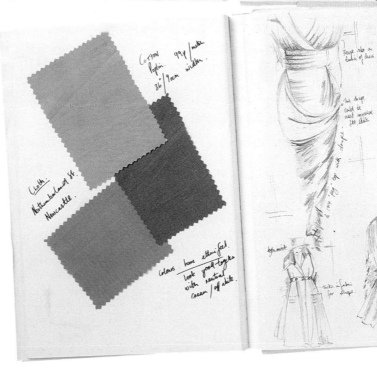

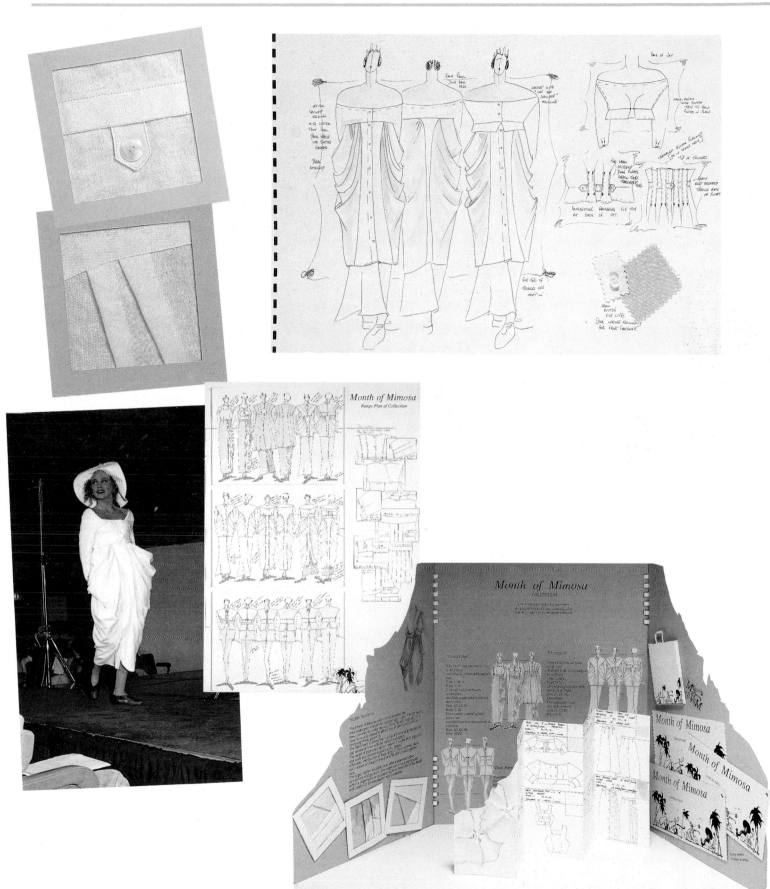

The timing of the different aspects of this work is usually indicated to students in advance and according to course requirements. Organisation of time is a very important factor in the success of such a project, especially as it is common practice to show only completed work at fashion shows.

The promotion of a collection should be based upon an appropriate name, a logo, swing tickets, market research, alternative fabrics and colour stories. A presentation package should be aimed at prospective buyers and a fashion show may finalise a student's work, especially as it is a vital aspect of a major fashion project and is the culmination of such a course.

A major project should include:

1. Research sketchbook.

2. Storyboard showing projected ideas.

3. Minimum of 40 outfit designs.

4. Ten design sheets of final outfits.

5. Minimum of three outfits (nine garments).

6. Patterns clearly marked with meterage, width and swatches.

7. Finished range illustration on an A2 format.

8. Promotional package.

9. Print ideas sheet, only if fabric printing.

These projects are more detailed than A-level projects, especially as students have more time to work on them. A-level students can produce fashion design projects that require all or only part of the activities outlined in the above project.

The major project collections are supplied by two BTEC National Diploma in Fashion Design students from South Tyneside College.

Gillian Branch's 'La Commedia' Collection: Gillian has successfully completed her second-year fashion design option. She will progress to a BTEC Higher National Diploma in Fashion Design at York College of Arts and Technology.

Susan Duguid's 'Month of Mimosa' Collection: Susan has also been very successful and will continue her design work at Newcastle Polytechnic where she will study for a B.A. (Hons) Fashion Design degree.

Both students' work contains examples of sketchbook notes, ideas sheets, storyboards, promotional packages, finished design range plans, working drawings, swatches and details and finished garments on a catwalk as used for a fashion show.

Background studies during the course included figure drawing, computer graphics and presentation designs for competitions.

Susan Duguid's swimwear prediction design project and her student design awards competition ideas for the Smirnoff competition 1990.

SMIRNOFF '90

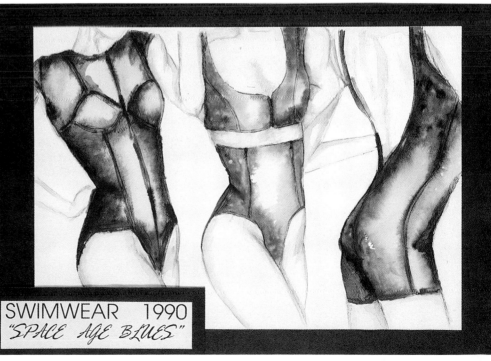

SWIMWEAR 1990
"SPACE AGE BLUES"

A-level fashion

Typical A-level fashion studies in art and design courses might, through certain two-dimensional projects, work on the following brief.

- Imagine you are a fashion illustrator working for 'Design International' in London. A national children's clothing company has commissioned you to predict a 'look' for the following spring or summer and requires you to design a fashion statement suitable for children aged two to five years and for a chosen season. Your designs will be printed as a double page layout in a forthcoming issue of 'The Clothes Show' magazine.

- Using one of the following themes as a research idea for inspiration, design three outfits for a specified market:
  a) The seaside.
  b) American football.
  c) A painter.
  d) Jungle animals.

- You must give careful consideration to the following practical issues:
  a) The clothes must be washable.
  b) Children tend to like bright colours.
  c) Garments should not restrict movement or endanger children, for example by using ties around the neck or by incorporating long wide sleeves or loose turn-ups on trousers.

- Creating a 'look' is your task. In order to achieve this you should aim to produce your own distinct original style and keep in mind:
  a) For whom you are designing.
  b) Which season the clothes might be worn in.
  c) On what occasions the clothes will be worn, including the time of day.
  d) Who your client is.
  e) The constraints of your brief.
  f) The themes or ideas that act as a stimulus to your work.

- Research is vital to this project, especially as this design activity should reflect a chosen 'mood' to suit the theme of your clothes. A storyboard that explores the mood of this design is also required.

- Study the work of other fashion designers and present some evidence of this in your folder by acknowledging their work in an appropriate way.

- All preparatory studies should be developed in your sketchbook or as part of your folder. Show clearly how your ideas progress and change as your research and thinking unfolds.

- Produce your finished designs on a bold format that is not smaller than A2. Use all your graphic skills of lettering and layout to create a visually exciting set of illustrations. Title your work and include a brief description of your overall presentation.

Technical illustration

General technical illustration

Good drawing comes from boldness and confidence; it is not born of hesitancy, nor is it a slapdash, inconsequential activity. Drawing can enable us to learn about things; we can also understand our design ideas by exploring their form, function and value through drawing. Be prepared to draw anything, anywhere, at any time because knowledge of drawing is crucial in design. A well-expressed sketch can often convey much more meaning than a great deal of verbal or written information. Drawing is a key to success in design, and drawing and observation are the essential skills for technical illustration and design in general.

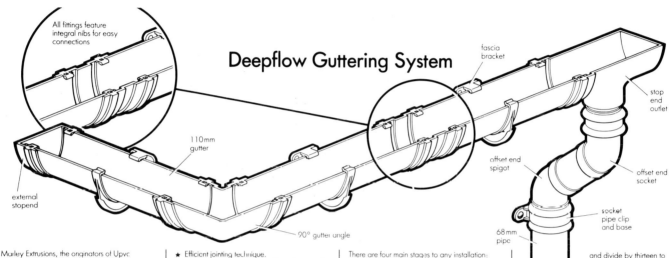

Deepflow Guttering System

All fittings feature integral nibs for easy connections

110mm gutter

external stopend

90° gutter angle

fascia bracket

stop end outlet

offset end spigot

offset end socket

socket pipe clip and base

68mm pipe

Marley Extrusions, the originators of Upvc guttering, have selected a range of guttering components especially for you, the D.I.Y. enthusiast, to fit yourself, quickly and easily.

MARLEY DEEPFLOW – HIGH CAPACITY GUTTER

The most important consideration when selecting guttering is to make sure it has the capacity to drain your roof efficiently.

Marley Deepflow Gutter, with its 110×75mm semi-elliptical profile, combines large capacity, excellent self-cleansing properties and aesthetically pleasing design. Used in conjunction with 68mm downpipes it will easily drain the rainwater from virtually any roof.

For smaller homes 100mm Half Round Gutter is usually adequate, or for sheds or greenhouses 75mm Miniline is ideal. Information on these gutter systems is available separately.

CONSIDER THE ADVANTAGES OF UPVC

All Marley Gutter feature the following:
* Never need painting.
* Easy maintenance – just the occasional wipe down.
* Its tough, light and strong.

* Efficient jointing technique.
* It all adds up to a true fit and forget system, that will protect your home for years to come.

The comprehensive range of fittings available allows you to overcome virtually any installation problem. From the typical gutter arrangement illustrated here you can see how and where some of the many components fit.

TOOLS FOR THE JOB

Normal fitting can be done with the most basic D.I.Y. tool kit.
The tools required are:-
1. Fine toothed saw
2. String line and plumb bob
3. Bradawl
4. Drill and bits
5. Medium flat file
6. Screwdriver
7. Spirit level
8. Tape Measure
9. Ladder

You may also need a spanner if you are dismantling old cast iron gutter. If so, be very careful as the cast iron is extremely heavy.

FITTING COULDN'T BE EASIER

An average sized house should take you no more than a weekend to fit the new guttering in place, a garden shed usually no more than a couple of hours.

There are four main stages to any installation:
1. Remove the old guttering and refurbish the fascia.
2. Fix the gutter brackets to the fascia with a slight fall towards the outlet.
3. Fit the gutter into the brackets, connect the gutter and unions together and install the outlet, stopend and any other fittings.
4. Fit the downpipes, securing and supporting each one with pipe clips fixed to the wall. Finish off with a 'shoe' or by connecting up to the original drainage.

Gutter joints cannot be pulled apart, they will also absorb contraction and expansion due to changes in temperature.

HOW MUCH GUTTER AND DOWNPIPE

Before going to your stockist estimate how much gutter you need by measuring the length of the wall at ground level under the eaves to be drained. Don't forget to add on any extra amount of gutter needed if the roof projects beyond the brickwork.

To estimate the amount of downpipe needed count the number of bricks from ground level to eaves and divide by thirteen to give the approximate height in metres.

WHAT YOU NEED . . .

Using the component chart overleaf select the items you need for your installation. Remember that fascia brackets must not be more than 1 metre apart. All angles and outlets need close supporting brackets not more than 150mm away on both sides, and unions need one bracket within 150mm.

If you're using the 2m downpipes you need one socket pipe clip and base to support each pipe. If you're using the 3m pipe an intermediate pipe clip needs to be fitted mid-way along each pipe.

Other fittings, bends, shoes or branches also need a socket pipe clip and base for support. If you need to make up an offset yourself to carry the rainwater from the gutter outlet to the downpipe don't forget you need a tube of solvent cement.

If you need any further advice or assistance please contact Marley Extrusions Marketing Department on the address shown overleaf.

Technical illustration is the use of pictures that clearly transmit and translate information in chosen contexts. Successful technical illustration requires design expertise. It has arisen from a multitude of communication needs throughout society; its main development is in industry. Technical illustration has developed because of the general advances and changes in technology, especially in engineering and mass production. It is used to promote the style, appearance and material form of many types of design, especially manufactured goods. Its function is to inform the public, or a specified technical audience,

Is a photograph of a Spitfire bullet sufficient information for an illustration of it?

visually about how various artefacts or systems are assembled, maintained and used.

Technical illustrations are very often used to promote and popularise new ideas and modified schemes. Examples may be concerned with major-achievements of public interest or matters that are considered to require wider understanding or appreciation. They are predominantly images that are formed after things have been made. Thus, the art of technical illustration is to make clear, through visual messages, certain items of information.

Such illustrations should be easily understood at a glance. Clarity of technical communication is derived from the practical needs of industry to involve workforces efficiently in their understanding of mass-production and manufacturing techniques. This need for effective communication to a wide audience came out of the urgent demands of manufacturing during the Second World War. The impetus of war stimulates many developments. What would you need to research to illustrate a bullet used by a Spitfire aircraft of the Second World War?

Many manufacturing, training and service industries require unskilled people to perform certain complex tasks. Such work can be achieved with the aid of three-dimensional representations in product development, assembly and the marketing of manufactured goods. There are many occasions when non-expert people are required to undertake quite complex and technical tasks without a full understanding of the process. For example, a non-technical workforce might be required to follow instructions to assemble multi-component objects, as well as to test or maintain them, without technical knowledge of the objects' function or use.

Instructional illustrations can be found in many forms, for example in repair manuals, museum exhibitions and technical presentations. Technical drawings and illustrations are also used for design and production control.

Study professional examples of technical illustration as much as possible. How important is consistency in the examples given? What is the value of a house-style of presentation? Use some Lego to make a machine and illustrate your device.

The combination of bold drawing and effective rendering techniques, for example painting or airbrushing, to give a finish to the image, is the essence of illustration. Often illustrations are clearer than photographs because, through the careful exploitation of line and tone, a great deal of structural information can be communicated. Photographs are still used a great deal in illustration work, but need to be of a high standard to be clear and successful.

The aim of an illustrator is to record objects and events accurately because the main intention is to see things exactly as they are. This is called the direct representational response to things through drawing in the formation of a 'likeness'. Sometimes you need to know what to look for and at other times you may be surprised by what you find.

A pattern drawing for a dress compared to a photograph from Simplicity pattern of the 1970s.

The following information was given by Simplicity in the 1950s to help people recognise what to look for when buying a dress. How does it relate to this photograph? Make a technical drawing for an example of 1990s woman's fashion. Does the information from Simplicity still apply?

Durable trimming which is easily cared for; neckline neatly finished; smooth shoulders; well-finished sleeves; well fitted; well-made jacket; fasteners sewed on securely; well-made belt; well-made seams with a good seam allowance; cut on the straight of the material; machine stitching is fine, strong and done with the correct shade of thread; fabric will not pull at seams; seams finished so as to prevent ravelling; even hemline; hem wide enough that the dress may be lengthened if necessary.

How many times have you experienced the strange feeling that you have never noticed something before although it has always been in common view?

Drawing can help you to explore the nature of things. Drawing can capture, in a still moment, a particular viewpoint or gesture that expresses the very nature of the subject matter. A photograph can also do this. But can something that intends to be very precise, as in the case of a technical illustration, ever catch the essence of something? Do not the precise measurement and accurate recording detract from the actual essence of the thing?

In a drawing, lines and tones refer to something in the real world or in our imaginations; the pencil lines are an analogy for something in the real world or in our mind's eye. Technical illustrations are two-dimensional designs that allow us to see things as they are.

Cartoon by Mordillo.

Not all drawings are representational. In design work we still need to explore imaginative drawing. Being imaginative means that we show and use our mental faculties to form images of things that are not present to our senses. We can thus produce ideas and images without direct observation of objects or actions. Technical illustration is a particular form of imaginative drawing; it requires us to be imaginative about our interpretations of reality. It also requires us to develop design ideas and to be creative in our use of tools, media and drawing techniques.

An illustration can be formed from records sketched on location, whereby sketches are made of the objects, actions or ideas where they operate and occur. The detailed development of a complex drawing should then be pursued in a studio setting. The production and use of orthographic drawings, in either first or third angle projection, may figure in the overall production of a technical illustration.

Sketching things as they occur requires skilful observation, based on adequate measurements and the recording of all essential details. The work in a studio can be supported by camera work, especially work that requires exploded views of the subject. Slides, prints and a light box will also be very useful.

Orthographic drawing is a skill in its own right. This applies as much to drawing in orthographic projection as it does to reading such drawings and taking action from them. A designer should be able to work from orthographic drawings and produce three-dimensional drawings from them, and vice versa. Being able to visualise the subject as a three-dimensional object is very important.

Look at the Stenhaus cube. Your task is to use drawing to communicate information about a puzzle with the objective of presenting a drawn representation of your solution to the puzzle. This activity will require you to make the pieces of the puzzle, solve it and to design an illustration of your puzzle's solution. This design study involves reading drawings, making something and designing an illustration for a chosen context. (*Mathematical Models*, H. M. Cundy and A. P. Rollett)

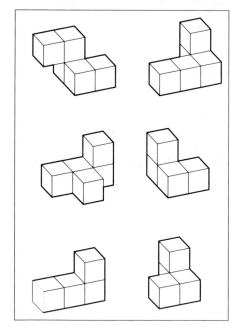

Stenhaus cube.

This puzzle is not easy. The six pieces are made up of three 5-unit cubes, and three 4-unit cubes. There are only two ways of fitting the pieces together to form a cube. There are three pieces that form a stepped pyramid and these same pieces can be put together in only two ways, hence the two possible ways of putting all the pieces together. However, the completion of the cube is unique.

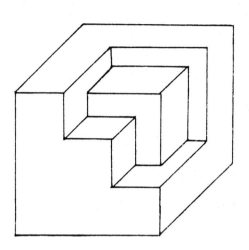

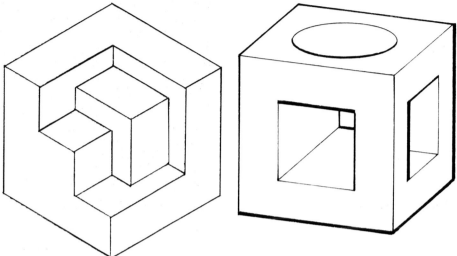

Line shadowing techniques using three thicknesses of line.

Study and use the techniques shown here in your illustration work.

How many ways can you see these drawings? Use rendering techniques for shadowing and colour work to interpret the different possible images that you can see. You should be able to see more than three different possibilities. Why is this?

Make a study of the history of technical illustration. When do you think it began as a recognised aspect of design? Who uses it and why? There is an infinite variety of purposes for drawings. In an article concerning 'Engineering Drawing: Origins and Developments' the following categories were offered concerning the use of drawings:

Designers' drawings
Project drawings
Production drawings
Presentation and maintenance drawings
Technical illustrations.

How has design drawing been developed in education over the years? What do we do, as a society, to educate our designers? What has been the influence of world wars in these regards? The education of designers and engineers, as well as specialist illustrators, especially in relation to the development of computers, is of some significance today. However, there is some concern that our graphic heritage needs wider recognition.

The drawing-step method
A guide to dimetric drawing

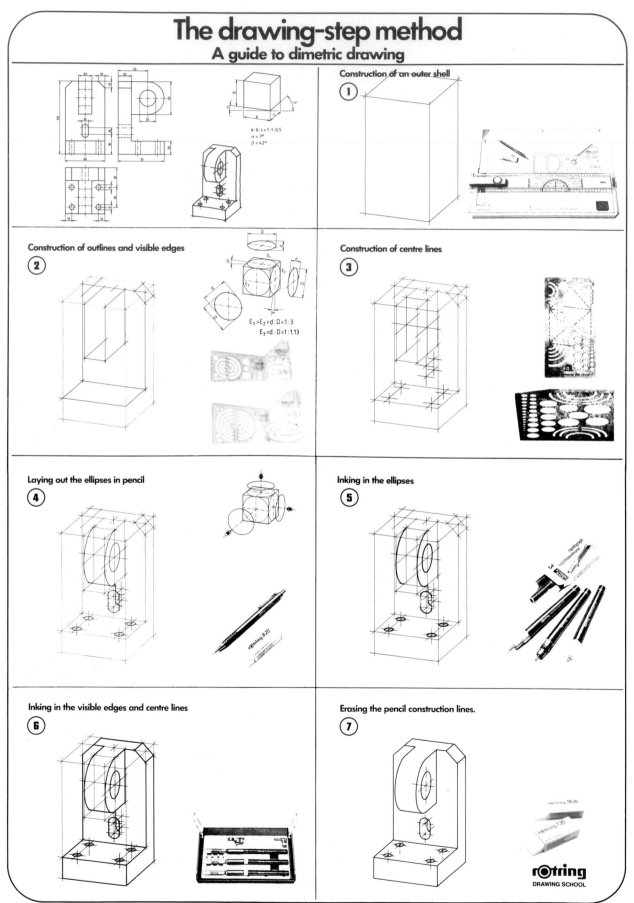

$a : b : c = 1:1:0,5$
$\alpha = 7°$
$\beta = 42°$

Construction of an outer shell
1

Construction of outlines and visible edges
2

$E_1 = E_2 = d : D = 1:3$
$E_3 = d : D = 1:1.13$

Construction of centre lines
3

Laying out the ellipses in pencil
4

Inking in the ellipses
5

Inking in the visible edges and centre lines
6

Erasing the pencil construction lines.
7

rOtring
DRAWING SCHOOL

rotring-werke Riepe KG · B.O.Box 54 10 60 · D-2000 Hamburg 54

97 339 120 Printed in W. Germany 6/85

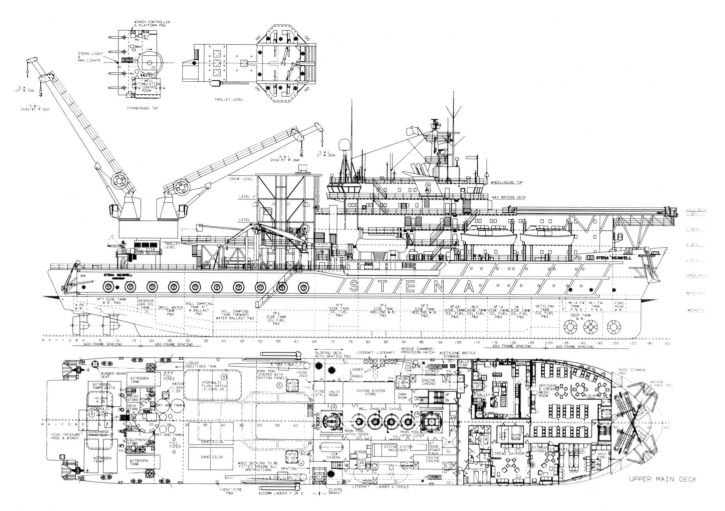

General arrangement drawing: Stena Seawell
Sunderland Shipbuilders Ltd.

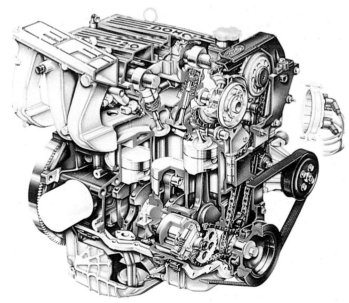

Ford engine showing all the techniques,
including line work, airbrushing and painting
and context. 'The new Ford DOHC engine has
been specifically designed to meet the
low-emission requirements of the 1990s'.

. . . drawing – by man or machine – is still central to our ability to design, to
foresee how things might perform, to imagine how they might appear, to
control their production and to look after them when they have been made.
(*The Art of the Engineer*, Welsh Arts Council)

Technical illustrations are usually not complete without certain graphic design elements within an overall presentation. Graphic design is an important ally, as it is essentially the production of designs through combinations of lettering and pictures.

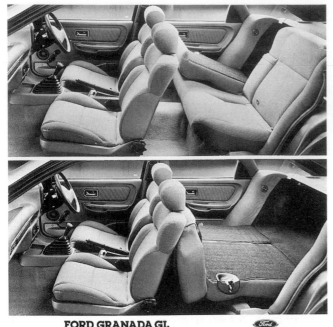

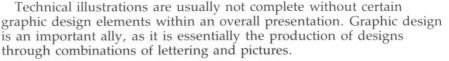

FORD GRANADA GL
Not for publication before March 19, 1985

Ford Granada interiors, sketches and photographs.

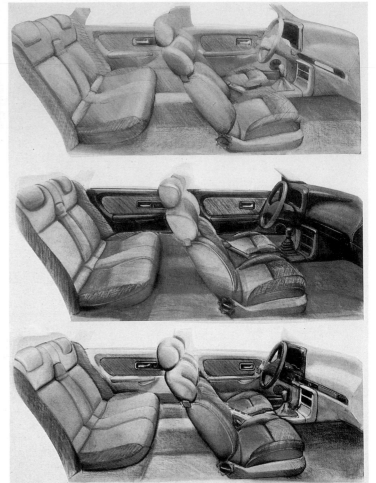

Illustrations can be exterior views of objects or buildings. They are designed to show the appearance of things by exploiting line and tone and using certain media to render surface textures and so on. Cutaways, overlaps, sectioning and ghosting are illustration techniques, often rendered in technical pen, that are devised to reveal internal views of things; these drawings also relate the inside to the outside, and show the relationship of parts in assembly, as well as how things work.

How is a technical illustration commissioned? There are many difficulties associated with coping with deadlines and learning how to work in a team, especially in situations removed from real design needs. It is not always possible to offer realistic working situations in this form of study but it is important that you aim to understand some of the problems of deadlines, teamwork and establishing costings, which are the most problematic issues that face designers, aside from their creative endeavours.

Determine for yourself the essential techniques for drawing small and large objects. Know when to use freehand drawing or mechanical drawing; seek out the basic techniques of perspective, ellipse drawing and orthographic projection. Recognise your opportunities to draw:

● things that exist;

● things that can be modified;

● ideas within your own imagination.

What things look like, how they work, what they do, how they can be used in different ways, by whom, and so on, are the essential items of information that require to be visualised in a technical illustration.

Use the information about an Alfa Romeo car to produce your own full colour illustration of this vehicle. The objective of this exercise is for you to employ an appropriate style of drawing. Mechanical drawing may be useful in this case. Use all your graphic and presentational skills for this study.

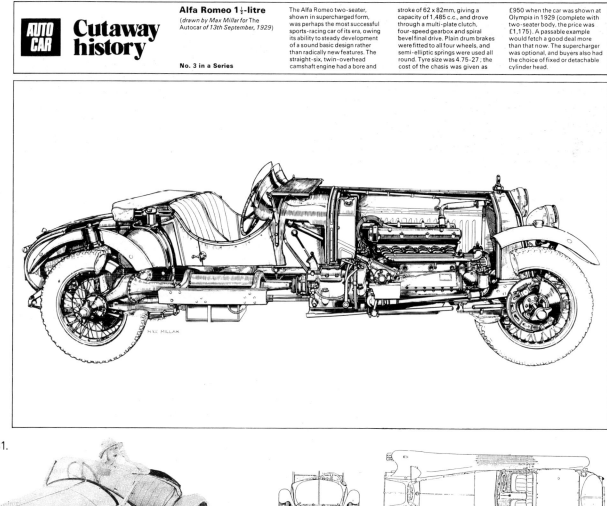

AUTO CAR **Cutaway history**

Alfa Romeo 1½-litre
(*drawn by Max Millar for* The Autocar *of 13th September, 1929*)

No. 3 in a Series

The Alfa Romeo two-seater, shown in supercharged form, was perhaps the most successful sports-racing car of its era, owing its ability to steady development of a sound basic design rather than radically new features. The straight-six, twin-overhead camshaft engine had a bore and stroke of 62 x 82mm, giving a capacity of 1,485 c.c., and drove through a multi-plate clutch, four-speed gearbox and spiral bevel final drive. Plain drum brakes were fitted to all four wheels, and semi-elliptic springs were used all round. Tyre size was 4.75-27; the cost of the chasis was given as £950 when the car was shown at Olympia in 1929 (complete with two-seater body, the price was £1,175). A passable example would fetch a good deal more than that now. The supercharger was optional, and buyers also had the choice of fixed or detachable cylinder head.

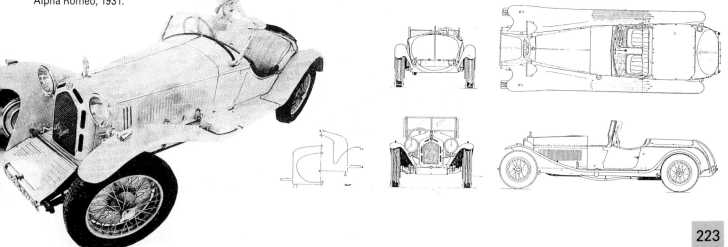

Alpha Romeo, 1931.

Imagination and illusion

A great artist invents a type and life tries to copy it . . . the proper school to learn art in is not life but art. (Oscar Wilde)

Are the graphic arts, drawing and illustrating simply concerned with ways of imitating solid objects upon flat surfaces by means of different media? Is this all that can be said about graphic arts? Such work, whether executed for its own sake or a commercial purpose, does, in fact, command our attention beyond our technical appreciation of the marks that are made to form an image. We do comprehend visual messages in pictorial images, whether or not a picture is intended to be purposeful, commercially or aesthetically.

Is technical illustration mere imitation of things that have been made and used; is it simply copies of nature and manufactured things or is it something else? Our understanding of the value of the graphic arts can most fruitfully begin with a study of our own reactions and feelings towards images and pictures. This can be of value for our study of design in imaginative artwork as much as in technical illustration. It will always be useful to know something about the many purposes to which we put artwork.

Recall certain television news images, for example of the Ethiopian famines during the 1980s. These images aroused emotions and fuelled tremendous endeavour to overcome the problems. However, do we

BE A FAMINE SUPERSTAR

Taking part in the 24 Hour Famine could get you in the papers, on the radio or even on the box.

What you have to do is think of an original and unusual way of spending the famine day or a novel way of recruiting sponsors - and let us know about it.

If it's a really good idea, we'll contact the media and who knows? You could be a superstar.

We'll also send a record token and a 24 Hour Famine T-Shirt to those who come up with the best ideas.

So don't forget. TELL US WHAT YOU'RE DOING.

Contact:
Claire Salter
24 Hour Famine Office
World Vision
Dychurch House
8 Abington Street
Northampton NN1 2AJ
Or phone us on 0604 231199

MAKE A DAY OF IT
Going without food for a day is not as easy as it sounds. Keep yourself occupied to take your mind off the meals you're missing. If you think about food it'll only make the temptation to eat greater. So get out the Scrabble or take the dog for a walk. Do anything but - just for a day - DON'T EAT.

What Jonathan Did

Jonathan Bownan from Hampshire, who's 11 and his brother Alexander, cousin Rebecca and two other friends walked for six miles as part of their effort to raise funds for the '24 Hour Famine'.

It was no ordinary walk. They decided to copy the African water carriers - except it wasn't water they carried on their heads but lemonade.

Their novel effort raised nearly £200.

In Uganda, the Homepak Programme helps provide shelter for many families

WORD SEARCH

Find the 12 hidden words listed below. They can run horizontally, vertically and diagonally, forward or backwards.

1. FAMINE
2. THIRD WORLD
3. BANGLADESH
4. ETHIOPIA
5. LIFESAVER
6. UGANDA
7. GHANA
8. HUNGER
9. SUDAN
10. SPONSORS
11. FOOD

FORM A GROUP

It is much more fun to do the 'Famine' with a group of friends than to do it on your own. Every extra person who joins in means more lives can be saved.

If you belong to a youth group, tell your Leader about it - perhaps the whole group could become involved.

Form a group in the street where you live - get all your neighbours to join you. Ask your teacher to register the school and form lots of groups within the school. You could do all sorts of activities to keep yourselves going and support each other and keep yourselves occupied.

fully grasp the significance and reality of these edited images. The danger is that we might become too abstracted from the scene, despite the power of our imaginations to reveal for us the true desperation of other people's plights through such images.

We have our actual life and our imaginative life, according to Fry, writing an essay on aesthetics in *Modern Art and Modernism*. In our actual life our instincts protect us and our conscious senses are constantly alert for action or danger. However, in the imaginative life no such action is necessary; we are free to place ourselves in danger without being hurt.

In the imaginative life, our 'whole consciousness may be focused upon the perceptive and the emotional aspects of the experience. In this way we get . . . a different set of values, and a different kind of perception.' Thus, we may see the famine in the film, but how can our feelings for this tragedy be brought out in a work of art?

A still photograph captures a precise moment in time, but a drawing can, through imagination, reveal the essence of things or actions. Using still photography, research and illustrate a precise moment in a particular sporting or entertainment event. Aim to capture the awkwardness of the action, including any tensions or contentiousness. This project could be used as a half-tone image for an article publicising a forthcoming television programme in a well-known television programme guide. Lay out your artwork in relation to a suitable typeface and in the style of your chosen magazine. Make your drawing work in a full page and possibly alongside a photograph of another aspect of the action you are illustrating. Also consider the technical qualities of your work in relation to it being printed.

Illusion

We may, then, dispense once and for all with the idea of likeness to Nature, of correctness or incorrectness as a test, and to consider only whether the emotional elements inherent in natural form are adequately discovered, unless, indeed, the emotional idea depends at any point upon likeness, or completeness of representation. (Roger Fry)

Draw what you see in your mind's eye, based upon your experience of nature and the things around you. Art is the 'expression and stimulus of [this] imaginative life, which is separated from actual life by the absence of responsive action'.

Henri Matisse was once asked whether a tomato looked the same to him when he ate it as when he painted it. 'Of course not,' he barked, 'When I eat it, I see it just the same as everyone else'. We learn to see in different ways, directly and through imagery.

Still Life with Oranges by Henri Matisse, © Succession H Matisse/DACS 1994.

Produce a colour illustration of tomatoes growing under cultivation. Remember that colour has a material quality, given to it by the particular medium used. You might use pastels, oil pastels, crayons, coloured pencils, markers or felt-tip pens, drawing inks or paint. Consider which medium can best help you to describe tomatoes. Start by sketching from memory, to see what you really know about a very common object, then work from observation.

Thus, seeing, coupled with the knowledge that we should be attentive to what can be drawn, is vital to any progress in design. Paint and draw what you see, but also look at what you draw and paint as well.

This study is concerned with how an artist converts solid things into two-dimensional images. Naturally, selection of what is seen is crucial to design and composition, as well as to the message of an image. '. . . you can't just see things, you need to reason out your perception of the world; drawing is not just a problem of seeing, but of representation'. (E. H. Gombrich)

These concerns tend to be the preoccupations of artists and designers involved in illusionistic painting and drawing, in their development of an 'eye witness' approach to painting and drawing. The complex skills of perception are utilised to the full when converting what is seen into still pictures. How can what is seen be interpreted in another form, for example as a drawing? How will the view in front of you project onto canvas? How is it that anything can represent something else? Recall the notion of our direct representational reaction to drawings. Did you see Magritte's pipe or his painting of a pipe, in *Ceci n'est pas une pipe*? Make a mark on a sheet of paper and assign a meaning to it.

The psychological notion of constancy in seeing is also an important issue when learning to draw or paint. It has been found that we tend to see things for what they are all the time. Find 1p and 10p coins and state which is the bigger. Then place the 1p in front of the 10p coin and move the coins so that the 1p coin covers the 10p coin. You should reason that the effects of perspective will come into play and that the further away from you things are the smaller they appear. Therefore you should be able to reason that it is possible for the 1p coin to be the same size as the 10p coin in this experiment. But what happens when you move the 10p coin to one side after covering it with the 1p coin? Does it appear the same size as the 1p coin? Try this activity with one eye open, as well as with both eyes open. What do you see?

Because you know that the 10p coin is the larger coin, it appears larger, even after you have reasoned otherwise and physically moved the coins to coincide at the same size. This is the effect of constancy; you see things for what they are all the time. The 10p coin is the larger coin. This idea should be acknowledged in your drawing. But how can this knowledge and contradictory information help in learning to draw? This is the point where people advise that you should draw what looks right, but drawing with knowledge is better. Draw the two coins the same size.

You need to draw what you see and to learn how to represent things by knowing about perspective and the art of illusion, based on the psychology of perception.

Art being a thing of the mind, it follows that any scientific study of art will be psychology. It may be other things as well, but psychology it will always be. (M. J. Friedlander, in *Art and Illusion* by E. H. Gombrich)

However, art and design have no franchise on creative activity in general, despite popular opinion. Design and art are inextricably linked historically and practically.

Italians have kept alive the Renaissance appreciation of the benefits of crossing disciplines, and of a good training in fine art or drawing for designers of all kinds. A radar and missile company engaged on secret work, for example, actually employs fine arts graduates, cartoonists and illustrators to work alongside the engineers on drawings derived from production models. These can be as imaginative as they wish, and are used to excite and stimulate the work of the technicians. (P. Sparkes)

This attitude can only be applauded as it is effective proof of the value of collaboration in design.

'Art for art's sake . . . money for God's sake.' Art and design cannot exist in a vacuum, nor should they be justified as only having commercial value, despite many examples to the contrary in design fields, for example, graphic design, fashion and product design. Art and design are not merely of value to the artistic, but to everyone. The skills and techniques that make them distinct are not merely therapeutic or esoteric.

The perception of art and design activity as a humanistic endeavour can be seen as a fundamental concern of art and design education across the world. (*Art and Design Education*, B. Allison)

Art and design are influenced by history, culture and society; they are a powerful means by which many of our values are formed, revitalised and focused upon. They are very important in the development of personal and social skills as well as contributing to our understanding of human endeavours, predicaments and achievements. One way this can be done is to learn to 'read the images of our culture'. Such learning is intellectually demanding, but the problems and issues raised by art and design are part of this rich cocktail of learning.

- Produce a landscape tapestry as though you had drawn it in wool. Exploit the many colours and textures of different weights of wool. Research, through photography and drawing, the horizontal nature of a landscape image, then draw an outline of your chosen view to act as a template. Use this drawing underneath a wooden frame to help you establish the warp and weft of your design. (The weft is the horizontal component from left to right ('weft' to right!) and the warp is the vertical component.) Make a frame to hold a string weft and establish a suitable way of maintaining the tightness of your weaving. Devise a way of framing your completed work.

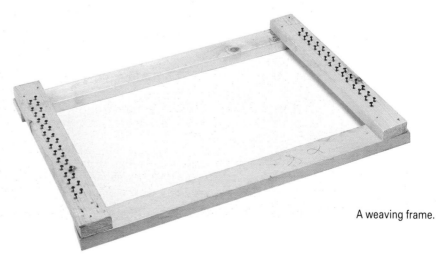

A weaving frame.

Tapestry landscape and supporting sketch by Jean Stokes.

Consider the following extract from a statement by eminent scientist Professor Fynman, where he said:

> . . . an artist might hold up a flower to see how beautiful it is, and say, 'I, as an artist, can see how beautiful a flower is, but you as a scientist, would take it all apart and it becomes a dull thing'. But the beauty the artist sees is available to the scientist . . . to everyone . . . despite the scientist not being quite as refined aesthetically as the artist. We can all appreciate the beauty of the flower.
>
> But, at the same time, I see, as a scientist, much more about the flower than the artist. I can imagine its cells, the complicated actions which also have a beauty, the inner structure, the processes . . . its colours which have evolved to attract insects to pollinate it. All of which are interesting because it means that insects can see colour . . . it adds a question . . . Does this aesthetic sense also exist in the lower forms of life? . . . Why is it aesthetic, and so on . . . All kinds of interesting questions can be asked . . . which scientific knowledge only adds to the excitement, the mystery and the awe of a flower. It only adds . . . it doesn't subtract!

Sensitivity to our experiences of things can be brought into focus through drawing. It is important that you recognise your disposition to things. The fact that some people respond to fluffy baby animals in a different way to a creature often considered to be strange, like a bat, is an example of contrasting dispositions towards things. You should guard against a clichéd response. A bat is usually regarded as an ugly creature and an ideal model for a gargoyle, but it is a beautiful animal. It is well adapted to its environment and has evolved very sophisticated means of survival, due to its abilities in echo location, surviving everything except the harsh effects of mankind on its habitat. Living things are to be marvelled at, and our different responses to them can be expressed powerfully through drawing.

Draw and design an illustration which presents a pipistrelle bat in a relevant context.

A pipistrelle bat in flight.

Hot-air balloons

Design brief

Produce and present an illustration, in full colour, of any contemporary:

Balloon   (lighter-than-air craft, consisting of a bag of gas that displaces a volume of air of greater mass than the total mass of the balloon and its contents);
or,

Airship   (dirigible balloon that obtains its thrust from a propeller).

Use your illustration to support a folder of work that assesses the technological significance and value of balloons and/or airships.

Your folder should explore the essential processes involved in your personal design awareness and capability. Ensure that your preparatory sketches and notes feature in your folder. This activity is devised to develop your skills in researching information for an illustration, as well as your experience of executing and presenting an illustration in a chosen context. Where would your illustration be best placed and used?

Technological assessment of balloons and/or airships

Hot-air balloons

There are several ways to become airborne. Heavier-than-air machines, such as gliders and aeroplanes, create a lifting force by moving through the air. An aeroplane exploits the aerodynamic forces of an aerofoil, and the lift developed by a conventional aircraft wing depends on the angle of attack of the wing and the velocity of the air in relation to the wing. Thus, it is necessary to provide forward movement for an aircraft to gain lift. A helicopter is equipped with one or more power-driven rotors, in the shape of horizontal propellers instead of fixed wings, and these obtain the necessary lift when the relative air velocity is produced by rotation of the rotor blades; when the angle of attack attains an appropriate value, the lift overcomes the weight of the machine and the helicopter takes off vertically. A rocket uses thrust to gain height; it is a jet-propelled missile that carries the source of its own propulsive energy. Rockets exploit Newton's law of 'action' and 'reaction', whereby every action produces a reaction of the same magnitude but acting in the opposite direction.

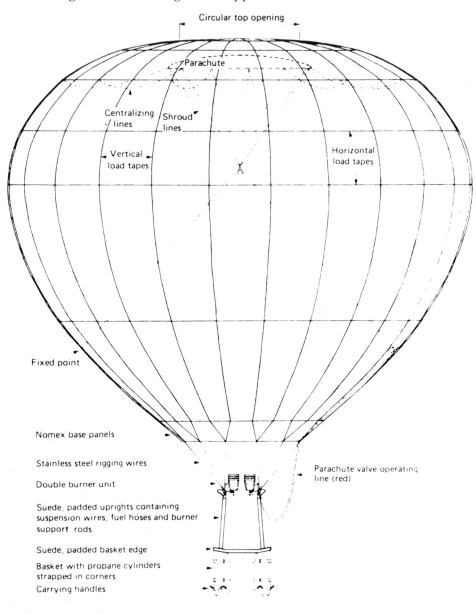

A hot-air balloon is a lighter-than-air vehicle. These vehicles span the whole history of manned flight. Balloons move *with* the air and not *through* it; they obtain their lifting force by means of displacement. This means that a balloon displaces a volume of air that is then replaced by something that is lighter, for example hot air. Archimedes' buoyancy principle applies to balloon flying, as when a body is immersed in a fluid, in this example air, at ambient temperature, it experiences an upthrust equal to the weight of the fluid displaced. The air pressure that held up the air is now holding up something that is lighter, and it is the pressure of the air that provides the upward thrust.

What technology is involved in producing controlled flight using hot-air balloons? What are their essential uses and functions? These balloons are safer than gas-filled balloons and tend to be a lot cheaper and easier to operate. Hot-air balloons of the future might use solar power to obtain the necessary heat energy.

A written exposition should accompany your folder and should feature: your technological assessment of balloons and/or airships; and your sketches, notes, drawings and researched information, especially those that relate to the context of use for your illustration. You should specify precisely any relevant background details concerning designers, technologies, manufacturers, technical or sales information and trade names, as well as the uses and qualities of the balloons or airships you are depicting.

Issues that can structure your technological assessment of ballooning are based on a series of questions for you to consider. Use them, as well as your own questions, to help you present your evaluation of balloons and airships today. Your studies should aim to reveal:

- The scientific and technical principles that underlie the design of balloons and airships (your illustration context might concentrate on the presentation of an information graphic which explains this).

- Establish a systematic method of technological assessment concerning the technologies developed, the users of balloons and airships and their interaction with the environment, including their effects on employment prospects and the quality and standard of work required in their manufacture and sales. (Your illustration context might be that of describing the uses to which such vehicles are put, including the historical developments of ballooning, or the manufacturing processes used in their general development. Consider the use of solar power in hot-air ballooning.)

'The Battle of the Balloons', an early fantasy of air warfare, 1784.

Key issues for the technical development of balloons and airships are centred on the following questions. What are the component parts? How do they work? How reliable and safe are they? How well made is the vehicle? What inherent capabilities, requirements and limitations does the technical development have? Use the concepts of innovation and diffusion to explore the value of balloons as vehicles.

Key issues for the user include: What purpose does the vehicle serve? How effective is it at fulfilling each purpose for which it is used? How much does it cost to use, and therefore how cost effective is it? Who controls it?

Key issues regarding the development's interaction with the environment are explored in the following questions. Is it appropriate? Who or what in the environment does it affect? What purpose does it serve? Who gains and who loses from its adoption and in which ways?

Key issues that affect those involved in running the development are concerned with the following notions. How does it affect work prospects? How does it affect the character of the work? These questions are not intended to provide a formula for correct answers. Why is this?

Student example by Tony Semans.

Illustrating balloons and/or airships

Illustration
In what ways does an activity like this develop your illustration skills as well as your understanding of design? The following questions are offered as starting points for you to consider certain aspects of illustration design for your folder and exposition.

Need
What is the working context for your illustration, and who will use it? Make a list. Which aspect of balloons or airships will you illustrate? Make a list of possibilities.

Brief
What brief could be written for your chosen illustration? How precise should it be? Compare it with the example given at the beginning of this exercise.

Investigation
Do you need to see a real balloon or airship? What factual research is required for your illustration, and for establishing drawing and illustration techniques? Make sure you fully understand this item! Which elements of this work will require you to develop a precise or complex drawing, or to use freehand and mechanical drawing, especially in the creation of surface textures depicting specific materials, shadows and light and dark? How will the selection of a suitable view of a balloon or airship be chosen and for which reasons? How will you use colour? How will your research be presented so as to include initial sketches, drawing experiments and relevant information or photographs? What part does design play at this stage of your work?

Proposition
Which is the best view of the vehicle you have chosen to draw? What should you do with the alternative schemes and ideas that you thought about and worked on? What is the creative narrative within the illustration, especially in relation to how it will be used? Are you depicting the appearance of a balloon or airship or anything else?

Realisation
How will you execute your illustration? Will the chosen media reflect the form or concept of the subject of your illustration?

Evaluation
Why is your illustration successful? What could you add to or subtract from your work to make it better? How effective is your presentation? Does the illustration work well in your chosen context or setting? What can you say about the quality of the finished work? Does your illustration fulfil your brief?

Any source of information about balloons or airships should be acknowledged.

Advertising with balloons or airships

Since the beginning of modern hot-air balloons in the 1960s, there has been a steady increase in their use in advertising and publicity. Prior to the 1970s almost all of the balloons constructed by Cameron Balloons were in simple colour schemes, and intended for private sport only. Today, at factory sites in Bristol, England and Ann Arbor, USA more than 350 balloons a year are

constructed, and all but a few of these carry commercial artwork.

Balloons offer an unequalled sporting experience. This low-speed, open-air form of flying to an unknown destination, combines great beauty with a sense of excitement and danger (which is fortunately illusionary as the very good safety record proves). But it is the great size and bright colours of balloons, in addition to their image of adventure, which make them so attractive to everyone who sees them and their use for publicity grows naturally from this.

The best style of operation depends very much on the owner's publicity needs and type of business. (Cameron Balloons)

Publicity applications can be based on 'general exposure'; by simply flying frequently in an area, especially over a town or city, a balloon will quickly become known. What other applications are known to you, or might be a commercial consideration?

Design brief

Design an advertising campaign using a balloon. This will require several avenues of research, the most important being the overall concept of the campaign. It is possible to design different balloon shapes, and to generate many forms of artwork for the respective shapes. Consider the design ideas and produce visual concepts for a chosen scheme, and also indicate how the artwork can be placed on your balloon shape. Use the design blanks provided by Thunder and Colt to assist your design format. Illustrate your final idea.

Review the technical requirements of actually placing a design on a balloon. How is it done?

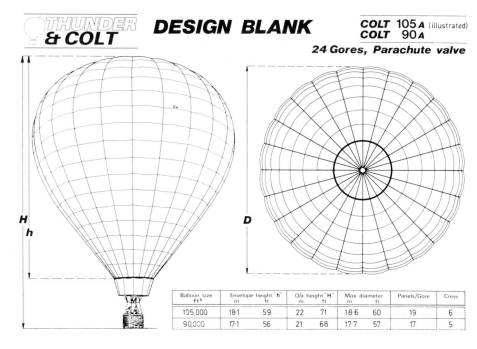

THUNDER & COLT **DESIGN BLANK** COLT 105 A (illustrated) COLT 90 A

24 Gores, Parachute valve

Balloon size ft³	Envelope height "h"		O/a height "H"		Max diameter		Panels/Gore	Crew
	m	ft	m	ft	m	ft		
105,000	18·1	59	22	71	18·6	60	19	6
90,000	17·1	56	21	68	17·7	57	17	5

Visual information design

Illustration for information

Look at the photograph that was used to support a newspaper article about unemployment in Merseyside. The images in the two posters contrast in quite marked ways; what do you think they are? Was the information in both posters intended to be presented this way?

Our way of life surrounds us with information of many kinds and forms, sometimes not always to our betterment. Many organisations, institutions and companies use visual information design; and we all use, read and follow such designs in our everyday lives.

Making a collection of many different examples of designs is a useful way to begin to understand this field of graphic design. Have you ever assembled something by following a diagram, and found, halfway through, that things have gone wrong! Was the fault with you or the instructions?

Naturally, information can be based on many things. It can be collected from statistics or technological data, or derived from our specialised knowledge of things. Occasionally, information may be presented in a poor way, as in the case of difficult assembly instructions (sometimes called 'destructions'). Have you ever found yourself lost in a computer manual?

The aim in visual information design is to make ideas and facts clear, easy to read and understand, as well as interesting. In recent times many graphic designs of high quality have come into being and these have increasing influence on our way of life. This is in part due to the high commercial value placed upon graphic design, especially since a great deal of graphic artwork is at the forefront of techniques and designer skills; photography and computer graphics are interesting examples.

The task of a visual information designer and illustrator is to make information visible and accessible to the reader or user. This can be achieved by designing illustrations so that they attract attention, make clear at a glance the subject matter, and get across the information, no matter how detailed or complex.

A sound visual design will be useful and will also carry within it a 'creative narrative'. It should tell a story. It should bring out the essential quality and feeling of the information and make it accessible to the user. This is where the designer relates the form of the work to its meaning.

This design work requires you to produce individual schemes based on experimental approaches towards a clearly defined structure and story line. Your work should aim to inform and project the atmosphere of the issue under review. A fact is a belief in what 'is', and a value is a belief in what 'ought to be'. You should know the difference between facts, values and beliefs in order to handle the complexity of your work confidently.

When studying and developing design skills, it is useful to be able to distinguish between different types of visual information design. There are those designs that are factually based on quantitative details and concerned with presenting precise, measured information. There

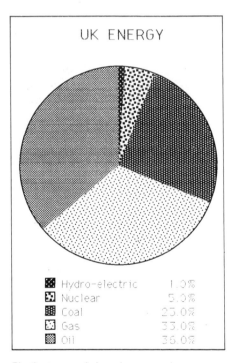

Pie chart example based on general information for UK Energy:
computer graphics using Framework One spreadsheet and graph drawing facility;

(right) The equipment used to cut out the different slices for a pie chart.

are contrasting designs that deal with non-quantitative information. They are intended to enable the user to explore and understand particular relationships or changes in things.

Typical graphic examples of quantitative designs are usually called bar charts or histograms, pie-charts, line graphs or tables of values. Examples of non-quantitative designs are flow diagrams, schematic diagrams and maps. They deal with issues concerning time, place and relationship.

In order to develop an effective portfolio of design ideas you should aim to:

1. Collect examples and systematically note which type of design each one is, including your sources of information.

2. Study particular examples, noting the time and place of each example and especially researching information concerning the design's background and how the designer thought through his or her ideas.

3. Work some examples.

4. Research information for a visual information design that explores an issue or concern, especially one that relates to 'cause and effect'.

5. Write a design brief, noting the context for your work.

6. Develop a folder of design ideas showing clearly your selected proposition.

7. Execute your design and present it to an appropriate audience.

8. Evaluate your work.

Visual information design briefs

The following examples are devised to encourage you to think about the content, structure and presentation of visual information designing. Use them to produce design ideas as well as finished graphic designs.

A folding paper-dart promotional 'freeby' from Vauxhall Astra.

- Select or create an example of paper folding and modelling, for example a paper dart, and design, draw, lay out and present a set of diagrams that depict its construction and use stage by stage. Your illustrations should be presented as camera-ready artwork suitable for a specified book.

  You might like to prepare your design in the manner of a 'Blue Peter' presentation. You should practise folding paper; if you have folded something incorrectly, start again with a new piece of paper, so as not to leave unwanted creases on the finished model.

  Use paper that has differently coloured sides, and make up a series of symbols for the various processes and techniques required to make your model. For example, you will need signs for the following items: 'turn over paper', 'fold', 'the direction of a fold', 'make a crease' and 'convex' or 'concave' fold. Provide an example of the finished model, as well as the illustrations for the essential stages in its manufacture.

- Design an illustration that will communicate the following information in a context specified by you.

  Using the title 'A Long, Long Way to Go', consider the enormous distances from earth to the stars. The sun is 93 million miles away and light takes eight minutes to reach earth. The light from the next nearest star, Proxima Centauri, takes four and a half years to reach us.

- Devise a set of illustrations that present the French game of 'boules', more properly called 'pétanque', and discuss the working context of your scheme.

- Using the title 'Children, Never Go with a Stranger!', design a leaflet for young children to explain how they should conduct themselves with strangers, getting across the point that most strangers are nice, but some strangers are nasty and like to hurt children.

- Research data for a visual information design that explains a particular environmental issue or concern. Consider producing three distinct designs that depict:
  a) 'What the facts are?' (a factual statement about the issue or problem);
  b) 'Cause and effect' (opinions and reasons for the issue/problem);
  c) 'What ought to be done?' (a value judgement showing ways to alleviate the problem).

An example might be to explain what the 'greenhouse effect' is and consider its possible impact on daily living. Study the information supplied by *Which?* magazine to discover what is happening to the ozone layer of the earth.

A group of chemicals called chlorofluorocarbons (CFCs) used in the manufacture of some aerosols, plastic foam and refrigeration equipment is now widely accepted to have an effect on the earth's atmosphere. This could cause serious health risks and changes in climate.

The chemicals in question
Chlorofluorocarbons were first developed in the 1930s. Their main use then was as refrigerants – chemicals used in fridges and air conditioning plant. Since the 1950s they've come to be used for lots of other things, especially in spray cans

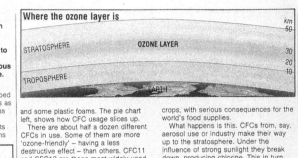

Where the ozone layer is

STRATOSPHERE   OZONE LAYER

TROPOSPHERE

EARTH

km 50 / 30 / 20 / 10

and some plastic foams. The pie chart left, shows how CFC usage slices up.

There are about half a dozen different CFCs in use. Some of them are more 'ozone-friendly' – having a less destructive effect – than others. CFC11 and CFC12 are those most widely used at present, as well as probably the most destructive of the ozone layer. But CFCs have several advantages too; they're odourless and have low toxicity and flammability.

Halons are chemicals used in some fire extinguishers which are also thought to damage the ozone layer.

The ozone layer
The ozone layer is vital to life on earth; it shields us from the most harmful types of ultraviolet (UV) light given off by the sun. If more of this UV light gets through, the number of skin cancer cases will increase (though increased sunbathing and holidays abroad may also be a factor). There's also strong evidence that increased UV exposure would harm

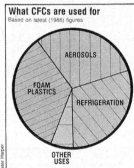

What CFCs are used for
Based on latest (1986) figures

AEROSOLS

FOAM PLASTICS

REFRIGERATION

OTHER USES

Peter Harper

crops, with serious consequences for the world's food supplies.

What happens is this. CFCs from, say, aerosol use or industry make their way up to the stratosphere. Under the influence of strong sunlight they break down, producing chlorine. This in turn converts the ozone gas into oxygen. The chlorine isn't destroyed in the process, so a little chlorine can do a lot of damage. Ozone concentration is steadily depleted.

There's another reason to worry about CFCs: their accumulation in the troposphere – along with other gases we produce, like carbon dioxide – may be causing the earth's average temperature to rise slightly. (This is often called the 'greenhouse effect', because the sun's heat is allowed through and then trapped.) Some scientists think this could change our climate and lead to a rise in sea level, causing major flooding.

The story so far
The CFC/ozone depletion theory was first

continued overleaf

Which? magazine extract, July 1988

STOP ACID RAIN

The Stop Acid Rain Campaign, Norway
STOP ACID RAIN

Norwegian Government/Embassy information on acid rain.

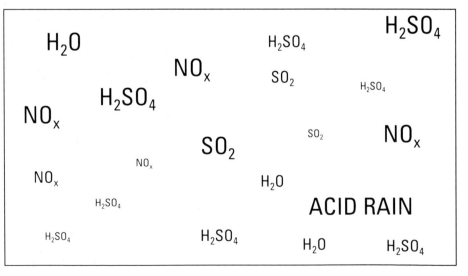

H_2O H_2SO_4 H_2SO_4

NO_x SO_2

H_2SO_4 H_2SO_4

NO_x H_2SO_4

SO_2 NO_x

NO_x SO_2

NO_x H_2O

H_2SO_4 ACID RAIN

H_2SO_4 H_2SO_4 H_2O H_2SO_4

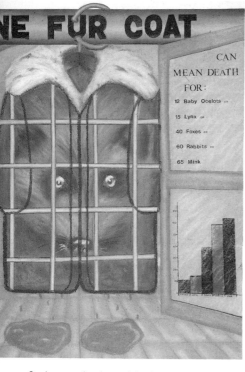

Oxclose student's work by Amanda Haggath.

Drawing and visual information design

Drawing is a process that enables you to find and communicate facts and feelings about all manner of information or knowledge. It is a matter of thinking about messages. In many ways, drawing is the most efficient and clear means by which information, feelings or insights about designs may be translated, represented and transmitted. There is an infinite variety of drawn forms that can be used. It is your skill and creativity that come to bear in your selection of the form of your design sketches and layouts.

1980s professional use of drawing in a graphic design context for a cover design.

Before you start to draw or design, think about what it is you want to 'say', or what it is you are feeling. Make sure you know what your task is, or at least what you should do to become fully involved in it. Define the issue or problem to yourself and consider both the practical and symbolic implications of your research. Generally, you should aim to devise highly innovative visual designs. For example, if you study

the visual information design required to depict the French game of 'boules', then it is vital that you familiarise yourself with the game.

As soon as you have decided what information you need to communicate, begin to choose the lines, tones, textures, patterns and compositions or layouts that will help you to articulate your design. Pay particular attention to layout techniques and lettering skills, especially the use of cutouts, overlays and lettering styles.

Use whatever may seem appropriate to your design in order to create the effects you require. Remember the notions of form and meaning. Think about colour, as well as black and white, in your sketches and drawings. Consider the style of your drawing and the atmosphere it may generate or detract from. You should use all the information you find through sketching to help you to decide the best place or context for your work, if you have not done so already. Be confident, and do not worry about initial mistakes.

Visual information design generally requires you to know the source of your information, to make judgements concerning the graphic techniques most appropriate for the presentation of your design, and to know the audience or recipient of your design.

In order to communicate information or a 'message', you will need to explore the background of your design task. Where does the information come from? Who needs to know it? Why should people be informed about your chosen or given topic or issue? How reliable is the information? Are you going to research an issue or is the information given to you in the form of a brief?

1950s illustration of the Tower of London.

URVIVAL AREAS

of each nuclear explosion would
but the extent of the damage
ies would be affected by a number
For example, apart from broken
he maximum extent of damage to
used by a 10 megaton bomb would
at between 20–25 miles from the
st.

CENTRAL AREA
few survivors

FRINGE AREA
many survivors

ide this area would not be affected
heat from this explosion but if they
wind of it they would be exposed to
fall-out.

1960s information on what to do in the event of a nuclear war.

SURVIVAL!

**We all want to prevent
nuclear war.
But, if it ever came, we
would all have to know the
do's and don'ts that could
help many families to survive.
This series of five diagrams
explains the facts about
our protection in the
survival areas.**

OF11   PREPARED FOR THE W.V.S. BY THE CENTRAL OFFICE OF INFORMATION

1970s graphic design. 'Facts of Life', *The Sunday Times*, 22 September, 1974.

What is the source of the population information given in the graphic from *The Sunday Times*?

The decision about the graphic techniques you will employ should be based upon your understanding of the value and meaning of your visual design. How is the information communicated? Which form of illustration best puts over the essential meaning of the information to be presented?

Being aware of the context in which the design will be used also aids the effective development of your design ideas. Who is the audience for your work? Is your design for yourself, and thus private to you, or is it more public and designed for a wide audience? Your design could also be for a more technical audience, and should be designed appropriately.

National Dog Registration Scheme information

The following design task involves research and the use of graphic techniques for visual information designs that will present your views concerning the promulgation of responsible dog ownership in Britain.

This design activity is centred around the problems and issues of mass dog ownership and is devised for you to explore the difficulties of distinguishing between facts, values and beliefs for this particular public issue, which affects us all in one way or another. You are invited to use the information supplied and to generate your own research for this topic. Use your findings to produce two designs, based on your creative judgement, concerning:

- A visual portrayal of quantitative information about dog ownership.

- A design that presents non-quantitative visual information concerning the different problems of controlling dogs.

Information about dog registration

One particular national scheme that has been widely promoted and supported by the RSPCA, the police and local authorities is the National Dog Registration Scheme. However, this scheme has met with disapproval by some politicians, who feel that it would not stop irresponsible dog owners from continuing to be neglectful in the proper care of their pets. Issues concerning costs and who pays for the scheme are also central to this discussion.

Dog ownership and care is an emotive subject. Separate schemes are proposed by government to cope with dangerous dogs, stray dogs and dog mess in public places, which might cause health hazards. This approach tends to separate the different issues requiring attention rather than providing an overall package to deal with the factors concerning dogs.

While the Government looks the other way, another 350,000 dogs look like this.

RSPCA

Registration, not extermination.

This doggy bag contains a dead doggy.

Thousands of them go to the incinerator every week.

The dogs are healthy but unwanted.

If they can't be placed, local vets, the RSPCA and other animal charities are forced to put them down.

When the Government killed the dog licence they left us to kill the dogs.

Urge your MP to press for a dog registration scheme.

For it is a sick nation that kills healthy dogs. **RSPCA**

Registration, not extermination.

The problem of how to deal with thousands of stray and abandoned dogs is acute. Greater restrictions and controls on dog ownership are required, especially through tougher enforcement measures concerning the use of dog tags and collars, laws against letting dogs stray and muzzling dangerous dogs. All those concerned with these problems are interested in promoting responsible dog ownership and care.

A registration scheme would require an annual fee of approximately £15–20. It would pay for the dog wardens required, hold each dog owner accountable for how he or she looked after his or her pet and identify each dog with its owner. Critics gripe that this system would be incomplete, bureaucratic and ineffective, but treating the problems we all face concerning dogs on a piecemeal basis is not necessarily effective either. For example, enforcing dog-collar use is only part of the problem. A broad framework is required in order to identify a dog permanently with its owner. Thus, the most practical way to prevent some dog owners from neglecting their pets is by compulsory registration on the acquisition of a dog.

A small microchip, about the size of a grain of rice, can be implanted in a dog painlessly and in a matter of moments. The chip is covered in silicon, which enables it to attach itself to the dog's tissues and prevents it from moving. The chip is a transponder. It is inert and can only be activated externally. It also has an aerial which receives a signal so that it can be read electronically rather in the manner of a bar code system in a supermarket. Each number is unique and is preset by the manufacturer. Thus, each dog and owner can have an individual code, which can be checked on a computer quite readily; they are thus permanently linked.

The £15–20 cover charge per year for the National Registration Scheme would cover the costs of running the scheme and enforcing it. This fee is seen as high enough to discourage casual dog ownership. With half a million dogs straying or loose on the streets of Britain, such a scheme would go a long way towards controlling a problem already addressed in many other European countries.

A lost pet needn't be a lost cause.

NOW INCLUDES THIRD PARTY LIABILITY INSURANCE

*id*ENTICHIP

Pets are lost without it.

A sentimental image of a dog.

Does freedom require discipline? Are we free to 'own' animals, through an unwritten right? Should we take such rights for granted?

Ornamental birds, pet dogs and domestic animals are common features in our way of life. Do we tend to treat some animals as though they were living pictures on a wall (examples being a goldfish in a bowl or a bird in a cage)? Does caring for animals require us to declare that we are capable of looking after them properly?

It is possible that a registration framework can be accompanied by supporting measures so as to give every assistance to sensible ownership and proper regard for dogs. Insurance and training in dog handling could most effectively complement registration and identification systems, especially at the outset of the relationship between a person and his or her dog. Why is it difficult to instigate a registration system and how have such systems been treated by politicians?

Packaging design

Environmental issues

Among the factors that have contributed to the development and wellbeing of our modern way of life, packaging can claim to be of special importance. In providing effective protection against spoilage and waste, the packaging of food and consumer goods has played a key role in maintaining health and distributing the products of industry more widely. Modern developments in packaging procedures have had a major impact on reducing the cost of preserved foods and consumer goods in terms of production, storage and distribution and have thus contributed to a rise in the standard of living in most parts of the Western world.

However, once having fulfilled its very necessary and desirable function, a package immediately becomes a disposal problem. This has, in recent years, become the subject of considerable public concern because of the sheer increase in the volume of packaged goods and an increasing awareness of the impact of packaging from the point of view of the consumer and the environment.

Although the packaging industry is primarily concerned with the provision of adequate and attractive packaging it has for some time been active in reducing the amount of packaging materials used and minimising instances of overpackaging which both wastes resources and creates litter once the initial purpose of the packaging is completed. One thing that ecologists have taught us is that no system related to human activity can be considered in isolation. Each human activity must be contemplated in relation to our total environment. We as designers must also extend our considerations of packaging practice to include source reduction and the ultimate disposal or recycling of the material from which the package is made.

'Green' design

- Identify a package in commercial production, which, in your opinion, is overdesigned or too elaborate for the purpose for which it is intended. Some of these features may include excessive use of different layers of packaging, excessively large packaging which reveals much smaller contents, or the use of expensive and sophisticated materials when more economical, and perhaps more readily disposable, alternatives would suffice.

- Redesign the package and model the solution.

- Produce a written justification for your new packaging design, outlining your decision-making process (500 words).

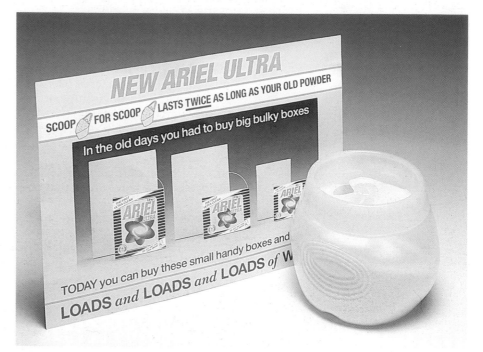

The new Ariel Ultra system – some manufacturers are reducing the quantity of their packaging. Is this solely for environmental reasons or just another marketing ploy?

Identifing a new market . . . links with industry

For packaging projects to be realistic, they should be linked to a company that has a specific set of requirements for the storage, handling, transportation and display of its particular packaging needs.

One particular company is Grundfos Manufacturing Ltd. The company manufactures water pumps for numerous applications in the construction industry, for industrial and commercial use, and for central heating in commercial and domestic properties.

The Selectric domestic circulator (pump).

The original Grundfos packaging.

Research: where will the product be sold?

A vacuum-formed pack complete with simple pressed tools and information to help in installation.

Letting the customer view the product.

Foam storage pack with information to help in installation contained in the outer sleeve.

It is of prime importance that all of these products are adequately protected during handling and transportation, to ensure that they arrive in an undamaged condition and fit for use. This particular design project was linked to a domestic central heating circulator pump, of which Grundfos is the largest producer. The company manufactures over three million units per year and these are traditionally sold to wholesalers, plumbers' merchants, central heating contractors, the gas industry and local authorities.

Market opportunities

This particular design project has been based on the presumption that the company aims to develop the growth of its business in sales to the DIY market. It has been identified that there is a growing demand among DIY enthusiasts who are now installing their own central heating systems or replacing faulty equipment in already established systems.

A DIY enthusiast may not be an expert plumber or electrician, although he or she may have the necessary technical expertise to fit such a unit providing he or she is given adequate information, support and confidence, which must all feature as an integral part of the marketing strategy of the new packaging. This 'added-value' appeal of the product must be conveyed to the consumer through the packaging. This has the added advantage and security from the customers' point of view that they are purchasing not only a pump, but also the additional expertise that will enable them to fit the product successfully.

As part of their submission for the project, students were expected to present the following design features:

- Following the exploration of a number of different ideas, design and produce a range of packaging/promotional/informational material specific to the Grundfos Selectric pump, such that the message conveyed to the DIY purchaser emphasises the quality of the product and promotes confidence in the potential installer.

- An essential part of the project is to ensure that the necessary information for fitting the pump is conveyed to the DIY enthusiast in a clear and precise way, using the most appropriate forms of communication.

- The packaging should be attractive. As a rigid structure, it must be strong enough to support and protect the pump, allowing for individual units to be stacked and shrink-wrapped onto pallets for dispatch, as is the company's current practice.

- Your submission should include an analysis of the market needs of the product, and proposals for a range of designs, which should all be carefully evaluated.

- You should explore the various structural qualities of different types of card and board to ensure that your package meets the minimum 'drop-test' standards as laid down by the company.

- You should produce a full-size prototype of your final design, supported by card developments, models, layout designs and informational text where this is required.

Bottle-counting technology

Design electronics

Bottles passing through a counting device.

Applied design problems

You are employed by a company to investigate the feasibility of ideas that are potential solutions to manufacturing problems.

This company wishes to install a monitoring process that checks whether bottles of known mass and size are being correctly filled with either the correct quantity of liquid or small solid objects, such as pills, on an automated dispatch system. The monitoring process has to be capable of giving a visual and/or audible warning of any malfunction in the system. It has to work at high speed. The system also has to count the number of bottles that have been filled in any given period of time.

Devise a simple monitoring system that can be reliably and cheaply introduced to achieve any or all of the above operations.

On the face of it, this problem seems fairly straightforward.

As the automated dispatch system runs at high speed, your product monitoring system has to be capable of counting the number of bottles that pass a point at any given time prior to packaging, as you cannot expect any human operator to be capable of counting such a process. It is inevitable that some bottles could receive more or less contents than they should. How could this particular problem be monitored?

When installed, your devised monitoring system has to be capable of giving a clear indication of any filling errors. How could this be brought to the attention of the operator at the time when the error occurs? Which fault indication process(es) would you recommend: a buzzer, flashing lights, automatic shutdown of the conveyor belt system?

Having identified a number of functions that need to be achieved, consider the variables that need to be monitored. There are a number of such variables:

- Varying mass of glass container and contents.
- Level of liquid in the bottles.
- Number of bottles passing a point at any given time.
- The counting process.
- The fault-indication system.

Having considered all the required functions, an overall solution is not as straightforward as it initially appeared, especially when a number of functions/variables have to be integrated within an overall monitoring system.

Let us therefore initially consider two elements of the problem and leave the others for your future development.

Diagram A

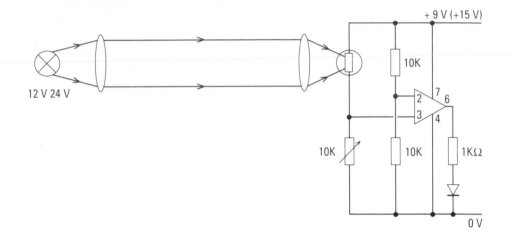

The process of identifying bottles passing a given point in any period of time can be easily realised. A simple circuit can be used (A).

When the beam of light is not interrupted, the LED glows. When the beam is interrupted, the LED goes out for the period that the beam is interrupted.

Diagram B

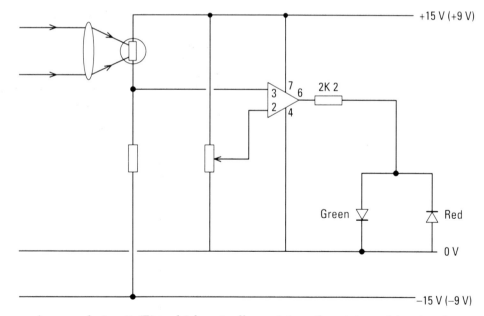

A second circuit (B), which actually registers the status of 'no bottle passing' – 'bottle passing' – 'no bottle passing' can be developed.

With no bottle passing, the green LED glows; when a bottle interrupts the beam, a red LED glows.

The use of an operational amplifier enables high speed detection of status to be possible. But can the operator observe the change in status as indicated by the LED glowing or not glowing (A)? This may be easier in (B), but it doesn't actually *count* the bottles, just indicates that a bottle has passed a point. Can you devise a counting system?

Instead of using visible light, the same system can be operated using infra-red (C).

Diagram C

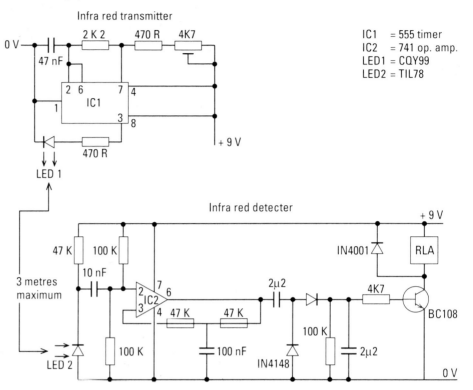

Whether visible light or infra-red radiation is used, we now have a reliable method for detecting the passage of bottles at any point on the conveyor system.

Can we detect the level of liquid in a bottle, or the number of pills that have been put in the bottle?

In considering this problem, let us consider a similar problem.

A system is needed that can be used to count high-sided trucks that pass along a busy road. The system must be able to count low-level, medium-level and high-level trucks.

Diagram D

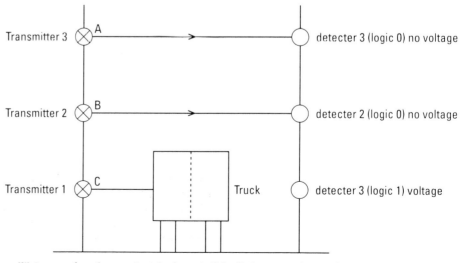

This can be done simply by visible light or infra-red radiation falling on detectors to give a voltage output (LOGIC 1) when the beam is broken (D).

The following 'truth table' can be completed and a circuit designed by deriving three logic statements for the three counters (E).

How can this now be realised. Devise a simple circuit(s) and test your theories. Can these ideas be transferred to our bottle problem?

Table E

Top beam A	Middle beam B	Bottom beam C	High truck counter	Medium truck counter	Small truck counter
0	0	0			
0	0	1			
0	1	0			
0	1	1			
1	0	0			
1	0	1			
1	1	0			
1	1	1			

However, this is just the beginning of the design and realisation process. What other opportunities are there for solving the identified problems? Can the problems be solved by non-electronic systems?

When you have considered the problems encountered, make a final mock-up of your solution? State clearly what you intend your developed solution to achieve. Can your solution be caught out by misuse or abuse? If it is to be totally reliable, it has to be capable of being used in a variety of situations. Is it cheap to make and install?

A simple counting process with an LED display can be added using commonly available ICs. As an object passes the sensor it increments the display by one.

Diagram F

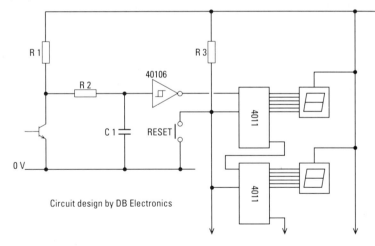

Circuit design by DB Electronics

R1 replaces the relay although the relay can remain if necessary.

The first part of the circuit is a switch debouncer (RC plus schmitt trigger), the RC slowdown network R2, C1 drives a CMOS schmitt trigger (40106) it smoothes the bouncy waveform on the input so that the schmitt trigger gate makes only one transition, a 10mS to 25mS RC time constant is generally long enough, though by replacing C1 with a larger electrolytic capacitor the counter will ignore smaller items passing the sensor.

The second part of the circuit uses a CMOS decade counter/display driver (CD4011B). For each pulse on the input it adds one to the display, counting up to 9. By using the carry on, and adding another CD4011B it will count to 99 and so on. A switch is added to set the display to zero.

Low-relief modelling

Design brief

Design, model and present a low-relief image of a building, or a part of a building, based upon your own observational drawing or photography. Your image should use a range of multi-media effects and techniques. Your choice of subject should be an example of architecture that you feel makes a valuable visual contribution to its environment. A suitable critique should accompany your folder of work so that you demonstrate and justify your views concerning the building's design. You should fully evaluate the effectiveness of your completed image.

An example of fully worked low-relief modelling and drawing.

There are many possible starting points to this activity. There is also a variety of alternative topics that you can consider, and these are explored in the information given in this study. Part of your task is to discover the different ways in which your work is either a 'photographic likeness' or an example of an imaginative interpretation of an observed architectural feature. To what extent is your picture real?

You may wish to present your image so that it demonstrates your skills in the use of different media or materials. This approach would engage you in exploring ways of creating certain effects, for example how would the surface of hammered glass be depicted? Would this be drawn or created by the use of a suitable material, cut or drawn upon to create such an effect? Such exploration is at the heart of this activity because it is designed for you to make suitable judgements concerning media and materials.

A gothic arch rainbow. A rainbow is a natural arch reaching out to the heavens, but a gothic arch is an incomplete arch made by humans. Both types of arch are used symbolically by Lawrence's characters in 'The Rainbow'. What do they symbolise?

However, you may feel that you can extend or change your design through a freer interpretation based on your sketches and notes on architectural features as an imaginative composition.

You could pursue an even more esoteric approach to this study by considering the notion of a building being a symbol for something. For example, what does a cathedral symbolise? Consider the following quotation if you wish to consider symbolism in your drawing and require a literary starting point from which to work.

The last few lines in D. H. Lawrence's *The Rainbow* state:

> And the rainbow stood on the earth . . . she saw in the rainbow the earth's new architecture, the old brittle corruption of houses and factories swept away, the world built up in a living fabric of Truth fitting to the over-arching heaven.

A symbol represents something other than itself, it embodies a meaning that has to be learned. Literary symbolism generally, and Lawrence's imagery in particular, do need to be studied further, although it is quite likely that you will know something of his work or that of other writers from your studies. In this context, much more needs to be explored with regard to symbolism in literature and its possible links with visual design. However, the purpose of including such a discussion here is to demonstrate the many ways in which you may begin a design topic, and that this activity can be realised through many different forms of visual expression.

Description of the activity

This design activity is based on the observational and imaginative drawing and modelling of a building or part of a building. It is a low-relief modelling activity, designed for you to demonstrate your skills in the use of drawing techniques and the selection of the materials and media best suited to communicate your feelings about your subject, as well as your presentation of a folder of work and a completed image.

If you choose a whole building to draw, then ensure that you will have enough time to execute the complete project. A feature of a building can be very effective: a roof with chimney pots and television aerials; an old doorway into a barn; or the steps of a prominent public building.

Any study can explore a grandiose example of architecture or a humble shed or barn. An essential aim of this activity is for you to capture the atmosphere of your chosen building, its period, its use today, its ruin or misuse, its power to attract attention, its character and so on. Through this form of study, you will not only extend your skills but also your knowledge and understanding of things.

The closing scene from The Searchers, starring John Wayne and directed by John Ford. Ford began the film by looking through a doorway on to a Texas scene and ended it looking through a similar doorway at the 'searcher'. This example highlights the idea of the external and internal features of a scene, and is essentially a film technique requiring a zoom shot as well as the use of a silhouette.

Observation, sketching and note-taking are the essential skills and research techniques required in this activity. You should aim to record colours, textures, materials and proportions in your sketches. They are the means by which your various design ideas will progress. They are also the essential means by which you can demonstrate your personal research skills, individuality and style.

Norwegian study –
a fully worked example
by Frank Hudson, using photography for research.

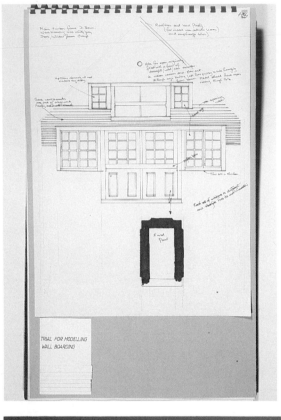

In addition to your own drawing, you can also develop your study by using established illustrations, photographs or technical drawings for a low-relief image of a made structure. Your study could be from different viewpoints. It may be inside looking out or vice versa; it may be night or day. Make a point of noting the atmosphere at the time when you are sketching.

When looking up at a building you will see reflections in the windows as well as shapes and forms through the windows. How can such layers of visual information be drawn? Which materials will you use? Will you draw the first-floor windows in the same way as the ground-floor windows?

Make a note of the different layers in your image. Some will need to be drawn in relief and some will need to be constructed with cards, and so on. Low-relief modelling of this kind involves you in understanding how to depict depth in a picture; by noting the possible visual layers in a scene, you can develop a very effective item of artwork.

Original work is best obtained through personal experience and discussion. Gone will be the comforts of working in a familiar room where everything is at hand. Issues concerning light, colour and composition come into sharp focus and are made more complex because you will also have to deal with movement and the atmosphere of your subject, including its setting. Buildings do not move but people do, sometimes in a busy and ever-changing way. Therefore, start carefully and modestly, and establish for yourself a comfortable working situation when drawing outside. Use basic drawing equipment and, most important, your sketch book.

When drawing outside, a useful gadget is a postcard-sized piece of card, with a rectangular opening cut into it, of suitable proportions for your work. This, if held up in front of the subject you select, will help you to find out how much of the scene you need to make a good composition involving the components of your image. Try it in both landscape and portrait positions. Also experiment with different proportions for the rectangular shapes involved, as well as other possible ways of framing your image.

Consider the 'golden section' proportions. Tastes concerning shape and proportion vary according to people's needs. Invariably, people select rectangular shapes in the following proportions: if the height is called 'h' and the width 'w', then $w/h - h/(w+h)$. This proportion, in which the smaller is to the larger as the larger is to the sum of both, is called the golden section.

This study can be most effective if drawn using an orthographic format, especially front elevational views. This style of drawing will enable you to represent your view of a building accurately, based on measurements, scale and proportion. You will probably find that a certain amount of interplay between orthographic projection and freehand perspective drawing will take place as your work unfolds. Is it possible to maintain only one fixed view of something when drawing, modelling or painting?

Study various still-life works to see how other artists approach this aspect of composition and visualisation. Cézanne tended to reflect different viewpoints in his still-life painting and a study of his work can be a useful starting point in this discussion.

You should note proportions and actual measurements if possible, in order to effect a scaled drawing. Employ multi-media effects imaginatively throughout this study, so as to establish the visual impact and appearance, textures, colours, surfaces, light and dark, materials, structure, environment, external appearance and any other visual information that may be communicated in your presentation.

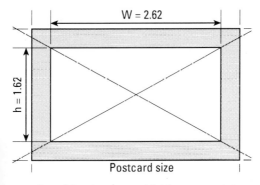

A useful gadget for establishing a general view and composition of a scene.

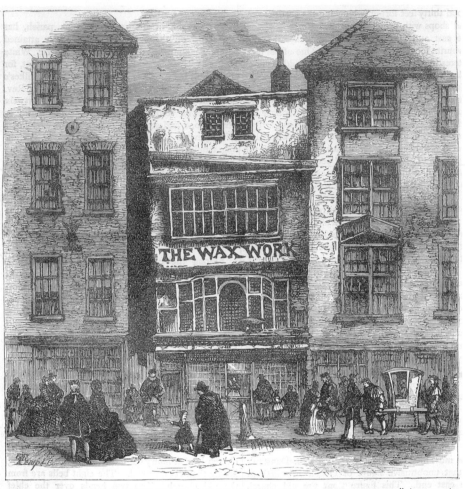

MRS. SALMON'S WAXWORK, FLEET STREET—"PALACE OF HENRY VIII. AND CARDINAL WOLSEY" (*see page* 45).

Use coloured cards and papers, as well as any suitable media, including both freehand and mechanical drawing techniques.

This activity is designed for you to explore both your drawing and presentational skills. Your sense of line, colour, proportion, composition and aesthetic judgement will be used in the development of your low-relief image.

Into what context would you place your completed work?

Evaluate the impact and quality of your work personally and with the aid of an independent critical judgement from someone else. What was it that you designed in this exercise? Which new skills did you learn? What is the relationship between form and function in this study? How would you judge the technical and aesthetic qualities of your image?

Local environment study

This design activity will require you to move out of the studio situation to complete your research and will satisfy many examination boards' requests for students to study their local environment. Preparatory studies of houses and their setting can be carried out using media and styles freely; and you should aim to appreciate that inanimate things, like groups of houses, exude character and atmosphere to which individuals can respond in many ways. You should experiment with different techniques, so as to capture and analyse your response to the built environment. Find personal responses that communicate foreboding, gloom, delight, pride or solitude.

It is impossible to predict the function of a building? Why is it important that architects design dwellings that do not alienate the people who use them? It is equally important that people use and treat their surroundings with care. How much of your view of your locality is determined by other people's opinions? Why are you attached to your home town?

Create a low-relief representation of a doorway in your locality, employing different thicknesses, textures and colours of paper and card, as well as using other media to build up an illusionistic image of a doorway. Where does it lead to? Study aspects of linear perspective as a means of creating the illusion of depth in artwork.

A door at South Shields: drawings and photography by Jean Stokes.

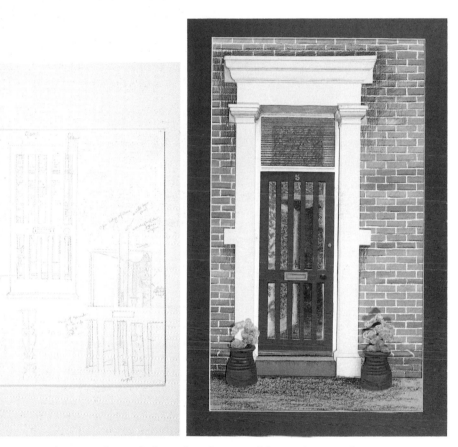

These exercises are intended to develop confidence in visual composition and design, whereby pictorial depth is created by overlaying the visual components of a chosen image. Use depth to create depth in an image. Relate your experience of low-relief modelling to your painting and drawing. Notice how Norman Rockwell creates depth in his illustration *What Makes it Tick?* and consider the technical skills required to paint the glass screen surrounding the watchmaker's work desk.

'What makes it tick?' Printed by permission of the Norman Rockwell Family Trust.

Ambiguous images

This art and design project invites you to study the many aspects of ambiguity that can be found, or placed, in visual images. Always consider the importance of your own ideas and aim to reflect upon what it is that you can see in things. What have you seen in the clouds?

Hamlet: Do you see yonder cloud that's almost in shape of a camel?
Polonius: By the mass, and 'tis like a camel, indeed.
Hamlet: Methinks it is like a weasel.
Polonius: It is backed like a weasel.
Hamlet: Or like a whale?
Polonius: Very like a whale.

(*Hamlet*, Act III, scene 2, lines 366-372)

Students of A-level Art and Design at South Tyneside College and Harton Comprehensive School are following a JMB syllabus. This course, modelled on recent GCSE developments, is largely coursework-based, with strong historical and appreciation input.

War Scene in Lieutenant Deschanel's Face by Salvador Dali. © DEMART PRO ARTE BV/DACS 1994. This image appeared on the cover of *Paris Match*, 12 October 1939.

In the first year of the course, students undergo an intensive analysis of their perception of art and design through a series of planned assignments, often linked to art-historical themes, techniques, processes and concepts. In the second year of the course it is anticipated that students will, to some extent, have achieved a degree of self-motivation and be actively encouraged to pursue personally chosen themes and interests.

The coursework is not undertaken by the students solely for the purpose of assessment but should be part of a teaching and learning process. Important criteria for the award of marks for the coursework are based on students demonstrating their abilities to:

1. Conceive, organize, develop and evaluate various elements in a continuum to produce a coherent visual statement.

2. Identify, analyse and explore design problems, using appropriate strategies, techniques and materials.

3. Use the formal elements with understanding.

4. Show evidence of a personal response to an idea, theme or subject.

5. Work from observed phenomena as an aid to the development of ideas or for their own sake.

6. Organize and present research from both primary and secondary sources.

Advertisement for the painkiller Nurofen.

To achieve maturity in the above objectives, the student should develop in three basic stages. The first stage is the struggle to acquire technique and an independent attitude towards art. The second stage is one of experiment, in which students seek to find what they might express, endeavouring to refine and intensify their vision of the world in order to improve their art. The third stage demands rare qualities. It begins at the point where technical proficiency has been acquired and students know what they want to say, seeking only the power to communicate directly what they know.

The first stage is the only stage that can actually be taught. Students can learn about technique and how to modify some of their attitudes to art, but after this they are alone with only the art of the past and their own sensibilities to guide them. At this point they can move on to the second and third stages and start the search for expression.

An early theme of portraiture in the course at South Tyneside College and Harton School was chosen to take students from a formal rendering technique through a descriptive self-portrait illustrating their likes, interests and attitudes and then to a project based on the transformation of a head or portrait using natural elements.

This project, entitled 'Ambiguous Portrait', was given to the students in the form of a fairly detailed brief, set out below. It was hoped that the procedure, beginning with objectivity, and the subsequent problem-solving activity, leading to a personal conclusion, would clarify the objectives laid down by the JMB.

Study the artwork produced by two students to see how the following brief was executed.

Theme: ambiguous portrait

Introduction

Purchase several types of fruit that are different both in size and shape from one another. You will use the fruit to produce a series of observational drawings. The drawings made will then be used to produce a design-orientated image involving fruit in an anthropometric state.

Method

1. Make a carefully considered set of studies of the fruit you have obtained, analysing surface textures, shape and other details. Approach your fruit from unusual angles as this will help you in the final part of the brief.

2. Use the drawings and cut-out shapes to produce a portrait by articulating and overlapping your images. Identify those drawings which resemble, in your own mind, facial features.

3. Make a pen and ink line drawing of your 'composite' portrait.

4. Produce a colour rendering of your final image in an appropriate colour medium. A mixture of media may be very suitable for this activity. At this stage you may wish to add other elements to your design to develop and improve its composition.

265

Spring and *Summer*, Giuseppe Arcimboldo
(1527–1593).

Refer to your drawings, collages an compositions of fruit as well as to examples of artwork that support this activity. Several examples are given here, but you could also usefully study many other works, especially those of Archimboldo and the use of ambiguous images in modern graphic art and advertising.

Aim

To introduce students to a range of materials through creative application and to encourage the discipline of drawing and observation as a basis for design interpretation.

Example 1 is by Lynn Stephenson, who worked in a systematic way. First, she produced a wide range of observational drawings from different angles to suggest facial features. Enlarged or reduced photocopies of her drawings were collaged to arrive eventually at her conclusion. She produced a line drawing in pen and ink to clarify her composition and finally the water-colour rendering required Lynn to return to observation, in order to analyse colour and texture.

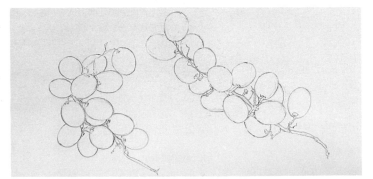

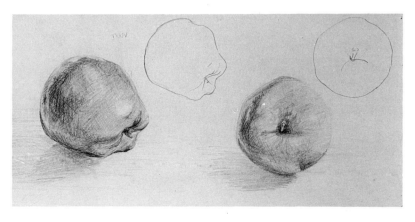

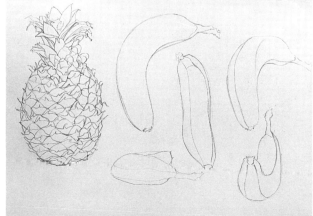

Example 2 is by Ian Drummond, who worked initially with objective drawing but relied largely on imaginative arrangements in sketch form before arriving at his final statement.

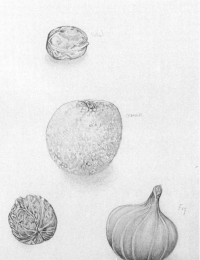

Vierge a l'Enfant by Salvador Dali © DEMART PRO ARTE BV/DACS 1994.

It was important throughout this project that the students made reference to existing works on a similar theme of ambiguity. The work of the seventeenth-century artist Archimboldo, who is most likely to have originated the ambiguous or double image, exploited the idea of two totally different interpretations of the same composition – a man's head could equally well be a pile of fruit.

Leonardo da Vinci referred to the use of chance configurations and the variety of pictures to be seen in crumbling walls, stones and clouds in his *Treatise on Painting*. 'You should look at certain walls stained with damp, or at stones of uneven colour.'

In the early twentieth century Max Ernst was affected by this statement and discovered the possibilities through his technique of 'frottage'. In his *Histoire Naturelle* of 1926, Ernst took crayon rubbings from wood grain and gave the result new interpretations. He altered and edited the rubbings to invent birds, insects, fish and plants. The metamorphoses he obtained owed much to his observations of illusionistic natural phenomena.

A few years later Salvador Dali exploited the dual interpretation to be seen in his *Paranoiac Visage* in *Surréalisme au service de la révolution*.

Visage Paranoiaque by Salvador Dali © DEMART PRO ARTE BV/DACS 1994.

THE MANAGEMENT OF A MAJOR DESIGN PROJECT

As part of the examination requirements for many syllabuses, you will be required to initiate, design and realise an extended project of up to one year's duration. These projects are usually tackled towards the end of your course, when you will already have had a variety of design experiences through your preliminary supporting project work.

The major project gives you the opportunity to practise your skills as a designer over an extended period of time, and the choice of a suitable topic should give you the opportunity to demonstrate both the cognitive skills of designing, such as research, analysis, generating proposals and evaluating, as well as the practical skills of design presentation and realisation, enabling you to complete an advanced piece of work which stretches your ability in all of these areas, and many more.

A musical activity centre for children with special needs was designed by Kathryn Shann, and was a winner in the Schools Design prize.

Rebecca Worsley's design for a feedback analyser to warn people when they are suffering from stress was also a winner of a Schools Design prize.

Selecting a suitable topic

Design – the problem is the problem.

One of the most difficult tasks you face is identifying an appropriate topic that will sustain you own personal interest and enthusiasm, as well as meeting the specific examination assessment criteria of the course you are studying. To help you focus your thoughts around a suitable topic, you will find, listed below, suggestions culled from examination boards, examiners' reports and experienced teachers who have been involved in the supervising of major project work.

- Your study should begin with a real design need that gives opportunity for extensive initial research leading to the formulation of a design brief and specification.

- Avoid the idea that you 'want to make a specific preconceived product', and therefore try to twist the assessment procedure to fit your own personal requirements. There is a considerable difference

THE DESIGN BRIEF

"The Hard Shoulder Of A Motorway Is Possibly The Most Dangerous Stretch Of Roadway In The World". This Was The Comment Made By An A Spokesman In September 1982 After An Horrific Accident In Which Seven People Lost Their Lives. The Incident Occured When A 32 Ton Lorry Crashed Into The Back Of A Hired Minibus Which Had Broken Down On The Hard Shoulder Of The M6. Only The Father And 16yr Old Daughter Survived The Accident And It Was Their Grief I Thought About When I Decided Something Had To Be Done.
    A White Line Only About 1ft Thick And Often Obliterated By Tyre Marks, Seperates The Vehicles Travelling On The Carriageway From The Stationary Vehicles On The Hard Shoulder. This Makes It Necessary For Drivers To Be Made More Aware Of The Hazards On The Hard Shoulder. Hazard Warning Triangles Are Already In Existance But I Felt They Had Fundamental Faults Which Could Be Improved Upon e.g. Too Small, Not Very Clear And Not Illuminated. For These Units To Fulfill There Purpose I Believe It Is Necessary For Legislation To Be Brought In To Make Their Use Compulsory In The Event Of A Breakdown On The Hard Shoulder Or Any Other Stretch Of Road.

DESIGN REQUIREMENTS

THESE ARE JUST SOME OF THE POSSIBILITIES I HAD TO CONSIDER WHEN DESIGNING THE UNIT.

POSSIBLE POWER SOURCES:

1. CIGARETTE LIGHTER SOCKET (12V BATTERY)
2. FROM HAZARD WARNING UNIT (INDICATOR UNIT).
3. STRAIGHT OFF THE BATTERY.
4. FROM REAR LIGHT BULB SOCKET.
5. INDEPENDANT BATTERIES (SMALL TORCH BATTERIES OR 6V MOTORCYCLE BATTERIES BUT THERE COULD BE PROBLEMS WITH ACID LEAKAGE.

POSSIBLE SHAPES:

1. TRIANGLE.
2. CIRCLE.
3. ADVISORY ARROW TO THE LEFT OR RIGHT.
4. COMBINED TRIANGLE AND CIRCLE.

POSSIBLE ADVISORY WORDING:

1. "OBSTRUCTION".
2. "STATIONARY VEHICLE".
3. "KEEP RIGHT".
4. "BEWARE".
5. "HAZARD".
6. "SLOW".

Traffic Hazard Warning System.

Title. The Brief

Sheet No. 2.

Date.

The City Of Leicester School.

between starting with an initial statement such as, 'Looking into the problems of storage that teenagers face in their bedrooms', or 'I want to make a wardrobe'. In practice, the two design routes implicit in these statements are likely to be very different. The first is divergent and looks out from the point of view of the needs of the user; the latter is largely convergent and is based around a stereotyped image of a piece of furniture.

- Your topic should give you sufficient scope to allow you to be able to demonstrate a variety of ideas including a degree of originality, as well as illustrating your knowledge of appropriate materials and processes and the economic implications of selection.

- Ensure that your project has been realistically chosen, taking into account your own expertise, as well as your capacity to develop with the project.

- Consider the amount of time you have available for commitment to this course as well as the other subjects you might be studying. What percentage of the marks does it carry? Set your targets realistically with these points in mind.

- Do you have the available resources at your centre to match the likely outcome of the project, i.e. in both expertise of staff and production facilities? Are there any industrial or commercial interests you can approach for assistance or sponsorship?

- There may be considerable financial implications if you embark on certain projects. Have you considered these points fully?

- If you embark upon a design project for someone else, for example a nursery school, local hospital or disabled neighbour, the organisation or individual concerned may contribute some financial assistance with the project, in addition to providing you with excellent objective feedback as your ideas develop. You should be able to build good user–client relationship, culminating in an independent evaluation of the final artefact.

- However, you need to avoid the scenario where you think you are designing for a third party, only to find that they tell you exactly what they want and how you should do it. You need to explain to potential collaborators the educational and assessment background against which your project is taking place. This ensures that both parties are aware of their responsibilities and rights in connection with the project.

- Carefully study the assessment schedule relating to your examination course and ensure that your topic gives you the opportunity to fulfil and score highly against these published criteria.

- You need to plan your project carefully to pace yourself throughout the year. There is always the danger that you underestimate the amount of time required to realise the project and do not actually build in additional time for things to go wrong, as they almost invariably will, given the nature of the research and developmental work you will be tackling.

- Your project will usually be assessed in May of your final year (check specific syllabuses for dates). This is also the time when you will be revising for written examinations in this subject and others. Do leave yourself time and energy to prepare yourself thoroughly for these other commitments. Ensure that you plan to complete your project allowing yourself sufficient time for thorough testing and evaluation, in addition to completing your design folio and project report.

- It is never too early to think about your major project. Indeed, it is a good idea to try to have more than one proposal to discuss with your project supervisor before you narrow it down to a final choice. In particular, use other students in your group as a 'sounding board' for your ideas. They can sometimes be brutally honest! Your teacher may ask you to complete a project proposal form and this is good means of focusing your mind on the project's essential structure. Whether specified on a form or in discussion important elements to consider are:
- the starting point of the project;
- the sources of initial research you will explore during the summer vacation, eg contacts, organisations, visits, reference material etc;

1. *Identifying needs and problems within a context*

   This group concerns the initial selection of a situation/area which contains a possible need or opportunity, together with the further elaboration of a more specific task.

   The criteria are:
   - the range of possible outcomes and their potential for extension;
   - matching the choice to the resources available to the candidate;
   - matching the choice to the examination assessment framework;
   - finding (or generating) and organising relevant information;
   - soundness of investigational strategy;
   - specifying the design requirements.

	Teacher's comments or statement of key evidence	Teacher's mark
HIGH ABILITY (*8 – 10*) – identifies a good range of possible outcomes, many of which are capable of extension; – shows clear and reasonable view of available resources, own abilities, and demands of the project; – acquires wide range of valid information from a variety of relevant sources, using a range of methods; – evolves a sound personal strategy for investigation; – produces a comprehensive and detailed product design specification. **MEDIUM ABILITY** (*4 – 7*) – identifies several questions, with rather limited vision of their further potential; – shows reasonable ability to recognise resource and ability limitations, but with significant omissions; – discovers an adequate range of relevant information; – can. create a reasonable strategy for investigation given some assistance; – can recognise the more obvious design requirements, but overlooks a number of important considerations. **LOW ABILITY** (*1 – 3*) – identifies few possible outcomes, of limited potential; – unable to recognise resource and ability limitations without considerable assistance; – discovers only limited amount of relevant information; – needs considerable help to create a strategy for investigation; – unable to specify realistic design requirements.		.... OR [*If more than one teacher is assessing candidates enter agreed mark below.*] .... Moderator's mark ....

- main areas of expertise with which you feel you may need assistance, eg product design and manufacture, graphic design, electronics, computing etc. This will help in placing you with a suitable adviser. While you need persistence as a designer, avoid being foolhardy. If everyone you meet is unhappy about your proposal, always consider that they may be right and you may be wrong.

Making a start

While most design educators would argue that there is no set sequence to the various activities that make up the process of designing, the dilemma faced by examination boards is that, as administrators and custodians of educational standards, they must publish and conform to a set of agreed criteria, which can, they hope, be flexibly interpreted by students, teachers and moderators. On the one hand, they have to provide an assessment framework to encourage individual creativity, while on the other they hope to avoid prescription and the stifling of individuality. An example of the criteria used for assessment in the University of Oxford Delegacy of Local Examinations Design and Technology (Design) A Level examination are shown below. These criteria are used for the assessment of the major project and the five elements are 1. Identifying needs and problems within a context', 2. Generation of ideas, 3. Planning and realisation, 4. Evaluation and 5. Communicating. In addition to these general criteria for the assessment of the project section 1 is further detailed to give an indication of the range of marks students would attain based on the evidence of work presented.

2. *Generation of ideas*

This group concerns the generating of an overall design concept; it builds on the investigation, but can also modify the outcome. It concerns the handling and organisation of ideas, judging and testing them, and building a secure base for more detailed work.

The criteria are:

- creating an overall concept or 'model' (including spatial, mathematical, and conceptual models);
- the construction of hypotheses, and handling orders of magnitude;
- discovering, creating, organising, and recording ideas;
- optimising within the conflicting needs of manufacture and the user, as well as the requirements of design;
- experimenting, and assessing risk on a numerical as well as on a judgmental basis;
- judging the strengths and weaknesses of ideas, and justifying decisions;
- the ability further to modify ideas.

3. *Planning and realization*

This group concerns the creation of the outcome. It involves the planning of a strategy for producing the outcome, as well as the making itself. It builds on 'the generation of ideas', but experience as production proceeds may require further modification to the concept.

The criteria are:

- defining the product/outcome in appropriate detail;
- making economical use of materials, components, and time;
- planning a strategy, including sequence and length of tasks, and procuring resources and assistance;
- acquiring skills and knowledge necessary for manufacture, determining necessary finish, accuracy, etc;
- taking responsibility for work done other than by the candidate;
- bringing to bear knowledge, understanding, and skills from other subjects, as well as the theoretical content of the syllabus itself.

4. *Evaluation*

This group concerns the way that candidates and others review the work. Evaluation occurs continuously during, as well as at the end of, the work. The evaluation reflects the outcome, the context, and the candidate's approach.

The criteria, applied frequently during the course of the work, are:

– the ability to review the outcome and its possible consequences against the original design specification;

– the ability to use judgment, and the results of formal testing to suggest further improvement;

– the candidate's ability to evaluate his/her strategies and approaches;

– the ability to consider, and respond to, the evaluation of others.

5. *Communicating*

This group concerns the way that candidates report and present their work as a whole; this includes producing a unifying document which is either a traditional report or an integral series of charts with associated text. It also includes the outcome of the project itself.

The criteria are:

– the coherence of explanation and reporting, including the strategies and methods used, and the interpretation and validity of information acquired and used;

– the quality of communication, including the use of an adequate range of appropriate styles and media, and matching the communication to the purpose and the audience.

A major project – the 'safety nest'

One way of attempting to devise a major project is to listen to public opinion and comments. This is what Richard Webster did when he identified a common complaint of parents with young children concerning the transporting of young children from a baby buggy into a safety seat in the back of a car. From an initial market survey, he

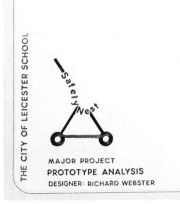

Baby Nest logo.

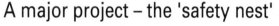

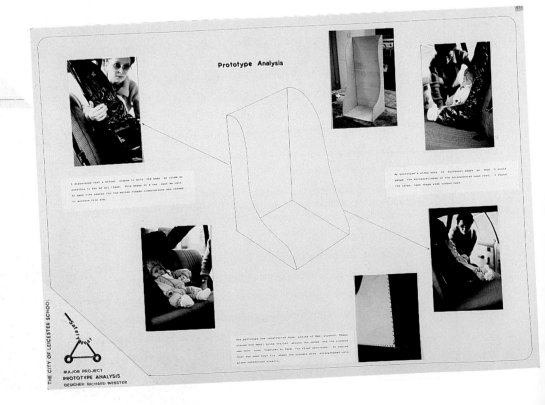

Design sheet – prototype analysis.

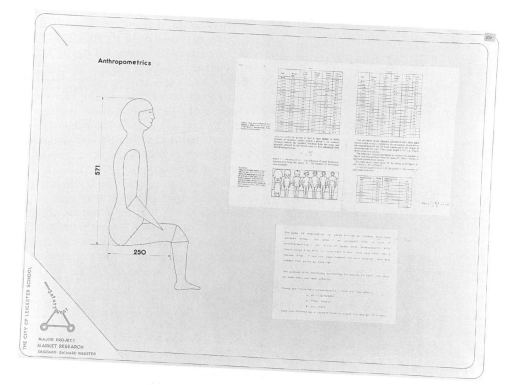

Design sheet – anthropometrics.

GRP split-mould for the seat and wooden 'plug'.

Plywood prototypes.

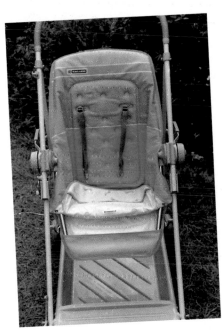

The general arrangement of the seat in the buggy.

A 'clip' attachment moulded as an integral part of the seat frame.

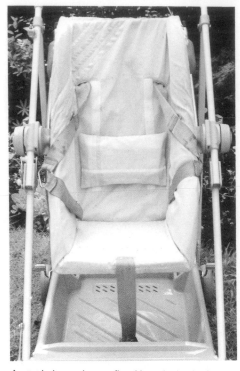

A seat belt attachment fitted into the back of the shell.

Attaching the top/central seat belt anchor into the car.

discovered that there were either baby buggies or safety seats, but not a dual-purpose product that could be used for both. At an early stage in the project he contacted Andrews Maclaren Ltd., a company that specialise in baby buggies. Richard realised that there was nothing wrong with the buggy design; the main problem was the ergonomics and structure of the seating element within the design that had to be capable of operating within the buggy frame and, once removed, attaching quickly into the car. Andrews Maclaren generously allowed Richard to design his project around their 'Dreamer DeLuxe' buggy, and the race was on to find a solution.

At an early stage of the design, a number of plywood prototypes were tested to assess the anthropometrics of different babies, as well as their fixing and handling characteristics in both the buggy and the car. Following further analysis and evaluation, Richard decided to make the shell of the seat from glass-reinforced polyester, and he experimented with a number of different seat belt fixings to optimise the speedy transfer of the 'safety nest', as it had now been named.

The transfer of the baby from the buggy to the car.

Getting organised!

One of the most demanding qualities required by students engaged in advanced design work is the need to deploy efficient organisational strategies to assist, and indeed ensure, progress in their chosen major project. These kinds of problems are not new to industry and commerce, and a number of techniques have evolved to support the needs of project leaders involved in complex organisational management. In particular, critical path analysis, also known as critical path method, network planning, and the related system PERT (programme evaluation and review technique), evolved from pressures generated during the Second World War to deal with the most efficient means of supplying military equipment against the background of the unfavourable industrial conditions of the time.

An understanding of critical path analysis will be useful in your own practical project work, as well as helping you to understand the complex procedures adopted in industry and commerce. However, it must be remembered that design is inherently unpredictable and

Critical path analysis using MAC Project software for lighting project.

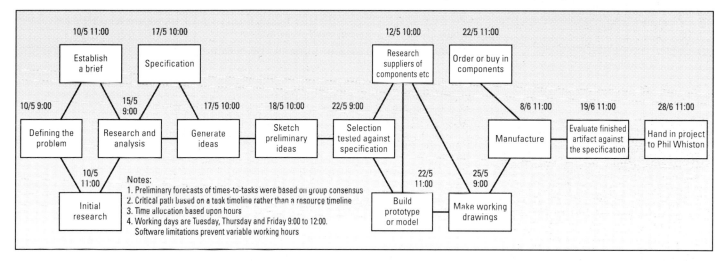

	Task Name	Hours	Earliest Start	Earliest Finish	Latest Start	Latest Finish	Fixed Cost	Resource Cost	Fixed Income	Resource 1
1	Defining the problem	2	10/5/90	10/5/90	10/5/90	10/5/90	0	0	0	
2	Establish a brief	2	10/5/90 11:00	11/5/90 10:00	11/5/90 10:00	15/5/90 9:00	0	0	0	
3	Initial research	4	10/5/90	15/5/90	10/5/90	15/5/90	0	0	0	
4	Research and analysis	4	15/5/90	17/5/90	15/5/90	17/5/90	0	0	0	
5	Specification	1	17/5/90 10:00	17/5/90 11:00	18/5/90 9:00	18/5/90 10:00	0	0	0	
6	Generate ideas	3	17/5/90	18/5/90	17/5/90	18/5/90	0	0	0	
7	Sketch preliminary ideas	2	18/5/90	22/5/90	18/5/90	22/5/90	0	0	0	
8	Selection tested against	1	22/5/90	22/5/90	22/5/90	22/5/90	0	0	0	
9	Research suppliers of	1	22/5/90	22/5/90	22/5/90	22/5/90	0	0	0	
10	Build prototype or model	4	22/5/90	25/5/90	22/5/90	25/5/90	0	0	0	
11	Order or buy in components	8	22/5/90 11:00	29/5/90 10:00	5/6/90 9:00	8/6/90 11:00	0	0	0	
12	Make working drawings	20	25/5/90	8/6/90	25/5/90	8/6/90	0	0	0	
13	Manufacture	12	8/6/90	19/6/90	8/6/90	19/6/90	0	0	0	
14	Evaluate finished artifact	12	19/6/90	28/6/90	19/6/90	28/6/90	0	0	0	
15	Hand in project to Phil	1	28/6/90	29/6/90	28/6/90	29/6/90	0	0	0	

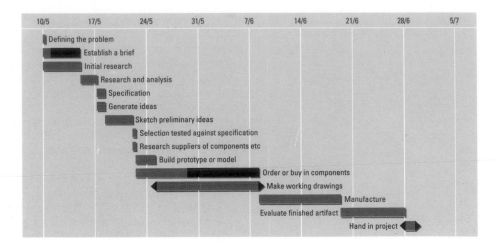

difficult to quantify except in the broadest terms. Consequently, its management must be flexible and you must accept that some decisions, which may be made on the basis of incomplete data, will need to be monitored and updated as necessary. The following quotation illustrates the logic of the scheme:

> Many industries have preconceived ideas about how projects should be run and which are the important tasks. One of the earliest industries to take up CPA was the shipbuilding industry. For them the key event which marked the progress of a new ship was the launch. The early networks showed a maze of activities conducted on the slipway all culminating in the all-important launch; then a second phase which took place in the dock. It was soon realised that many activities, such as the installation of electrical wiring, plumbing, air-conditioning and other services and the work of carpenters and painters, did not have to reach a specific point before the launch. Work simply stopped for the launch day then carried on in a different location. Soon the picture of the project had changed completely. The launch became a minor activity which could take place anytime after the hull was watertight and painted. Other activities were more important and the discipline of simply examining the logic of building a ship gave greater understanding of the process than had been derived from thousands of years of history. (*Engineering Design Teaching Aids* 'Design Management' Colin Ledsome)

Critical path analysis can be defined as a method of planning and maintaining control of the most logical and economically efficient sequence of operations for the purpose of completing a project. The technique may be applied to industrial applications where the provision of materials, labour and industrial components may have to be brought together to produce a new product, or it may be concerned with bringing together an administrative procedure as part of the setting up of a new organisation.

This management technique is widely used to organise and control a project where a number of participating demands such as the supply of materials, and availability of labour and plant have to link and interface with one another at critical points in time to ensure that the project advances within an agreed schedule.

The purpose of CPA can be summarised as follows:

- To design a sequential programme to enable an individual or organisation to achieve a specified outcome.

- To identify all the inputs that are required within the project, such as labour, materials, expertise, equipment and finance.

- To establish and monitor the time requirements for these inputs, both in terms of 'when?' and 'how long?', and to allocate and deploy the resources to the project as required.

- To identify agreed areas of responsibility within the project and monitor performance and progress, appraising and updating the schedule if necessary.

Planning a network diagram

The network diagram is produced to illustrate the flow of the project from its beginning, or 'start event' to its completion, or 'end event'. Essentially, the network diagram is a graphic that illustrates every stage or 'activity' essential to the successful completion of the project. Each activity is represented by an arrow constructed from a solid line with a simple note to describe the activity. The arrowhead points towards the completion of the activity and the chart reads from left to right.

The arrows connect at points that indicate stages in the sequence of operations. These points are known as 'events' and are represented on the chart as circles, which are then numbered to represent the logical sequence in which the events take place.

Produce a network diagram for the following:

1. Repairing a puncture in a bicycle inner tube.

2. Defrosting and cleaning a fridge.

3. Preparing a breakfast consisting of cereals, toast and coffee.

4. Changing the engine oil and filter in a car, and replacing and resetting the spark plugs.

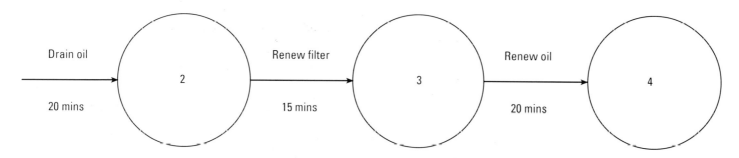

Identify tasks – allocate time – select calendar dates

In the initial stages you may draw the network a number of times before you select the best plan, so quick sketches are recommended before a neater version is drawn up. Remember to involve in your discussions other individuals who may influence your planning.

All the activities in the diagram represented by a solid line require an allocation of time to allow for their completion. However, broken lines may appear in the diagram, which serve to illustrate the relationship between one activity and another. These are referred to as 'dummy' activities.

However, to maintain flexibility, it has to be recognised that while some activities cannot begin until the proceeding activity has been completed, certain activities can be continued independently of one another and can proceed in parallel. They only need to link up with one another in the main network diagram when they assume reliance on another activity in order to proceed.

As the project progresses, there will be a frequent need to update the diagram, particularly if the project is an original piece of design that is being undertaken for the first time. Can you imagine the logistics of building the Channel Tunnel and trying to identify all the potential engineering problems inherent in this type of grand scheme? How realistic is it to expect this type of project to be built on time and to an agreed budget? This type of project is different from an operation that may have been carried out many times before, for example the servicing of an aircraft, where most activities and events will have been clearly established by previous experience.

The Channel Tunnel Development: Lower Shakespeare Cliff.

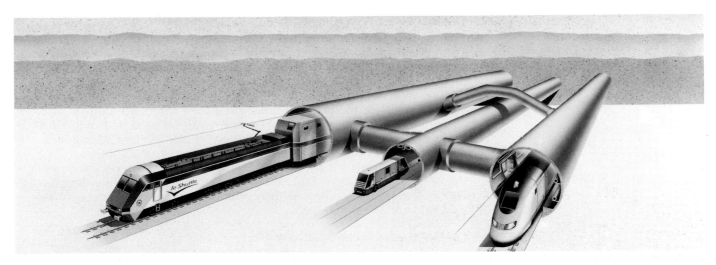

Diagram of the tunnel, showing service tunnels.

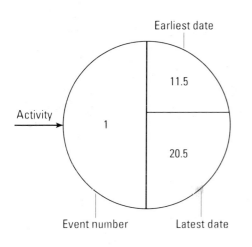

Earliest date

11.5

Activity

1

20.5

Event number   Latest date

Time analysis

Once the sequence of operations is identified, it is necessary to estimate the amount of time required for each activity and add this to the relevant activity arrow. Deciding on time durations for tasks is a difficult part of project planning for the novice. It is only through experience that people get to know how much time to allocate. If you are uncertain about task durations, you should seek advice from others who have experience of that type of activity.

When this time factor has been added to the overall plan, it is possible to see which aspects of the plan need to be carefully controlled or even modified to ensure that the project will be completed on time. To help the planner build some flexibility into the network diagram, any spare time or 'float' must be identified. The identification of this spare time may prove extremely valuable if the network has to be updated. When the 'float' has been identified, this information is included in the event circle.

In the diagram illustrated, the planner has identified nine days float that might prove very useful if problems occur during the activity and result in that activity overrunning the schedule.

Before an event can be reached, all supporting activities must be completed. Where an event is reliant upon more than one activity, then the longest path determines the earliest date. An activity that overruns and is delayed beyond its latest finishing date will extend the total project duration and perhaps create problems for other activities and events that have already been planned unless some redistribution of resources or labour can be deployed in other activities to shorten their timescale.

The critical path

If all the events without float are linked together, the sequence will form the longest path through the network and reveal the project duration. Any delay along this path will extend the project and this route is therefore known as the 'critical path', represented by . . . . on the network diagram. However, complex projects may include more than one critical path.

Whatever planning technique is adopted it should be used as a guide rather than deployed as a rigid scheme. Consequently, the planner must continually appraise and adjust the network in order to produce an acceptable framework within which the desired outcome can be achieved.

The Channel Tunnel – project management on a grand scale. Do you think the Channel Tunnel will provide more efficient links with Europe? What about its impact on the environment and on ferry design? Will you use it, or travel by ferry?

Calendar dates

The final stage of the planning process is to set the network diagram against real calendar dates to enable the plan to be assessed within an operational context where factors such as weekends and holidays may influence the progress of the project. When these dates are established, you are in a position to order materials and services, and to inform subcontractors of the point in time when their input is required. This co-ordination is very important because it will be seen that theoretical networks cannot be designed in isolation by one planner sitting at a desk. If the network is to be credible, then participating individuals must be aware of their place in the scheme. The interdependence of the network means that individuals who cannot meet agreed targets will jeopardise the validity of the network and the final success of the project.

Computer-aided network planning

So far the planning scheme has involved the use of manual calculations and while this is easily controlled on medium-sized projects, for longer and more complex operations computer software programs are available. In addition to handling the complexity of the project, this software can quickly reassess any changing circumstances and update times and events simultaneously.

Further information

The above offers only an outline of the techniques of network planning; for further, more detailed, information, reference should be made to specific texts or software packages that deal with project management. These include the British Standards Institute's publications:

BS 4335 *Glossary of Terms Used in Project Network Techniques;*
BS 6046 Parts 2–4 *Use of Network Techniques in Project Management.*

The earliest known English patent of invention was granted to John of Utynam in 1449. The patent gave John a twenty-year monopoly for a method of making stained glass that had not been previously known in England.

Design protection

As your major design project evolves, you may realise that you have produced a very original piece of work which you feel needs to be legally protected in some form or other. You may feel that perhaps there could be some commercial worth in what you have produced and that you ought to take the opportunity to exploit this if possible.

You will not be alone in coming to this conclusion; indeed, each week over 500 applications for new patents alone arrive at the Patent Office. This section explores the variety of ways in which you can protect your work, and begins by exploring the reasons for this ancient, but very necessary, practice.

> The creation and development of new technologies and industries, and the encouragement and growth of commerce, are essential to the economic well-being of the United Kingdom. To achieve advances in these areas depends not only on the ingenuity of scientists, engineers and others, but also on the investment necessary to develop new ideas and set up new enterprises as well as the ability to market them effectively. Intellectual property rights, that is patents, registered designs and the design right, registered trade marks and service marks, and copyright, play an important part in bringing these various factors together. In all cases, they give legal recognition to the ownership of new ideas or brand names and give the proprietor the right to stop other people exploiting his property. So they create for the innovator a system by which he can benefit from his ingenuity, be it the invention of an electronic timer, the design of a fashion shoe, the marketing of chocolate bars under a new brand name, or the creation of a new musical. Typically, the rights will be sold or licensed to others or will be used to safeguard investment in new ventures, so that the ideas they represent may be developed and exploited to the ultimate benefit of us all.
> (*What is Intellectual Property?*, the Patent Office)

This quotation illustrates the important role played by legal protection for all aspects of invention, design and marketing. However, first impressions can prove confusing and complex when you try to

Towards the end of the reign of Elizabeth I, the granting of patents of invention had become a common practice. However, the Queen did refuse to grant patents in certain cases. For example, in 1596, Sir John Harrington's request for a patent on his design for a water closet was turned down on the grounds of propriety.

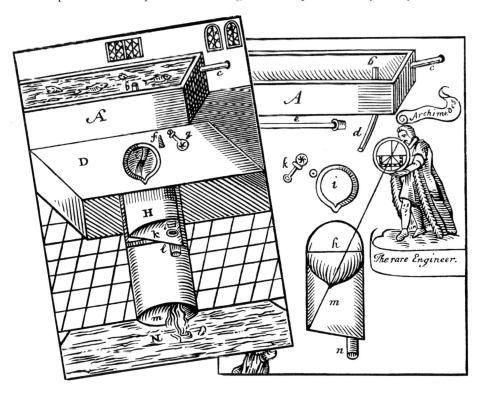

work out whether your idea should be patented, copyrighted, registered as a design or protected in some other way. If invention in design and industry is to be encouraged, it is vital that the individuals and organisations who expend a considerable amount of time in developing new ideas receive both the intellectual credit and any financial rewards that may accrue from their success. However, it must also be remembered that if protection is obtained to cover a piece of work, it is still up to the individual to safeguard his or her own interests. No organisation exists to police patents; consequently, if you believe you have a claim against another party who has copied your work, then it is your responsibility to initiate litigation and defend your patent. This can be both expensive and time consuming and should not be entered into without considerable legal advice. You will have to decide whether you can risk the financial outlay and whether it will be worth it in the long run. Making this decision can be far more difficult for private individuals than for larger commercial concerns who are often far better prepared to defend their interests against would-be predators. If you find the idea of defending your work a rather daunting prospect, then you may choose to sell, hire out or license your protected design like any other business commodity.

James Watt's patent for the improvement of the steam engine, 1796, was the subject of extensive litigation which eventually established that valid patents could be granted for improvements to a known machine.

Patents

The Patent Office receives over 30,000 applications per year covering a diverse range of proposals and products including games, mechanical engineering, photography, electronics, medicines and many more. For an invention to be patentable, it 'must be concerned with the composition, construction or manufacture of a substance, article or apparatus, or with an industrial type of process' that is new, must be inventive and must be capable of industrial application. Exceptions include artistic creations, mathematical methods, computer programs, business schemes and new methods of medical treatment.

1880 – 'Great minds think alike'. It is rare that identical inventions should come about at the same time. But that is what happened with the electric light bulb, which was patented almost simultaneously on either side of the Atlantic by Edison and Swan. To avoid patent squabbles, the two business interests combined in England to produce the lamps under the name of © Ediswan', which is still registered as a trademark.

1930 – 'It'll never work'. Patents are granted for inventions that can be made. But that does not mean that the products should be capable of being mass produced. Whittle's patent for the jet engine described a system that would work but which, at the time, would not work efficiently and could not be manufactured on an industrial scale. In fact, the RAF, Whittle's employers, had so little faith in his proposals that they allowed his first patent to lapse.

Design registration

While patents are used to protect the unique and novel aspect of a piece of equipment, product or process, and are therefore more concerned with the function of the proposal, it is also recognised that the visual appearance of an artefact may prove to be a vital selling point due to its unique outward form or decorative treatment. Consequently, while a new form of shutter release in a camera may be patentable, the exclusive form of the whole camera body can be protected by a registered design or design right. Prints used for textiles and wall coverings may also be registered.

Important changes in the law, regulations and forms relating to design registration were introduced on 1 August 1989 by the Copyright Designs and Patents Act 1988 and by the Registered Designs Rules 1989. These are outlined simply in the document *Introducing Design Registration – Supplement*, produced by the Patent Office in which it is stated:

Under the new provisions, the protection afforded to three-dimensional articles by copyright in the original designer's drawings or plans is removed. Equivalent protection of three-dimensional articles is now provided by a new, 'DESIGN RIGHT' which, like copyright, is automatic (i.e. requires no application to the Patent Office). The duration of protection is 10 years from the first marketing of articles made to the design subject to an overall limit of 15 years from the creation of the design. Design Right protection does not prevent additional protection being obtained for the design by registration (provided the design otherwise satisfies the criteria for registration).

Copyright

Copyright gives rights to the creators of original material such as music, sound recordings, films, video, written work, artistic work and drawings. These rights enable the creators to limit the use of their original work or to obtain royalties for its reproduction. Thus, the authors of this book, being the originators of the work, will obtain royalties from Longman Group UK Limited, who, as publishers, own the copyright. As an individual, you may copyright your own drawings by placing a © on the work and adding your name and the date.

Registered trade marks and service marks

This form of protection is aimed at maintaining the goodwill and reputation of a firm and its products or services. Many companies have trade names and logos which the consumer readily identifies, and which promote a company's image in the way they wish. These trade marks may be registered or unregistered and this may be the single most important marketing tool a company has. Many companies register their trading identity to prevent others from trading under their name. Counterfeiting of goods can be a very sophisticated form of deception, where the reproduction of a company's trade mark is used to market often cheap and inferior items of similar products. These products are then purchased by unsuspecting consumers under the assumption that they are buying a quality product, only to discover at a later stage that they have been 'conned'.

Protection issues

The laws surrounding design protection are complex and detailed and the notes in this section should be seen only as a brief introduction to this topic. Any type of protection you may take out will be supported by a legal document which, if it is to stand up to possible challenges in court, must be very carefully drafted. A patent agent will compile and file your application using the recognised formal terminology and appropriate drawings. He or she will offer professional advice and give you the confidentiality and security that a DIY approach cannot provide.

One key issue is that of confidentiality. If you have an invention or design that you wish to exploit, you should not discuss it with, or show it to, anyone who is not under a legal obligation of confidentiality by contract or by nature of your relationship with them.

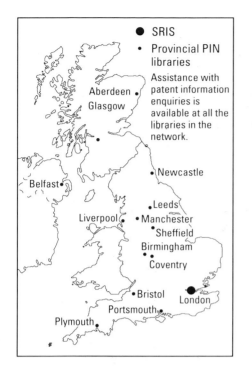

The UK Patent Information Network. In addition to the resources available in London at the SRIS, patent information facilities are provided at thirteen public libraries around the country. Each of these PIN libraries has substantial holdings of British and foreign patent specifications, abstracts and indices.

Housed in the building constructed at the turn of the century for the Patent Office Library, the Science Reference Information Service contains not only patent publications, but also a vast range of other scientific and technical literature.

If you disclose your invention to anyone else, or put it on display before you file your application for a patent, then the law constitutes this as a prior publication which will disqualify your application.

If you are employed and your design or invention is produced as a result of your work for that company, the exclusivity of your contract with an employer usually means that the invention or design belongs to them. However, if you feel that the patent is of outstanding benefit to the company, it is possible to claim compensation from your employer above and beyond normal remuneration. In some cases, employed designers or inventors, even when working in their own time and using their own resources, may find that, contractually, their employer still has some claim on their work.

Patent search

The Science Reference and Information Service (SRIS) forms a major part of the British Library and is based in London. It holds the specifications and abstracts of every British patent going back to 1617 when the series was first published. Today, the SRIS receives patents, trade marks and design publications from 38 countries and has a total of 23 million overseas patent applications. There is also the UK Patent Information Network, from where patent information facilities are provided at thirteen public libraries around the country. At an early stage in your work it is important to establish whether your idea is truly original or has already been registered. The following advice is recommended by the Patent Office:

. . . the Patent and registered trade mark and service mark database are publicly available to be searched, either by the applicant himself or with the assistance of a commercial search service such as the Search and Advisory Service of the Patent Office. Moreover, the applicant can ask the Design Registry to conduct a search on his/her behalf. In addition there is a Patent Information Network of libraries in many of the principal cities of the United Kingdom, and the libraries will be glad to assist any enquirer to locate the relevant prior art. Your local business libraries should also be consulted as necessary.

The use of databases to research around your subject may also prove helpful in identifying a variety of ways in which different problems have already been solved. This, in turn, may advance your own thinking on a particular subject and assist in developing your own proposals.

The original patent Office Library, which was situated in a long, dark corridor, was soon nicknamed 'the Drain Pipe'. From the beginning, the Patent Office emphasised the importance of publishing patent information. At one point in the Victorian era, 400 provincial centres carried patent documents for the public to consult.

Both the Patent Office and SRIS have access to many computerised databases. For a scale of fees, patent examiners of SRIS staff can carry out extensive up-to-date sophisticated patent searches.

PRACTISING DESIGN – STUDENTS' COMMENTS

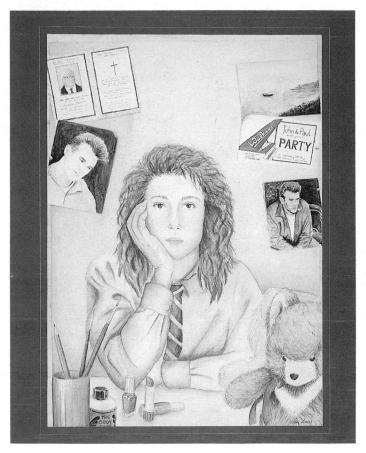

Self-portrait by Lisa Amos.

Lisa Amos

I found that some people have the idea that studying art is an easy option for A-level because they do not realise that it is as demanding as any other subject. The pupils who do opt for art because they think it is easy usually drop out of the course after a few weeks when they have found out just what is involved. A-level art is a lot different from O level; I became more dedicated and I was expected to do a lot of work in my own time in order to be successful. Our teacher constantly pushed and encouraged us to work hard and produce pieces of work reasonably fast. We became used to working quickly in order to complete our exam composition piece in the three weeks we were given, and those of us who wanted to go on to do an art foundation course had to build up a good portfolio.

We were given a new project every month or so, which was very like a brief that a professional artist or designer would get when being commissioned, for example to do a book illustration. In this way, we learned what it would be like to have a career in art, while at the same time we were building up a good selection of work. The rest of our time was spent learning about the history of art in preparation for our art history exam which had to be passed, and we had some practice at figure drawing, ready for our six-hour drawing exam.

I have always enjoyed art, especially being able to stand back and look at what I have achieved, and also knowing that others can see it and appreciate it as well. It gave me great satisfaction building up a portfolio over the two-year course. I only have to look back at the first few pieces of work I did at the beginning to see how much I have progressed during the A-level course.

I am currently doing an art foundation course at Sunderland Polytechnic and I have specialised in painting. It is completely different from A-level Art in many ways; it allows us to loosen up and be more expressive and therefore I found it difficult to adapt to the foundation course having just finished my A-levels.

I am hoping to be accepted for a BA Honours course at Sunderland Polytechnic to study fine art, in particular painting. I hope to complete this successfully and to find a career for myself in art. It has always been a competitive field, and therefore prospects cannot be brilliant for everyone. However, that is a chance that all students of art have to take and I would rather work hard at this subject than choose a career in some other field, to which I was less dedicated and found less enjoyable.

Loz Farmer

Loz Farmer studied design at O- and A-level before obtaining a BA Honours on the Design for Industry course at Newcastle-upon-Tyne Polytechnic. He is now an industrial designer working in London and recalls some of his learning experiences.

Having successfully completed and immensely enjoyed my O-level design course, the logical progression appeared to be the A-level course. I recall becoming disillusioned with traditional run-of-the-mill subjects which rarely, if at all, rewarded creativity and originality and I remember all too vividly my inept efforts at art. However, even at sixteen I could foresee my future in the design field. The A-level course particularly attracted my interest and I looked forward to the increased depth of project work, the freedom to develop one's own brief, the wider scope of the theoretical studies and the emphasis on personal design awareness across a wider spectrum of design.

As I progressed through the two-year course I gradually became aware of the tremendous amount of time I spent on coursework. The many evenings spent on O-level coursework became part of a habit that continued through A-level and remain with me today, along with the late-night panic before a deadline. Some people may regard such last-minute efforts as poor planning or a lack of organisation. I would disagree; design is a discipline in which there is never an ultimate solution to any particular problem and therefore one is continually striving towards the optimum solution and an eleventh-hour idea can throw even the most meticulous schedule into disarray. During the course, the setting of interim deadlines at regular intervals was central to the smooth running of my project work, and is now an integral part of any project in which I am involved. Such deadlines, either meetings with the 'client', discussions with outside specialists or purely the completion of stages of the project brief, also function as evaluation points – an opportunity to step back, take stock of the project to date and check that everything is progressing satisfactorily.

The major project in the second year of the course was my first real experience of a long-term design project running over a period of seven or eight months, and required the application of the whole range of skills and techniques that I had developed during the previous three years.

The project area I chose was home video security, a problem that I became aware of through incessant reports in the local press of video recorder thefts from houses. Over the following months the project included initial consultation with the Police Crime Prevention Squad, research into video security devices already available and market research among owners to establish whether there might be a market for such a product. I produced simple working prototypes of my proposals as well as developing my expertise in electronic circuits capable of being part of an integral alarm system. I found the major project a rewarding challenge and it was during this time that I became increasingly interested in using my skills as a vehicle to design mass-produced products and machines – to be an industrial designer.

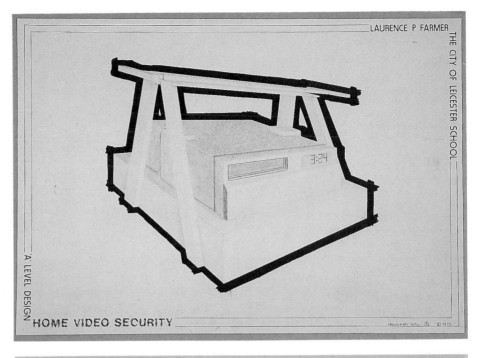

LAURENCE P FARMER

THE CITY OF LEICESTER SCHOOL

'A' LEVEL DESIGN

HOME VIDEO SECURITY

A-level Major project – the home security device employed mechanical and electronic features to keep its contents safe.

THE HOME VIDEO SECURITY SYSTEM.

Design features of the Home Video Security System.

After researching higher education courses, I decided my first choice would be the BA (Hons) Design for Industry course at Newcastle-upon-Tyne Polytechnic. A step I would recommend to any potential student looking for a course is to make informal visits to colleges to speak to staff and students. Such visits helped my selection process and staff comments on my portfolio were particularly helpful in preparing for interviews. I gained entry to the course direct from A-levels and found the transition from school to polytechnic an exciting and also intimidating experience. Suddenly I found myself in an unusual environment, among a highly competitive group of similarly motivated people. With hindsight, I feel that those people who

An extract from Loz's A-level Major Project design report, highlighting the testing of a wall support bracket.

make a concerted effort to get the most out of polytechnic life will undoubtedly gain from the experience; however, one shouldn't waste the opportunity to broaden your social, cultural and recreational horizons either.

The structure of the course included a number of introductory projects in the first year and then a variety of 'live' projects working with manufacturers, as well as a variety of industrial placements. These, in my case, included working for ICI as part of a multi-disciplinary design team, operating alongside an in-house design team as part of a manufacturing concern and finally working in a well-established design consultancy back in my home town of Leicester. It was during this last placement that I realised I wanted my design career to develop within a consultancy environment, providing a much wider mix of work and experience than can be found within the design department of a manufacturing company.

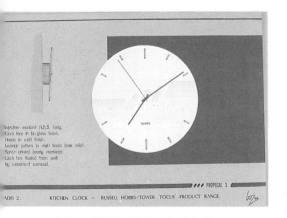

A Russell Hobbs kitchen clock design.

Office furniture design project realised to a model form.

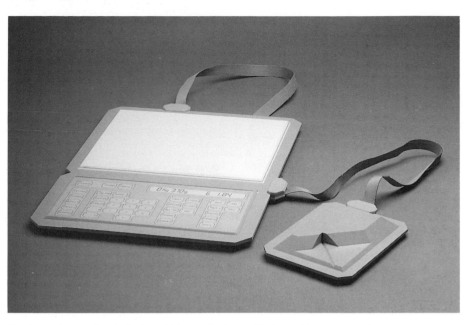

An electronic postal scale design which won for Loz an RSA travel bursary award.

It is true to say that a tremendous effort was required towards the end of the course to complete all the project work in time for assessment. Many of my colleagues joined me in fighting through several sleep-starved weeks. This workload was not lightened by the need to compile several detailed retrospective and analytical reports on the evaluation of my major project, a system of letter mail transportation, undertaken in conjunction with the Royal Mail. I was not to know that the need to present lengthy proposal reports and strategic planning documents is a growing aspect of professional practice and that to be at ease with written language is a great advantage.

Upon leaving the polytechnic I decided I would prefer to be a 'big fish in a small pond' rather than become lost among the layers of junior designers in a large, albeit high-prestige, consultancy. I took this view for several reasons:

1. More say in decision-making at an earlier stage.

2. My value may be more easily recognised and more likely to be fully rewarded.

3. More client contact and therefore a broader range of skills would develop at an earlier stage in my career.

4. Ability to grow with the company.

5. A clearer picture of how a consultancy works, as most designers harbour a vague future ambition to run their own professional practice.

6. Greater responsibility.

To this end I began my professional career working for two or three small design consultancies on a freelance basis. Within a matter of weeks I found myself a pivotal member to two companies, working across a wide range of markets and gaining firsthand experience of the complete design process. This initial experience has enabled me to widen my client base over recent years to include some of the major British design consultancies and additionally to act as a consultant to manufacturing companies and inventors direct. My freelance status permits a flexible and varied career, including part-time lecturing and speculative design work.

An example follows of a typical job from the initial years of my career, for which I was the sole designer responsible for the running and execution of the project.

The components to be designed around.

The machine awaiting client approval.

Prototype model under construction.

The British Airways self-service ticketing machine

One of the principal clients of Worlds Apart is British Airways, a company with a diverse range of internal divisions and operations.

The brief

I was briefed that British Airways Staff Travel, in conjunction with BA Distribution Services, had developed a self-service ticket machine (SST) for trials and now wanted to design the machine, initially for a prototype unit and then subsequent batch production.

Background Research

The existing ticket machine was analysed and the way in which it was used was noted.

1. Selection of flight details (timings, destinations, airport departure) via a touch-sensitive screen.

2. Payment by credit card, also involving touch-screen procedures.

3. Collection of tickets from the machine.

My involvement as designer would include the design of the exterior appearance of the new machine, the configuration of the interior components (screen, ticket printer, PC, credit card swipe reader), and the ergonomic configuration. The on-screen graphics sequence had already been created by BA Distribution Systems and the exact specifications of the electrical components had been finalised. It was proposed that the project be divided into four stages, with presentations to the client taking place between each stage.

1. Conceptual designs presented in visual form.

2. Design development of the preferred concept in two and three dimensions, taking into account all aspects of the unit's appearance, user interface and construction.

3. Production of a fully accurate visual prototype to illustrate to the client the exact design proposal, including surface finishes and graphics.

4. Production of a working prototype, including a comprehensive set of component drawings and artwork.

Design considerations

The following points acted as a guide in my original proposals:

1. The environment in which the machine would be used (perhaps friendly at first, changing to semi-hostile in the future after the concept of self-service ticketing had been proved).

2. User perceptions of the technology.

3. Methods of construction, including colours and finishes and the materials to be used.

4. A one-off unit required at first, batch production later.

5. Ergonomics relating to the person – machine interface, including screen visibility and glare, and the general ergonomic configuration taking account of screen height; credit card slot access and ticket retrieval; audible indicators for progress and rejection; and repair and maintenance considerations.

6. Access to the machine components, adequate venting and dust control.

7. Designed within the BA corporate image.

8. Safety and security considerations, given that the machine stores airline tickets that can be equated with blank cheques.

The machine is now in use on a trial basis. We look forward to its success.

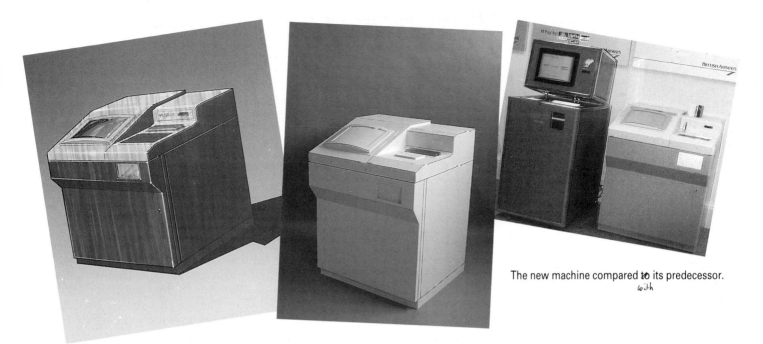

The new machine compared to its predecessor.
with

Design concept drawing.   A model prior to finishes and corporate identity.

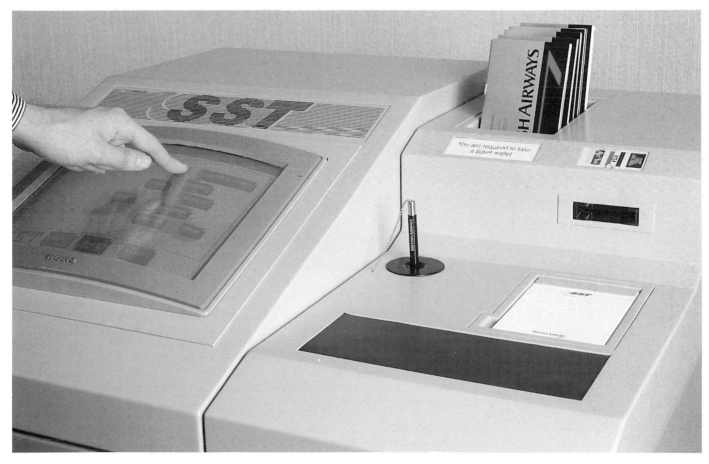

The self-service ticketing machine in operation.

5 Design Resources

SELECTED BIBLIOGRAPHY

Students following design-related courses require a broad range of reference material if they are to be exposed to a variety of influences and issues essential to the development of critical and analytical skills. The publications listed below are indicative rather than definitive of the type of material available. These resources have been used by the authors in their own teaching as well as in the preparation of this book.

Presentation techniques

Buchan, J., *The Graphic Artist's Handbook*, Macdonald, 1986
Camp, J., *Draw: How to Master the Art*, Guild, 1985
Critchlow, K., *Islamic Patterns*, Thames and Hudson, 1976
Curtis, S. C. and Hunt, C., *The Airbrush Book*, Guild, 1980
Dalley, T., *The Complete Guide to Illustration and Design*, Phaidon
Gill, B., *Forget All the Rules About Graphic Design*, Watson-Guptil, 1981
Holmes, N., *Designer's Guide to Creating Charts and Diagrams*, Watson-Guptil
Jennings, S., *The New Guide to Professional Illustration and Design*, Headline, 1987
Lewell, J., *Computer Graphics*, Orbis, 1985
Martin, J., *Drawing with Colour*, Studio Vista
Martin, J., *The Complete Guide to Calligraphy*, Quill, 1984
Padwick, R. and Walker, T., *Pattern, Its Structure and Geometry*, Ceolfrith Press
Powell, D., *Presentation Techniques*, Macdonald/Orbis, 1985
Powell, D. and Monahan, P., *Advanced Marker Techniques*, Macdonald/Orbis, 1987
Stribley, M., *The Calligraphy Source Book*, Guild, 1986
White, G., *Perspective*, Batsford, 1982

Ergonomics and anthropometrics

BSI, *Compendium of British Standards for Design and Technology in Schools*
Clark, T. S. and Corlett, E. N., *The Ergonomics of Workspaces and Machines – A Design Manual*, Taylor and Francis
Croney, J., *Anthropometry for Designers*, Batsford/Van Nostrand
Dreyfuss, H., *The Measure of Man*, Watson-Guptil
Galer, I., *Applied Ergonomics Handbook*, Butterworth
Grandjean, E., *Ergonomics of the Home*, Design Council
Pheasant, S., *Ergonomics — Standards and Guidelines for Designers* BSI
Pheasant, S., *Bodyspace*, Taylor and Francis

Source books

Agostini, F., *Visual Games*, Guild, 1986
Bayer, P., *Art Deco Source Book*, Guild, 1988

Bayley, S., *The Conran Directory of Design*, Guild, 1985

Berger, J., *Ways of Seeing*, Pelican, 1972

Burden, I., Morrison, J. and Twyford, J., *Design and Designing*, Longman, 1988

Clark, E., *The Want Makers*, Hodder and Stoughton

Cundy, H. M. and Rollett, A.P., *Mathematical Models* Tarquin Publications 1981

Dawkins, R., *The Blind Watchmaker*, Longman Scientific, 1986

Day, C., *Places of the Soul*, Aquarian

De Sausmarez, M., *The Dynamics of Visual Form*, Studio Vista

DES, *Safety in Practical Studies*

Edwards, B., *Drawing on the Right Side of the Brain*, Fontana

Effron, E., *Planning and Designing Lighting*, Windward, 1986

Fraser Reekie, R., *Design in the Built Environment*, Arnold

French, M. J., *Invention and evolution: Design in nature and engineering*, Cambridge

Gibberd, V., *Architecture Source Book*, Macdonald/Orbis

Goldsmith, S., *Designing for the Disabled*, RIBA

Gombrich, E. H., *Art and Illusion*, Phaidon, 1960

Harvie, C., Martin, G. and Scharf, A., *Industrialisation and Culture 1830–1914*, Open University, 1970

Haslem, M., *In the Nouveau Style*, Guild, 1989

HRH The Prince of Wales, *A Vision of Britain: A Personal View of Architecture*, Doubleday, 1989

Jones, J. C., *Design Methods*, John Wiley & Sons

Katz, S., *Classic Plastics, from Bakelite to High-Tech*, Thames and Hudson

Kitts, B. and McQuiston, L., *Graphic Design Source Book*, Macdonald, 1987

Landow, G. P., *W. H. Hunt and Typological Symbolism*, Yale University Press

Ledsome, C., *Engineering Design Teaching Aids*, Design Council

Leonardo da Vinci, *Leonardo's Notebooks* Yale University Press, 1989

Lynton, N., *The Story of Modern Art*, Phaidon, 1980

Macready, S. and Thompson, F. H., *Influences in Victorian Art and Architecture*

Martin Miller, J., *Period Details*, Mitchell Beazley, 1987

Naylor, G., *The Bauhaus*, Studio Vista

Norman, E., Riley, J., Urry, S., Whittaker, M., *Advanced Design and Technology*, Longman, 1990

Nuttgens, P., *Living in Towns*, BBC Publications

Oakley, K., *Man the Toolmaker*, British Museum (Natural History)

Packard, V., *The Waste Makers*, Penguin

Papenek, V., *Design for the Real World*, Paladin

Patent Office, *What is Intellectual Property*

Patent Office, *Introducing Design Registration*

Pevsner, N., *Pioneers of Modern Design*, Penguin

Prideaux, T., *The World of Whistler*, Time-Life 1970

Schumacher, E., *Small is Beautiful*, Paladin

Sparkes, P., *An Introduction to Design and Culture in the Twentieth Century*, Allen and Unwin, 1986

Sparkes, P., *Design in Context*, Bloomsbury

Sparkes, P. et al, *Design Source Book*, Macdonald/Orbis

Strut, G., *The Wheelwright's Shop*, Cambridge

Sudjic, D., *Cult Objects*, Paladin, 1985

Sudjic, D., *The Lighting Book*, Mitchell Beazley

Tjalve, E., *A Short Course in Industrial Design*, Newnes Butterworth

Twyford, J., *Graphic Communication*, Batsford, 1981

Vasari, *Lives of the Artists*, Penguin, 1965

Welsh Art Council, *The Art of the Engineer*, Science Museum

Wills, G., *Wedgwood*, Spring Books, 1988

Further sources

A Dictionary of Art and Artists, Penguin

The Open University Course T264 'Design Principles and Practice' consists of a number of course handbooks and video material which may be used to support a variety of design-related courses.

Dover Publications, Inc.
31 East 2nd Street
Mineola
New York
11501
A full range of design resource books many of which are copyright free.

Design Council publications
These include an extensive range of books, videos, slides, magazines and posters. For further information contact:

Sales Department
The Design Council
28 Haymarket
London
SW1Y 4SU

Monthly publications

New Scientist
Design
Which?

USEFUL ADDRESSES

As part of your research you may find it necessary to make direct contact with companies or professional organisations. Some of the following addresses may prove useful.

Advertising

The Advertising Association
Abford House
15 Wilton Road
London
SW1V 1NJ
Tel: 071 828 2771

The Advertising Standards
   Authority
Brook House
Torrington Place
London
WC1E 7HN
Tel: 071 580 5555

Design Protection

The Patent Office
25 Southampton Buildings
Chancery Lane
London
WC 2A 1AY
Tel: 071 438 4700

Chartered Institute of Patent
   Agents
Staple Inn Buildings
London
WC1V 7PZ

House Construction

Timber and Brick Homes
   Information Council
Stanhope House
Stanhope Place
London W2 2HH
Tel: 071 723 3444

National House Building Council
Chiltern Avenue
Amersham
Bucks
HP6 5AP

Materials

Timber Research and
   Development Association
Stocking Lane
Hughenden
Bucks
HP14 4ND

Education Service of the Plastics
   and Rubber Industry
University of Technology
Loughborough
Leicestershire
LE11 3TU
Tel: 0509 232065

The British Plastics Federation
5 Belgrave Square
London
SW1X 8PH
Tel: 071 235 9483

Lighting

Decorative Lighting Association
   Ltd.
Bryn
Bishop's Castle
Shropshire
SY9 5LE
Tel: 058 84 658

Osram
PO Box 17
East Lane
Wembley
HA9 7PG
Tel: 081 908 5111

Packaging

The Institute of Packaging
Sysonby Lodge
Melton Mowbray
Leicestershire

PAST A-LEVEL EXAMINATION QUESTIONS

Many design-based syllabuses require students to sit a timed theory paper as part of their final examination. The questions included in these papers are often of a diverse nature, related to design awareness in its broadest sense. The questions listed below are examples from a number of such examinations, which encourage candidates to make reference to specific examples from their own experience as well as illustrating their answers with suitable graphic techniques where appropriate. Where marks have been included in the question, they may prove useful in identifying the weighting of individual sections within the overall question.

Products

- Discuss the case for designing some products to have a limited life. What are the possible consequences of planned obsolescence? (20)
  (AEB, Design and Realisation, 1989)

- The influence of different cultures within our society is reflected in the range and design of its products. Discuss this statement giving appropriate examples. (20)
  (AEB, Design and Realisation, 1988)

- (a) Explain the essential features of the following methods of production, and give an example of a product which you consider suitable for each method:
    - (i) one-off production; (6)
    - (ii) batch production; (6)
    - (iii) volume production. (6)
  (b) State the costs which contribute to the selling price of a manufactured article. (8)
  (c) Discuss the relationship between the scale of production and the various factors that influence the selling price of a manufactured article. Use examples to illustrate the points you make.
  (Oxford, Design, 1988)

- (a) (i) Define the terms 'mechanisation' and 'automation'.
      (ii) With reference to specific examples of industrial processes, explain the difference between the terms.

  (b) Give reasons for the introduction in manufacturing of:
      (i) mechanisation;
      (ii) automation.
  (c) (i) Select a product and explain how either mechanisation or automation has been introduced into the manufacturing process.
      (ii) Identify any problems which may have resulted from this change of production method.
      (Oxford, Design, 1987)

- (a) Select a product and describe its development during this century. (12)
  (b) Explain how technological developments have affected the quality of the product. (8)
  (Oxford, Design, 1988)

- Discuss the ways in which the development of programmable machine tools influences the choice between individual, batch and mass production.
  (AEB, Design and Realisation, 1987)

- Explain the factors which have influenced the evolution of the design of one of the following:
  (a) a motor cycle crash helmet.
  (b) a pair of trainers.
  (c) a fibre tip pen.
  (AEB, Design – Communication and Implementation, 1986)

- To what extent is there still a role for the craftsmen/women in today's society of mass-produced consumer goods?
  (AEB, History and Appreciation of Art, 1988)

- Discuss the work of William Morris as a craftsman/designer.
  (AEB, History and Appreciation of Art, 1988)

- Discuss the aims of the Bauhaus, and its influence on a design area of your choice.
  (AEB, History and Appreciation of Art, 1988)

- (a) Discuss the implications of the word 'quality' in connection with:
     (i)   mass produced items;
     (ii) the work of an individual craftsman.
  (b) With reference to its development, comment on the 'quality' of the contemporary, mass-produced motor car.
  (Oxford, Design, 1987)

Architecture and planning

- Write an essay describing the main characteristics of an architectural style you have studied, making detailed reference to one building of the period.
  (AEB, History and Appreciation of Art, 1987)

- Describe the architectural character of either (a) the domestic buildings or (b) the public buildings in your locality. Make special reference to the design features and materials used in the construction of one building of your choice.
  (AEB, History and Appreciation of Art, 1987)

- The damage caused by the blitz during the Second World War gave a great opportunity to architects and planners. The new thinking inspired by Le Corbusier was evident and the popular idea was to 'Go High'. By the end of the 1960s the dreams had faded and the demand was for housing on a more human scale.
  (a) Discuss the 'new thinking' that led to the high-rise developments of the post-war period. (16)
  (b) Comment on the change of attitudes towards high-rise flats. (8)
  (c) With reference to an example with which you are familiar, describe how the needs and aspirations of the developer, residents and conservationists have been reconciled. (16)
  (Oxford, Design, 1988)

- Describe and evaluate the design of one contemporary domestic house you know well, referring to function, aesthetic qualities and the materials used in its construction.
(AEB, History and Appreciation of Art, 1988)

- The design of public environments such as shopping centres and transport terminals involves different considerations from those involved in private environments such as housing. Explain how these considerations can influence the design of public areas. (20)
(AEB, Design and Realisation, 1988)

- Discuss some of the ways in which contemporary artists, designers and craftsmen/women can collaborate with architects to provide enrichment to buildings. Describe two examples of this type of decorative work that you have studied.
(AEB, History and Appreciation of Art, 1987)

Advertising

- Advertisers have a number of ways in which they can communicate with consumers.
  (a) With the help of examples, discuss the advantages and disadvantages of the following methods of reaching the public:
      (i) television and radio; (5)
      (ii) newspapers and magazines; (5)
      (iii) posters such as those displayed on hoardings. (5)
  (b) To what extent can a product advertise itself? (5)
      (Oxford, Design, 1988)

- Discuss how and why advertising attempts to influence taste and fashion. (20)
(AEB, Design and Realisation, 1987)

- Discuss whether advertising, by itself, can create demand for a product.
(AEB, Design and Communication and Implementation)

- In relation to media advertising, what, in your opinion, is the role of the contemporary poster?
(AEB, History and Appreciation of Art, 1988)

- There is an acceptance by government and consumer organisations that advertising plays a significant part in keeping down prices by stimulating competition.
  (a) Describe an example of advertising (in any form) which has been of advantage to the customer. Explain the advantages.
  (b) (i) State the restraints which operate on the advertising of goods to the public.
      (ii) Identify the pressures that have resulted in the imposition of these restraints
      (Oxford, Design, 1986)

Graphic design

- The designer makes considerable use of graphic language.
  (a) Explain the meaning of the term 'graphic language'. (3)
  (b) Describe the purposes for which a designer uses graphic language, and indicate the form of graphic language most suitable for each purpose described. (12)
  (c) Discuss the ways in which the introduction of computers is affecting the graphic language used by designers. (5)
      (Oxford, Design, 1988)

- (a) Explain what is meant by 'the language of design'.
  - (b) Explain, using examples, how the introduction of computers has affected the language of design of each of the following:
    - (i) the designer;
    - (ii) the production engineer;
    - (iii) the designer's client.
      (Oxford, Design, 1987)

General

- Package design plays an important part in the presentation and sale of a product. With reference to actual examples, discuss the merits and demerits of packaging, bearing in mind the factors of visual appearance, over-elaboration, function and cost.
  (AEB, History and Appreciation of Art, 1987)

- Discuss the importance of preliminary drawings and research in the creative process with reference to both your own experience and the work of one noticeable artist, craftsman/woman or designer.
  (AEB, History and Appreciation of Art, 1988)

- Describe the ways in which consumers can influence the design of products. Illustrate your answer with reference to a specific example, indicating those features that are attributable to consumer pressure.
  (Oxford, Design, 1987)

- A work of art can be a record of the time, place and society in which the artist/designer lives. Select one example from any art form which you think performs the function well, and explain the reasons for your choice.
  (AEB, History and Appreciation of Art, 1986)

- Discuss ways in which public bodies can influence the environment. (20)
  (AEB, Design and Realisation, 1987)

- Discuss the relationships between market research, the design and the selling of a product. (20)
  (AEB, Design and Realisation, 1989)

- Manufacturing consumes natural resources. Discuss why and how this consumption could be minimised. (20)
  (AEB, Design and Realisation, 1988)

- 'Industrial designers, industry and governments must determine together what social and ecological harm we are doing to our communities. To say that there is something inherently wrong with technology is overly simplistic. We can no longer just rid ourselves of technology since the world depends on it.'
  Discuss this statement with particular reference to any two of the following: (10, 10)
  - (i) the pollution of the environment;
  - (ii) the use of non-renewable energy resources;
  - (iii) designing for a limited product life.
    (Oxford, Design, 1988)

- Write a critical appreciation of any one book or series of articles, which you have read recently, and is concerned with the history and/or the practice of painting, sculpture, craft or design. Explain how this publication of a general or specialist nature has helped you in your studies.
  (AEB, History and Appreciation of Art, 1987)

Index